THINKING CRITICALLY ABOUT
SOCIAL PSYCHOLOGY

JENNIFER BONDS-RAACKE
Fort Hays State University

Kendall Hunt
publishing company

CONTENTS

AUTHOR BIOGRAPHIES

Chapter One

Dr. Jennifer Bonds-Raacke is currently the Chair and Professor of Psychology at Fort Hays State University (FHSU). Her primary research interests are the psychology of mass communication, decision-making, and the psychology of teaching. Prior to joining the faculty at FHSU, Dr. Bonds-Raacke served as the Associate Dean of the Maynor Honors College and as a Faculty Teaching Fellow for the Teaching and Learning Center at the University of North Carolina at Pembroke. She has also been an Assistant Professor and Faculty Advisor of the Honors Program at Briar Cliff University. Dr. Bonds-Raacke obtained her PhD and MS from Kansas State University in Experimental Psychology and her BA from Christian Brothers University. She has been happily married to Dr. John Raacke for over 15 years and they have two daughters, Callie and Brooke.

Chapter One and Six

Chelsea Schnabelrauch Arndt is an experimental social psychologist interested in persuasion and social influence. She received her BA in Psychology from Calvin College in 2011, her MS in Experimental Social Psychology from Kansas State University in 2013, and will finish her PhD in Experimental Social Psychology at Kansas State University in 2016. Chelsea currently teaches online psychology classes as an adjunct faculty for Fort Hays State University. Though she enjoys teaching psychology in general, her favorite areas of psychology to teach are statistics and experimental research methods and design. When she is not teaching or researching, Chelsea enjoys spending time with her husband, David, and relaxing at the pool (during the summertime).

Chapter Three

Dr. Drew Curtis immensely enjoys teaching and igniting students' passion for learning. He is currently an Assistant Professor of Psychology and Director of the Counseling Psychology master's program at Angelo State University in San Angelo, TX. Dr. Curtis has taught a variety of undergraduate and graduate courses, for eight years, at universitiy and community college settings. He earned his BS in Psychology and MA in Clinical Psychology from Sam Houston State University. Dr. Curtis earned his PhD in Counseling Psychology from Texas Woman's University. His clinical experience has been primarily within university counseling centers and private practice. Dr. Curtis completed his predoctoral psychology internship at the Career and Counseling Services at the University of Houston Clear Lake in Houston, TX. His research interests have focused on deception: within health care professions, in the context of therapy, intimate relationships, and parental relationships. Seondary research interests are teaching of psychology and postpartum and perinatal psychology. Dr. Curtis has received the Texas Woman's University Excellence in Teaching Award and the Outstanding Graduate Student Award. As for his personal life, he is meaningfully married with four children. In his free time, he enjoys playing guitar, spending time with his family, and being a jungle gym for his children.

Chapter Two

Donna Stuber is a Professor of Psychology at Friends University in Wichita, KS. In addition to teaching, she has supervised the research of seniors preparing presentations or manuscripts since coming to Friends in 1996. She is the proud coadvisor of the Friends University Chapter of Psi Chi, which is the recipient of multiple regional and national honors, including the 2008 Ruth Hubbard Cousins National Chapter Award. Dr. Stuber received her BS from Missouri Western State College, MS from Emporia State University, and PhD from Kansas State University. Dr. Stuber's research interests include academic dishonesty in the virtual classroom and the relationship between hypercompetitiveness and supervisor worth ethics among women in power positions. Since 1992, she has published over 20 articles and chapters and has made over 20 presentations, many coauthored by undergraduates. Dr. Stuber's memberships include Association for Psychological Science (APS), the Society for the Teaching of Psychology, Southwestern Psychological Association, and the Association for Psychological and Educational Research in Kansas (PERK). She is twice a Past President of PERK, has three times served on the Board of Directors for the Great Plains Behavioral Research Association, and is a National Past President of Psi Beta. Once a presenter herself, she has served three times as convention coordinator for the Great Plains Students' Psychology Convention and has had numerous students win first- and second-place awards. Dr. Stuber was included in Who's Who Among America's Teachers and in 1998 was presented the Outstanding Recent Graduate Award from the Teacher's College at Emporia State University.

Chapter Two

Kristina Thielen earned her BS in Psychology at Friends University and a Master of Criminal Justice at Boston University. Kristina's research interests include subjects such as same sex marriage, stress responses in emergency responders, the effect of alcohol consumption on social capital, and the Internet's effect on human sexuality. Kristina has presented her research at a variety of conferences and has won several first place awards. Kristina served as the Psi Chi Vice President and Historian for the Friends University Chapter of Psi Chi and wrote the winning essay at the time the chapter received the Ruth Hubbard Cousins National Chapter Award. During her master's program at Boston University, Kristina was inducted into Alpha Phi Sigma, the criminal justice honor society. Currently, Kristina is an EMS Volunteer with the Halstead, KS fire department.

Chapter Four

Steven J. Hoekstra, PhD, is a Professor of Psychology and Interdisciplinary Studies at Kansas Wesleyan University. His research interests include mass media effects, relationship beliefs, interpersonal communication, pseudoscience beliefs, religiosity, and any other thing that he finds curious in the moment. He lives in Salina, KS with his wife Anne and daughter Thea, along with four loving dogs.

Chapter Five and Seven

Darin Challacombe is a graduate of and adjunct instructor for Fort Hays State University's Psychology Department. He has taught at Fort Hays for 10 years and is currently pursuing a doctorate in psychology. His broad research interests center around social and forensic psychology. He is particularly interested in law enforcement officers' personality changes due to their career and radicalization processes of domestic terrorists.

Chapter Five

Christopher Kiker-Beury recently obtained his MA in Clinical Psychology from Washburn University in May 2015. His thesis involved researching how heterosexism influences learning about LGB issues and has recently been updated and submitted for publication as *Learning through Heterosexism: Prejudice and Learning about Lesbian, Gay, and Bisexual Issues in Clinical Classrooms*. Along with his thesis, he worked on a research project assessing the Safe Zone programs at two different universities and presented a poster at the 2015 Great Plains Student Psychology Convention, where he won first place. He is continuing the Safe Zone research and will be submitting *Agency, Identity, and Diverse Community with Higher Education: A Multi-Method Safe Zone Program Assessment* for publication once research is finished. Prior to graduating, Christopher completed his internship as a therapist at Wyandot Center, where he worked with a diverse clientele and enhanced his therapeutic skills, particularly Cognitive Behavioral Therapy, Interpersonal Process Therapy, and Group Therapy. He has recently applied for his LMLP and he will be going back to school to obtain his PhD in Clinical Psychology where he will continue research on topics involving the LGBTQ community and mental health. Besides studying and researching, he enjoys quality time with loved ones, and he is often seen relaxing at home with his best friend and roommate, Asiland, who is a cat.

Chapter Eight

Dr. Fantasy Lozada is a National Science Foundation Postdoctoral Fellow at the Center for the Study of Black Youth in Context at the University of Michigan. She graduated with her PhD in Lifespan Developmental Psychology from North Carolina State University as an Initiative for Maximizing Student Diversity Scholar and a Center for Developmental Science Predoctoral Fellow. Her work explores predictors of the social and emotional development of ethnic minority children such as familial emotion and racial socialization and children's school and out-of-school race-related experiences. Dr. Lozada is also an adjunct instructor for the Fort Hayes State University Virtual College where she teaches undergraduate and graduate courses in developmental psychology.

Chapter Nine

Dr. Christopher Barlett is an assistant professor at Gettysburg College in the psychology department. He earned his BS and MS at Kansas State University and his PhD at Iowa State University in experimental social psychology. Trained as an aggression researcher, Dr. Barlett has published many articles focusing on the variables and psychological processes that increase and decrease the likelihood of aggressive behavior. Currently, his two independent lines of research involve the processes involved in cyberbullying perpetration and how mitigating information (e.g., excuses) can reduce aggressive behavior after a perceived provocation. His work has appeared in several journals, including *Personality and Social Psychology Bulletin*, *Journal of Experimental Social Psychology*, *Psychology of Popular Media Culture*, *Aggressive Behavior*, and *Journal of Cross Cultural Psychology*. Overall, Dr. Barlett strives to reduce aggression in society by understanding the psychological processes involved in such actions.

Dr. Natalie Barlett is an adjunct professor at multiple colleges and universities with a BA from Kansas Wesleyan University and an MS and PhD from Kansas State University in experimental social psychology. She greatly enjoys teaching courses in social and developmental psychology while pursuing her lines of research. Her research interests include understanding the correlates and predictors of relational aggression in childhood and adolescence and exploring the factors related to and the developmental process experienced with Emerging Adulthood.

Chapter Ten

Holly Krech Thomas began teaching in the Psychology Department at Bethany College in 2012, after moving to Kansas from New York City, where she taught at Kingsborough Community College, CUNY. She received her doctorate in cognitive science and linguistics from the University of Colorado, Boulder, in 2004. With research interests in cognitive psychology ranging from perception and attention to language processing, she finds many aspects of social psychology have fascinating connections to cognition and how the brain shapes our interactions with the world. When not on campus, she gardens, reads with her four children, teaches in the Christian education program in her church, and delights in riding her bicycle around town.

Andrea Ring received her Bachelor's of Science in Psychology in 2002 from Fort Hays State University and her Master's of Science in Clinical Psychology in 2005, also from Fort Hays State University. She worked as a Clinical Psychotherapist at Salina Regional Health Center in the Intensive Outpatient Program for four years. She began working as an adjunct professor at Bethany College in the spring of 2009. At that time she realized her love of teaching. In the fall of 2009, she joined the faculty at Bethany College full-time and became chair of the department in fall 2013. She still continues her clinical work. She maintains her clinical license and works evenings at the outpatient clinic with Salina Regional Health Center.

Chapter Eleven

Dr. Adair is an assistant professor of psychology at Lyon College. She completed her bachelor's degree in psychology at Florida State University, under the mentorship of Dr. Jon Maner and Dr. Michael Baker, exploring facultative shifts in memory performance as a result of the activation of mating motives. She completed her master's degree and PhD at Kansas State University, with Dr. Gary Brase, studying the nature of fertility decision-making in the individual, specifically exploring the sensitivity of fertility intentions to social and ecological cues. Dr. Adair's research primarily focuses on topics within the domains of evolutionary psychology and judgment and decision-making. Investigated topics within her research include mate choice, intrasexual competition, reactions to relationship threats and defection, stigma by association in intimate relationships, attitudes toward abortion and media representations of abortion, and reproductive decision-making. Dr. Adair also serves as an instructor of several courses relevant to sex and sexuality, including the Psychology of Women and the Psychology of Sexual Behavior. Dr. Adair has a passion for teaching, specifically sharing her love for psychology with her students and helping them find topics within the field of psychology that speak to them and their personal experiences. She believes that the keys to progress in psychology are a spirit of excitement, curiosity, and a healthy dose of skepticism.

Chapter One
An Introduction to Social Psychology

Dr. Jenn Bonds-Raacke and Chelsea A. Schnabelrauch Arndt

Fort Hays State University and Kansas State University

Learning Objectives

- Distinguish common sense from social psychology
- Define social psychology
- Identify major historical influences on the development of social psychology
- Describe social psychology's place in contemporary psychology
- Explain the topics covered and approach of the textbook

Chapter Outline

Common sense versus social psychology

Definition of social psychology

Historical influences on the development of social psychology

Social psychology in contemporary psychology

Overview of topics covered and approach of textbook

Opening

Social psychology might be one of the easiest classes that you will take in college. Let me assure you that you read the previous sentence correctly! That's great news as you embark on new semester, right? But, I should clarify. It is not that social psychology is easy because the content is simple or because the exams are easy or because you will not have to put forth effort. Some of these things may or may not be true. However, the reason I think social psychology will be the

easiest class you will take is because I believe you will find the content inherently interesting. You will not need a professor to explain to you why the information is important. In fact, it may even be hard to find a chapter in the textbook covering material or concepts you do not like or you find boring.

Concepts, terms, and theories from social psychology surround you every day, and consequently, you will be able to relate what you are reading about to things that matter in your life. You will likely even be able to apply what you are learning in class to help you out in specific situations. For example, we will discuss how to make a good first impression on a job interview and how to persuade people to do you a favor, which can be very useful information. We will also learn how to have a positive impact at the societal level; specifically, we will discuss ways to increase altruistic behavior and reduce prejudice thoughts and behaviors.

Social Psychology vs. Common Sense

One of the first things you will learn about social psychology is that what you think is common knowledge and how you think people will respond in given circumstances is not always true. In fact, some have argued that the results of many social psychology experiments could have been predicted in advance (Ross, Lepper, & Ward, 2010). In other words, people would hear about results of an experiment and say, "I knew that already" or "We knew that all along." Such comments imply social psychology is only common sense and research is not

needed to advance our understanding of how others and the environment can impact thought and behavior. But, you will learn this is not the case. We do not know in advance the outcome of social psychology research, and in many cases, we (people in society) believe the exact opposite of what research shows us. Let's look at one example.

Do you ever take quizzes on BuzzFeed or a similar website? I must admit that I do, especially when my friends post their results on Facebook and I want to compare my results to theirs. One very popular topic for such quizzes is relationships. There are relationship quizzes

Alexander Raths/Shutterstock.com

360b/Shutterstock.com

about finding the perfect mate, seeing if your mate understands you, or predicting how long your relationship will last. In fact, it seems you can't go a few days without seeing a quiz on the topic of relationships.

One particular area of relationships receives significant attention; this is the idea that opposites attract. I took a quiz just today titled, "What Opposite Personality Do You Attract?" (http://www.playbuzz.com/mirandar10/what-opposite-personality-do-you-attract) and the results revealed that I attract the opposite personality called, "The Dynamo." The Dynamo personality likes action-packed fun and prefers not to think. However, it is not just in romantic relationships where we hear that opposites attract. I found this article on BuzzFeed explaining, "17 Ways Introvert/Extrovert Friendships Rule: Opposites Attract!" (http://www.buzzfeed.com/alexalvarez/this-one-is-for-mario#.ogqeZDP2xz). As the name implies, this article contains 17 benefits to introvert/extrovert friendships. One example is that an introvert can show his/her extrovert friend the importance of one-on-one time. Can you guess the number one reason on the list? The top reason was that, "You are both living proof that opposites really do attract."

It is easy to look at the results of these types of quizzes and focus only on the aspects that are accurate for us. For example, of the list of the 17 benefits to introvert/extrovert friendships, perhaps only five of the listed benefits stand out to us as we read them. Even though out of 17 reasons, we only could relate to five of them, we finish reading the list with a feeling that we gained insight into our friendships. In reality, though, we ignored 12 benefits that didn't ring true to us and simply devoted our attention to the five benefits that fit our own introvert/extrovert friendships. We overall are left with a sense that the list was accurate and personalized to our relationships, when in actuality those five benefits probably fit most other friendships as well. Of course, we don't realize that the information we read was so general that it could apply to anyone and that most of what we read wasn't insightful. This tendency to believe personality descriptions are accurate (and ignore the descriptions which do not fit us) and specifically for us is known as the **P. T. Barnum effect**. Let's take a moment to talk a little about this effect, by reading the Thinking Critically Box on the top of page 4.

P. T. Barnum Effect
Tendency to believe generalized personality descriptions as highly accurate for oneself.

Before the Thinking Critically Box, we were discussing how relationships are a popular topic for online quizzes and in particular, our fascination with the idea that opposites attract. This idea that opposites attract is but one example that social psychology research is not always common sense. Lilienfeld, Lynn, Ruscio, and Beyerstein (2010) recently published a book examining myths in popular psychology. One of the chapters was titled, "Opposites Attract: We Are Most Romantically Attracted to People Who Differ from Us." Though the belief that opposites attract is popularized to the extent that we believe it is common sense, it is actually contradicted by research. We will discuss research in this textbook that explains it is not always the case that opposites attract nor that opposite personalities lead to increased relationship satisfaction or longevity. You might wonder how these myths develop or where they come from if they are not based in truth. Why it is that we think opposites attract? It could be that relationships are very important to us as social people. Because of

Ai825/Shutterstock.com

THINKING CRITICALLY

Have you ever wondered why people read horoscopes or why people believe information that a psychic tells them? One possible explanation illustrates the P. T. Barnum effect. It seems that we have a natural tendency to internalize generic personality descriptions as being accurate and unique to ourselves.

Take a look at the list of statements below. Forer (1949) found that students rated these descriptions as being highly accurate for themselves, even though the exact same descriptions were provided to all students in the class.

1. You have a great need for other people to like and admire you.
2. You have a tendency to be critical of yourself.
3. You have a great deal of unused capacity which you have not turned to your advantage.
4. While you have some personality weaknesses, you are generally able to compensate for them.
5. Your sexual adjustment has presented problems for you.
6. Disciplined and self-controlled outside, you tend to be worrisome and insecure inside.
7. At times you have serious doubts as to whether you have made the right decision or done the right thing.
8. You prefer a certain amount of change and variety and become dissatisfied when hemmed in by restrictions and limitations.
9. You pride yourself as an independent thinker and do not accept others' statements without satisfactory proof.
10. You have found it unwise to be too frank in revealing yourself to others.
11. At times you are extroverted, affable, and sociable, while at others times you are introverted, wary, and reserved.
12. Some of your aspirations tend to be pretty unrealistic.
13. Security is one of your major goals in life.

Do you think you would have evaluated these descriptions as accurate for yourself? I would like to think that I would not be susceptible to this. However, research indicates we are all vulnerable to this line of thinking. You can learn more about this tendency by reading about the P. T. Barnum effect (Dickson & Kelly, 1985; Furnham & Schofield, 1987).

this importance, we look around us and try to explain why some relationships work and others do not.

Although no one place is solely responsible, the media does provide some inaccurate information on psychological topics and media portrayals have helped reinforce popular myths, including the idea that opposites attract. For example, think about the countless romantic comedies depicting the struggles between a man and a woman who can't agree on anything but in the end, realize their love for one another. One of the first examples of this you might recall seeing as a child is from Disney's *Beauty and the Beast* (re-release 1991). There are even songs in the movie which highlight the differences between the characters of Belle and the Beast, before they fall madly in love. More recently, this plot continues with Margaret and Andrew from *The Proposal* (2009), Edward and Bella from *Twilight* (2008), Matt and Danielle from *The Girl Next Door* (2004), and Andie and Ben from *How to Lose a Guy in 10 Days* (2003). These portrayals could have contributed to the myth stating that opposites attract is a well-established phenomenon.

It is also common for people to believe that men and women communicate in completely different ways. We can refer again to the book by Lilienfeld et al. (2010), which contains a chapter titled, "Men and Women Communicate in Completely Different Ways." As we discussed with the notion that opposites attract, many factors could contribute to people believing that men and women communicate so differently. For example, there are posts on social media that reinforce this idea. I took a quiz recently to see if I communicated like a man or a women. You can take the quiz at: https://www.blogthings.com/doyoucommunicatelikeamanorawomanquiz/.

Or, what about media portrayals that exaggerate differences between men and women? One of my all-time favorite shows, *Friends* (1995), has an episode that highlights how men and women share information differently by showing how Ross and Rachel tell each of their friends about their first kiss. If you do not remember this scene, check it out: https://www.youtube.com/watch?v=iGoC8FTLKSI.

Bottom line: No matter what the source of the misinformation, social psychologists help society test everyday notions. After reading this textbook, you will have a much better understanding of what commonly held believes about behavior and thought are accurate and which ones are bogus. So, let's get started!

Definition of Social Psychology

Let's begin by defining social psychology and providing some examples of research that social psychologists have conducted. **Social psychology** examines people's behaviors and cognitions, with particular focus on how others and social situations impact these.

Two social psychologists, Festinger and Carlsmith (1959), wanted to know what happens to our beliefs when we are placed in a situation to publically say

Social Psychology
The study how others and the environment impact people's behaviors and cognitions.

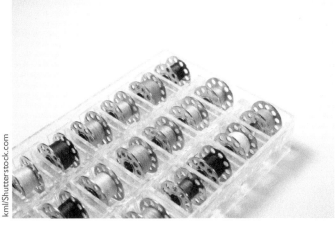

something that contradicts what we believe. To find out, the researchers had participants engage in a repetitive, boring behavior (i.e., placing 12 spools on and off a tray for 30 minutes and turning 48 square pegs a quarter clockwise for 30 minutes). Without going into all the specifics, some of the participants were later paid either $1 or $20 to describe the experiment as enjoyable to future participants. Those who were paid $1 to say something publically they disagreed with rated participation in the experiment as more enjoyable than those who were paid $20. This type of research demonstrates a concept we will explore later in the textbook known as cognitive dissonance theory and explains how people change internal beliefs to be congruent with public statements and behavior.

Social psychologists have also explored how doing a favor for a person impacts how much we like that person. Jecker and Landry (1969) had participants engage in a task that involved winning money. Following the conclusion of the task, some participants were asked by the researcher to return the money because he was running low on funds to conduct the experiment, some participants were asked by the secretory to return the money because the department was running low on funds to conduct the experiment, and some participants were allowed to keep the money. Next, all participants were asked to evaluate the researcher. The group asked by the researcher to return the money rated him the highest. These results might seem strange, but they demonstrate how our opinions of others increase when we do them a favor. Later in the textbook we will talk about why this happens.

A final example of research by social psychologists explores how we can increase our appearance of being trustworthy to others. Walster, Aronson, and Abrahams (1966) had participants read an interview with a boxer and convicted

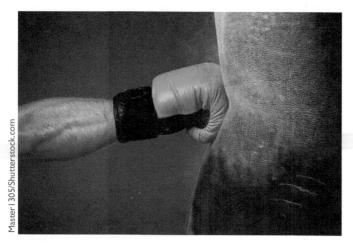

drug dealer, Joe "The Shoulder" Napolitano. In one version of the interview, Joe argued that the courts should be less strict and more lenient, and in another version of the interview, Joe argued the opposite. Specifically, he argued the courts should be stricter with more sever sentences. Results indicated that participants viewed Joe as more trustworthy in the latter condition when he was communicating against his own self-interests. This research is an example of how complex persuasion can be. Even an individual who is viewed negatively (such as a convicted criminal) can be an effective communicator if he or she is arguing against his or her own self-interests and appears to have nothing to gain.

In this section, we provided a working definition of social psychology. We also discussed three examples of social psychology research. These examples illustrate social psychology in action and hopefully you are now excited to learn more in these areas. In the next sections, we will discuss how social psychology developed within the historical context, as well as social psychology's place in contemporary psychology.

Historical Perspectives of Social Psychology

Psychology
Systematic investigation of human behavior and thought.

You might wonder how social psychology developed and, in particular, how social psychology developed in reference to psychology becoming its own discipline. To understand this, it is helpful to briefly review the origins of psychology.

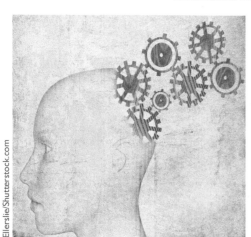

As you have probably learned from a previous class, **psychology** is the systematic investigation of human behavior and thought. This means psychologists study what people do and think and they study this in an organized and consistent manner. Psychology as a discipline is a paradox in that the field is both old and new. Although the formalization of the discipline did not occur until the latter part of the 19th century, the subject matter of psychology has been studied by many people for thousands of years. Historically, the origins of psychology have been grounded in two separate fields: philosophy and physiology. Philosophy is the field from which psychology gains much of the subject matter we study today, while physiology provided researchers in psychology the tools to study the subject matter.

Wilhelm Wundt (1832–1920) was one of the early aforementioned physiologists to study psychological principles. Following graduation from medical school in 1855, Wundt worked as an assistant in many early psychophysics and physiology research laboratories in Western Europe. It was during this time that Wundt began to develop his ideas for a new scientific discipline, psychology. Although others helped to contribute along the way, Wundt is considered the founder of modern psychology due to his publication of the first psychology book, *Principles of Physiological Psychology*, in 1874. Five years later, Wundt established the world's first psychological laboratory at the University of Leipzig in 1879, which remained active until 1910. It was from this laboratory that Wundt trained the first generation of psychologists who would go out into the world and make psychology the discipline it is today (Benjamin, 2008).

jurate140/Shutterstock.com

The start of social psychology occurred shortly after Wundt established his lab. In 1898, Norman Triplett published a paper in which he noted that bicycle racers had faster times when they raced with others versus alone. Triplett tested this observation in an experiment measuring how fast children turned a fishing reel. His results supported his earlier observation of the cyclists; children working beside other children turned the fishing reel faster than children working alone. Triplett's work in this area (discussed later in the textbook under social facilitation) is seen by many as the beginning of social psychology research.

Shortly thereafter, the first social psychology textbooks were published in 1908 by William McDougall and Edward Ross. McDougall's textbook focused on the topics of emotion, morality, and religion, which are very different than the topics covered in this textbook and other social psychology textbooks today. Though these early textbooks are not representative of what the field of social psychology would grow to become, they were nonetheless the first attempts at establishing social psychology as an academic field.

Though Triplett is acknowledged for conducting one of the first social psychology research studies, Kurt Lewin (1890–1947) is considered to be one of the pioneers in social psychology as we know it today. Shortly after graduating from graduate school with his PhD, World War I broke out in Europe. Lewin enlisted in the German army and served for several years. His experiences in the war and the outbreak of World War II sparked Lewin's research on leadership (Lewin, Lippitt, & White, 1939). He was also influential in social psychology because of his urging of other psychologists to apply psychological knowledge in order to solve social problems.

Lewin was not the only psychologist influenced by the events of the world wars. During World War II, Hitler forced Jewish psychologists out of academia, which led to many psychologists fleeing to the United States and other countries. As these psychologists settled into their new lives in foreign countries, their paths crossed with other academics that gave birth to research collaborations and new theories.

Accompanying this migration of great minds, the holocaust also sparked a great deal of research in social psychology. Many psychologists became fascinated how individuals' behavior changes when in the presence of others. As you will learn more about in a later chapter, some of these studies include Solomon Asch's (1955, 1956) conformity studies, Stanley Milgram's (1963) obedience studies, and Philip Zimbardo's Stanford Prison Experiment (Haney, Banks, & Zimbardo, 1973). The unexpected findings of these famous studies further increased the popularity of social psychology and caused the research on social psychology to explode.

Social Psychology in Contemporary Psychology

The development of social psychology, as discussed above, was heavily influenced by current events, and to some degree, this influence continues today. It is important to keep in mind where social psychology is in relation to the contemporary field of psychology.

Psychology is a diverse field, and as such, experts in the field approach the study of human behavior and cognition from a variety of perspectives. The American Psychological Association (APA) highlights the perspectives listed in the table below. In the table, you will find brief definitions. For additional information and examples of each, visit https://www.apa.org/careers/resources/guides/careers.aspx#. When reviewing the table, pay particular attention to how social psychology fits with the other areas within contemporary psychology.

Table 1.1

Clinical psychologists:
Work with individuals who have psychology disorders

Cognitive and perceptual psychologists:
Study human memory, thinking, and perception

Community psychologists:
Work to improve the lives of individuals within a community and assist individuals in locating needed community resources

Counseling psychologists:
Work with individuals to help with everyday life stressors

Developmental psychologists:
Study human development throughout the lifespan, from birth to death

Educational psychologists:
Study how people learn and ways to make teaching practices more effective for learners

Engineering psychologists:
Study how people work with machines, commonly referred to as human factors

Environmental psychologists:
Study the interaction of the person and the environment (including the physical and social settings)

Evolutionary psychologists:
Focus on how evolution impacts thoughts, feelings, and behavior

Experimental psychologists:
Use experimental methods to study a wide range of topics

Forensic psychologists:
Apply psychological theories and research findings to the legal setting

Health psychologists:
Study factors that impact an individual's health and wellness

Industrial/organizational psychologists:
Apply psychological theories, methodology, and findings to workplace settings and issues

Neuropsychologists (and behavioral neuropsychologists):
Study the brain and its relation to behavior

Quantitative and measurement psychologists:
Focus on designing experiments and analyzing data for a wide range of topics

Rehabilitation psychologists:
Work with individuals with disabilities to address rehabilitation needs

School psychologists:
Delivery a variety of psychological services to those in the school setting

Social psychologists:
Study how behaviors and thoughts are influenced by others

Sport psychologists:
Work with athletes, especially on motivational issues to improve performance

There are professional organizations devoted specifically to the study of social psychology. For example, the APA has two divisions of particular interest for those individuals in social psychology. These include Division 8: Society for Personality and Social Psychology (SPSP) (http://www.spsp.org/) and Division 9: Society for the Psychological Study of Social Issues (SPSSI) (http://www.spssi.org/). Another professional association for social psychologists is the Society for Experimental Social Psychology (http://www.sesp.org/). You can visit the websites provided to learn more about the organizations and stay up-to-date on current information, including upcoming conferences. By the way, SPSP welcomes undergraduate college students, such as yourself, to join and become a member (for an annual fee, of course).

This section of the chapter was brief but reviewed the diverse and broad nature of the field of psychology. We also looked at how social psychology fits within contemporary psychology, and we discussed professional organizations for individuals in social psychology. Before wrapping up the first chapter, I want to briefly mention the approach of this textbook.

Approach of the Textbook

Writing a textbook is a difficult and time-consuming task. Thus, you might wonder why we decided to do so. To begin, we frequently heard students express concerns about the length of standard textbooks on the market and the high price. We wanted our students to have a briefer textbook with accurate information at a reasonable price. Second, we wanted to have chapters written by faculty members who have extensive training, research experience, and/or teaching experience with the topic matter. Thus, you will find that each chapter is written by a different faculty member. We have provided a picture and a bio or fun facts about each faculty member. Finally, we wanted you to do well in the course. So, we have incorporated many student-friendly features in this textbook, which are presented in the list below.

Relevant and Interesting Examples

We provide you with many examples to help you understand key concepts. We use examples relating to your life and examples that are well known within the field of social psychology. We also offer examples appealing to students with a broad range of backgrounds and interests. We hope by giving such examples you will find it easier to remember and apply the information.

Easy-to-Understand Definitions

When introducing new terms, we avoid using technical or jargon-filled language. Rather, we explain the concept in easy-to-understand language. You will find new terms and concepts are presented in bold font within the paragraphs and new terms are also defined in the margins. This will help you to easily spot new information as you are reading the textbook.

Thinking Critically Boxes

Each chapter has a thinking critically box. In these boxes, you will be asked to think about a specific example or scenario. In some thinking critically boxes, there are correct answers provided at the end of the chapter. However, in other thinking critically boxes, they are not necessarily correct answers. Rather, the purpose of the box is to have you reflect on the topic in depth and think about how it could be applied in your life.

Connections to the Faculty

We want you to feel connected to the faculty members who contributed to this textbook. At the end of each chapter, you can learn more about the faculty member who contributed to the textbook. Although the faculty work at different institutions, we have one important thing in common: our belief in student success!

Please feel free to share your comments about the textbook with me via email (jmbondsraacke@fhsu.edu) and we hope that you enjoy thinking critically about social psychology!

Suggested Readings

Dickson, D. H., & Kelly, I. W. (1985). The "Barnum effect" in personality assessment: A review of the literature. *Psychological Reports, 57*(2), 367–382. doi:http://dx.doi.org.er.lib.k-state.edu/10.2466/pr0.1985.57.2.367

Fiske, S. T., Gilbert, D. T., & Lindzey, G. (2010). *Handbook of social psychology.* Hoboken, NJ: John Wiley & Sons.

Furnham, A., & Schofield, S. (1987). Accepting personality test feedback: A review of the Barnum effect. *Current Psychological Research & Reviews, 6*(2), 162–178. doi:http://dx.doi.org.er.lib.k-state.edu/10.1007/BF02686623

References

Asch, S. E. (1955). Opinions and social pressure. *Scientific American, 193*(5), 31–35. doi:http://dx.doi.org.er.lib.k-state.edu/10.1038/scientificamerican1155-31

Asch, S. E. (1956). Studies of independence and conformity: I. A minority of one against a unanimous majority. *Psychological Monographs: General and Applied, 70*(9), 1–70. doi:http://dx.doi.org.er.lib.k-state.edu/10.1037/h0093718

Benjamin, L. T., Jr. (2008). Psychology before 1900. In S. F. Davis & W. Buskist (Eds.), *21st century psychology: A reference handbook* (pp. 2–11). Thousand Oaks, CA: Sage Publications. doi:10.4135/9781412956321.n33

Crane, D. (Writer), Kauffman, M. (Writer), & Place, M. K. (Director). (1995). The one with the list [Television series episode]. In D. Crane, M. Kauffman, & K. S. Bright (Producers), *Friends*. Burbank, CA: Warner Bros. Studios.

Festinger, L., & Carlsmith, J. M. (1959). Cognitive consequences of forced compliance. *Journal of Abnormal and Social Psychology, 58*, 203–210. doi:http://dx.doi.org.er.lib.k-state.edu/10.1037/h0041593

Fletcher, A. (Director), Lieberman, T. (Producer), Bullock, S. (Producer), Hoberman, D. (Producer), Kurtzman, A. (Producer), Orci, R. (Producer), & Burr, K. (Producer). (2009). *The proposal* [Motion picture]. United States: Walt Disney Studios Motion Pictures.

Forer, B. R. (1949). The fallacy of personal validation: A classroom demonstration of gullibility. *Journal of Abnormal and Social Psychology, 44*, 118–123. doi:http://dx.doi.org.er.lib.k-state.edu/10.1037/h0059240

Greenfield, L. (Director), Gittes, H. (Producer), Gordon, C. (Producer), & Sternberg, M. (Producer). (2004). *The girl next door* [Motion picture]. United States: 20th Century Fox.

Hahn, D. (Producer), Trousdale, G. (Director), & Wise, K. (Director). (1991). *Beauty and the beast* [Motion picture]. United States: Walt Disney Pictures.

Haney, C., Banks, W. C., & Zimbardo, P. G. (1973). Interpersonal dynamics in a simulated prison. *International Journal of Criminology and Penology, 1*, 69–97.

Hardwicke, C. (Director), Godfrey, W. (Producer), Mooradian, G. (Producer), & Morgan, M. (Producer). (2008). *Twilight* [Motion picture]. United States: Summit Entertainment.

Jecker, J., & Landy, D. (1969). Liking a person as function of doing him a favor. *Human Relations, 22*, 371–378. doi:http://dx.doi.org.er.lib.k-state.edu/10.1177/001872676902200407

Lewin, K., Lippitt, R., & White, R. K. (1939). Patterns of aggressive behavior in experimentally created "social climates". *The Journal of Social Psychology, 10*(2), 269–299. doi:http://dx.doi.org.er.lib.k-state.edu/10.1080/00224545.1939.9713366

Lilienfeld, S. O., Lynn, S. J., Ruscio, J., & Beyerstein, B. L. (2010). *50 great myths of popular psychology: Shattering widespread misconceptions about human behavior*. Malden, MA: Wiley-Blackwell.

McDougall, W. (1908). *An introduction to social psychology*. Londres, Argentina: Methuen. doi:http://dx.doi.org.er.lib.k-state.edu/10.1037/12261-000

Milgram, S. (1963). Behavioral study of obedience. *The Journal of Abnormal and Social Psychology, 67*(4), 371. doi:http://dx.doi.org.er.lib.k-state.edu/10.1037/h0040525

Petrie, D. (Director), Evans, R. (Producer), Forsyth-Peters, C. (Producer), & Obst, L. (Producer). (2003). *How to lose a guy in 10 days* [Motion picture]. United States: Paramount Pictures.

Ross, E. A. (1908). *Social psychology: An outline and source book*. New York, NY: Macmillan. doi:http://dx.doi.org.er.lib.k-state.edu/10.1037/11416-000

Ross, L., Lepper, M., & Ward, A. (2010). History of social psychology: Insights, challenges, and contributions to theory and application. In S. T. Fiske, D. T. Gilbert, & G. Lindzey (Eds.), *Handbook of social psychology* (pp. 3–50). Hoboken, NJ: John Wiley & Sons.

Triplett, N. (1898). The dynamogenic factors in pace-making and competition. *American Journal of Psychology, 9*, 507–533. doi:http://dx.doi.org.er.lib.k-state.edu/10.2307/1412188

Walster (Hatfield), E., Aronson, E., & Abrahams, D. (1966). On increasing the persuasiveness of a low-prestige communicator. *Journal of Experimental Social Psychology, 2*, 325–342. doi:http://dx.doi.org.er.lib.k-state.edu/10.1016/0022-1031(66)90026-6

Chapter Two
Research Methods

Dr. Donna Stuber and Kristina Thielen

Friends University

Learning Objectives

- Identify and explain the goals of scientific research
- Understand the difference between basic and applied research and list the pros and cons of each
- Explain the steps in the research process
- Compare and contrast experimental and nonexperimental research and define the terms associated with each

Chapter Outline

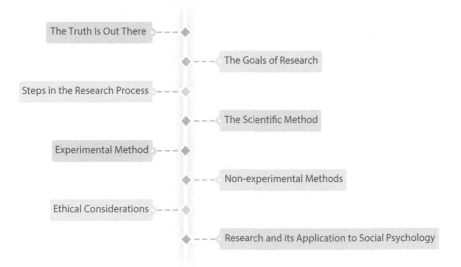

- The Truth Is Out There
- The Goals of Research
- Steps in the Research Process
- The Scientific Method
- Experimental Method
- Non-experimental Methods
- Ethical Considerations
- Research and its Application to Social Psychology

Bruce Rolff/Shutterstock.com

The Truth Is Out There

In watching the daily news, we often hear the phrase "Studies show . . ." followed by an assertion about the state of society. "Studies show at least 35% of American teenagers have used drugs or alcohol in the last year" or "Studies show 40% of college students suffer from depression during their freshman year." It is not uncommon to take these assertions at face value. After all, "studies" must prove whatever is being said, right? The answer to that question is yes, no, and maybe.

Psychological research is rooted in the idea that science-based answers are more reliable than anecdotes, intuition, and personal beliefs regarding societies. Although these methods of examining social structures are easier to access, they are unlikely to yield accurate results and do little to further actual scientific understanding. Nonscientific methods are prone to several known pitfalls, including **confirmation bias**, **stereotyping**, **hindsight bias**, and **anchoring bias**, to name a few. Rather than relying upon faulty or flimsy reasoning, research in social psychology seeks to use the **scientific method** to gather **empirical evidence** that supports or does not support a hypothesis.

Confirmation Bias
A type of cognitive bias that involves favoring information that confirms previously existing beliefs.

Stereotyping
Overgeneralized beliefs about a group or class of people; an experimenter's stereotypes can creep into the method, thus invalidating the results.

Hindsight Bias
Also known as the "I knew it all along" effect; the tendency to view events as being more predictable than they really are.

Anchoring Bias
A decision or evaluation based on the first piece of information received, even if the anchor contains incomplete or irrelevant information.

The scientific method is characterized by four essential components: objectivity, confirmation of findings, self-correction, and control (Smith & Davis, 2013). Objectivity means that the researcher avoids bias. This is important in all aspects of the study from its initial design to selection of participants to data collection to the final interpretation. Along with objectivity, psychologists must ensure that their findings can be confirmed. This is achieved by ensuring that their findings are both valid and replicable.

Perhaps the most significant component in this process is that science is self-correcting. Although most psychologists go to great lengths to design well-thought out investigations, errors can be made. Moreover, times and situations may change. For example, what was generalizable in the 1950s may not be in the 21st century. Ongoing research, often including modern studies that replicate earlier studies, is important for just this reason.

Finally, whether we directly manipulate or reduce extraneous factors, good control means the results accurately reflect the natural world.

The Goals of Research

The scientific method provides the foundation to systematically study human behavior and mental processes. It consists of procedures used to gather, analyze, and interpret information that leads to verifiable generalizations. Social psychologists are engaged in both basic and applied research. The purpose of **basic research** is to gain a greater knowledge or understanding. In contrast, the focus of **applied research** is to increase our ability to relate results to particular situations and find solutions to everyday problems. The knowledge gained from basic research provides applied researchers with a better understanding of how to solve real-world problems. Similarly, basic researchers can take what was learned through applied research and expand or refine for further study. These two goals do not compete but rather work hand-in-hand and are each equally important.

Table 2.1: Comparison of the Pros and Cons of Basic and Applied Research

Types of Research	Pros	Cons
Applied	Practical "real-world" value	Results may relate only to specific group studied Limited control of testing conditions
Basic	Good control of testing conditions Findings of significance and value to society in general	Results may have limited direct application

Although applied research usually offers immediate application, basic research leads to broader generalizations and found theoretical implications (Stanovich, 2010). Table 2.1 lists some of the pros and cons of basic and applied research. As can be gleaned, the pros of one type of research are often considered cons in the other.

Steps in the Research Process

Research ideas do not develop in a vacuum. Rather, inspiration can come from a variety of sources, such as an incident in the daily news, personal experiences, and even someone else's study. Once a topic of interest is determined, the researcher must follow a series of steps. First, the researcher must identify the problem. This is accomplished through a thorough search of the scientific literature to see what has previously been investigated. Psychologists can also find current studies through reputable Internet sites, by attending regional or national conventions, or through contact with colleagues at other colleges and universities. It is vital that the problem is testable; this means the research, whether basic or applied, can be studied through a series of systematic techniques. Extrasensory perception (ESP) might be an interesting topic; but with the technology available, it cannot be measured. However, belief in ESP is certainly a measurable topic.

After the problem has been identified, the researcher then formulates the hypothesis. The third step is to design the study to test the hypothesis. The study must be designed in a way that minimizes error and leads to dependable generalizations.

The next two steps require collecting and analyzing the data. Statistical methods allow social psychologists to determine whether the hypothesis can be supported.

The final step is to share the results with the scientific community through conference presentation and/or publication. Researchers are expected to report exactly what was done and what was found. The presentation of the material must be presented in a clear, unambiguous style so that others can replicate the study. See Figure 2.1 for a summary of this process.

Scientific Method
A way to ask and systematically answer questions through careful observations; it consists of procedures used to gather, analyze, and interpret information that leads to verifiable generalizations.

Empirical Evidence
Information acquired by careful observation or experimentation. The data are recorded and analyzed and is a central process of the scientific method.

Basic Research
Research is primarily directed toward greater knowledge or understanding.

Applied Research
Research is primarily meant to increase our understanding and find solutions to everyday problems.

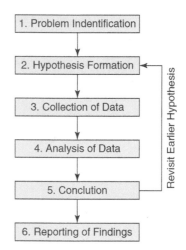

Figure 2.1 flow chart:

1. Problem Indentification
↓
2. Hypothesis Formation
↓
3. Collection of Data
↓
4. Analysis of Data
↓
5. Conclusion
↓
6. Reporting of Findings

Revisit Earlier Hypothesis

Figure 2.1.   Steps in research process.

Experimental Method
The prime method of inquiry in science. Its features are control over the variables, careful measurement, and establishing cause and effect relationships.

The Scientific Method

Social psychologists use two methods to study people—experimental methods and nonexperimental methods. The **experimental method** involves manipulation; the researcher changes and controls something in the environment or situation and then observes to see what happens. Experimental research allows the researcher to determine if there is a cause/effect relationship.

Nonexperimental methods allow social psychologists to conduct investigations in situations in which manipulation or control is impossible or unethical. For example, researchers cannot manipulate age or randomly assign participants to be older or younger. Instead, we might correlate the relationship between age and degree of loneliness. Additionally, it would be unethical to assign participants to live in isolation for 12 months simply to study how long it takes for them to get lonely.

scyther5/Shutterstock.com

Nonexperimental Methods
A label given to a study when variables cannot be controlled or manipulated; cannot demonstrate a true cause and effect relationship.

Theory
An organized set of concepts tied together in a logical way.

Experimental Method

As previously noted, if the experimental method involves purposeful modification, through manipulation and control, we can determine causality. Systematic observations involve a series of steps to ensure the method is clear and replicable. Often terms and concepts have broader meanings because they are based on different perspectives or approaches. In order to provide direction, researchers need to choose the direction. The way to find a focus is to first begin with a theory. A **theory** is a set of ideas or constructs tied together in a logical way. For example, a psychologist may want to ask why people change their minds. Approaching the study under the umbrella of Cognitive Dissonance Theory could provide direction to the study.

We've all heard the phrase, "it's just a theory." One common mistake people make is using the term "theory" when they really mean "hypothesis." A theory is more than a hunch; it is a widely accepted set of ideas based on repeated observation and testing. For example, in the 1950s, Leon Festinger (1957) developed his theory of cognitive dissonance. Cognitive dissonance is a state of uneasiness that develops when cognitions (or thoughts) and behaviors are contradictory. It creates an unpleasant psychological tension that subsequently motivates an individual to try to resolve this dissonance usually by changing his or her thinking rather than the behavior. Festinger and others conducted numerous studies that eventually led to a set of principles to explain the theory of cognitive dissonance.

A theory is based on a set of principles that provides direction, which leads to a hypothesis. In essence, hypotheses are generated from theories. A **hypothesis** is a testable prediction about a specific outcome. In experimental research, hypotheses are typically stated as if/then statements—it is hypothesized that if a specific stimulus is presented, then this will result in a defined reaction.

For example, we know that people are well educated about the long-term effects of smoking; they know smoking can lead to lung cancer and other serious health problems (cognition). However, many continue to smoke (behavior). Research in cognitive dissonance theory indicates that people are more likely to change their thinking rather than behavior in an attempt to create a state of harmony between the cognition and the behavior. Can we manipulate or change someone's smoking behavior? Past research has shown that one way to reduce dissonance is to acquire new information. Based on this information, let us hypothesize that showing a short video of real lung cancer patients who have suffered and died as a result of smoking will lead to a change in the participant's smoking behavior. In fact, the Center for Disease Control reports a substantial reduction in smoking through a series of hard-to-watch TV commercials (Park, 2013).

To begin, we must first identify a population. A **population** consists of members of an identifiable group. For example, it could consist of individuals who live in a specific geographic region, age group, economic class, education level, or other group of interest. The important thing is to first define the population. In our example, we might define our population as male, blue collar workers between the ages of 30 and 40. Logistically, it is impossible to attempt to study every man in this particular population. Thus, we would want to randomly select a sample of men from this population. **Random selection** is the process of gathering a representative sample; the randomness means that everyone in the population has an equal chance of being chosen for the study; it assures we are choosing participants without bias. Additionally, through random selection, we are able to generalize the results to the larger population. **Generalization** allows researchers to apply the findings from their sample of subjects to the larger population.

Let's assume there are 10,000 men available in the population. We decide to choose 1,000 participants in a defined geographic radius; in this example, we could choose every 10th person available. Once selected, we would randomly assign these 1,000 men to one of two treatment groups. **Random assignment** means that participants are assigned to either the experimental or control group. Simply stated, the **experimental group** experiences the treatment and the **control group** does not. In experimental research, something is manipulated or changed. The experimental group is exposed to that change. The control group allows researchers to compare the results to the experimental group. It is vital to use a comparison group; otherwise, any change to the experimental group could not be determined.

Hypothesis
A hypothesis is a prediction about a specific outcome; it is used in experimental research to define the relationship between two or more variables.

Population
A total group of individuals from which a sample will be drawn.

Random Selection
A process of gathering a representative sample from a defined population.

Generalization
The extent to which findings can be generalized or extended to the larger population.

Random Assignment
A procedure used to ensure that each participant has the same opportunity to be assigned to any group.

Experimental Group
Refers to the group of participants who are exposed to the treatment (independent variable).

Control Group
Composed of participants who do not receive the treatment. If selection and assignment procedures are properly done, they should closely resemble the experimental group.

IV ➡ DV

Figure 2.2.   Does the IV cause the DV?

Independent Variable
The part of the experiment that is manipulated or changed; it is assumed to have a direct effect on the dependent variable.

Dependent Variable
The measure; what is measured after making changes to the independent variable.

Extraneous Variables
Undesirable influences that can interfere with the outcome of a study.

Control Variables
Variables that are intentionally held constant to minimize the effects on the outcome.

Similar to the selection process, random assignment means that each participant has an equal chance of being assigned to either the experimental or control group. Random assignment attempts to ensure that the groups are equivalent and that there are essentially little to no differences between the groups. If proper selection procedures were used, we can be confident that the experimental and control groups are also equivalent.

As previously noted, the experimental group receives the treatment (i.e., the independent variable). The **independent variable** (IV) is the part of the experiment that is manipulated or changed. It is independent because it stands alone and allows researchers to determine if there is a change in behavior. The **dependent variable** (DV) is the measure. It is what is affected during the experiment. It is the behavior produced as a result of the presentation of the IV. The goal of the experimental method is to determine if there is a cause/effect relationship (see Figure 2.2).

A hallmark of the experimental method is to design the study with as much control as possible. Without good control, it is possible to inadvertently generate **extraneous variables**, which are undesirable, outside influences that can inadvertently affect the outcome, and thus, affect the interpretation of the study. It is necessary to remove as many unwanted influences as possible and keep the design and method consistent for both the experimental and control groups. We do this through **control variables**, which are constant, unchanging standards of comparison. Control variables are intentionally kept constant to minimize the effects on the outcomes. Essentially, both experimental conditions are the same for both groups except the independent variable. Figure 2.3 contains an example of a two-group experimental design.

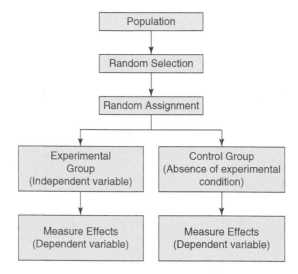

Figure 2.3.   Sample two-group experimental design.

Nonexperimental Methods

As previously noted, not all studies can or should be investigated through manipulation and control. Although nonexperimental research does not determine cause and effect relationships, these types of methods are often better suited to the types of questions being asked and can clearly contribute to the body of knowledge.

For example, there is a real-life "experiment" going on in Gloucester, MA, regarding opiate addiction (DiNatale, 2015). The Gloucester Police Department (GPD) has embarked upon a project to help its community with a crushing opioid overdose epidemic. The GPD has made it known that they will take any addict who appears in their stations to ask for help, assign them an "angel" to accompany them through treatment, and follow-up with them afterward. The addicts will not face criminal charges as long as they turn over their current "stash" (the amount of drug they currently possess) and "works" (the means to introduce the drug into their body, including needles, syringes, and spoons). This is nonexperimental because addicts are not randomly assigned to either an experimental or control group; it would also be unethical to deny treatment to those who seek it. Thus, the personnel who are monitoring the program cannot assign participants to "control" and "treatment" groups. The "control" group are inherently those who choose not to participate, and the "treatment" group are those who self-select to receive treatment. The GPD has had substantial success helping addicts recover from opiate addiction.

Correlational Research

Correlational research allows us to determine if there is an association between two variables, because if there is no manipulation, a cause/effect relationship cannot be made. Correlational research is an effective method to employ, especially if manipulation is not practical or ethical. Variables can be either positively or negatively related. A **positive correlation** means the variables move in the same direction. Conversely, a **negative correlation** means the variables move in opposite directions.

The illustration below can help you visualize these relationships.

For example, it can be conceptualized that 40% of inner city youth are convicted of crimes before their 18th birthday, and that part of the reason they commit crimes is that their families earn wages that fall beneath the poverty line. There is no real way to "test" the hypothesis, as we cannot ethically assign subjects to live above or below poverty-level wages. The best that can be done to

Correlational Research
A way to determine which two variables are connected.

Positive Correlation
The variables move in the same direction; both can either move up or move down.

Negative Correlation
The variables move in the opposite direction; the variables are inversely related.

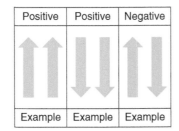

Figure 2.4.   Positive and negative correlation.

try to explain the high juvenile delinquency of the inner city is to find variables that positively correlate with the high crime rate. We might also investigate high school dropout rates, parental divorce rates, drug usage rates, domestic violence rates, rates of participation in after school programs or church programs, and teen pregnancy rates.

No matter what aspect is investigated, the reality is that we cannot draw cause and effect lines by the questions we are asking, as cause and effect can only be determined when we are able to completely control the variables that are being studied. One last example: we can conduct a study that examines the life satisfaction of people with high incomes versus low incomes; perhaps we find that people with high incomes report being "happy" more often than people with lower incomes. It would be tempting to say, given that outcome, that money buys happiness (money = cause; happiness = effect). As evidenced by miserable millionaires and the pleased but penniless, we know this is not the case. There are other variables at work, but they are not necessarily taken into account with correlational research.

Spurious Variables
Sometimes referred to as a "third variable." A correlation may at first seem to exist, but when further studied, it is clear that an unforeseen variable actually influences the relationship.

These other variables at work are called **spurious variables**, and they are the reason that we can never be sure that correlation equals causation. We can examine whether low high school graduation rates correlate with high juvenile delinquency rates, but we cannot definitively say that graduating high school insulates an individual from committing a crime as a juvenile. Juvenile delinquency rates are also influenced by parental divorce or abandonment rates, self and parental drug use rates, community crime rates, and a whole host of other factors.

Correlational research is generally a stepping stone toward finding actual cause and effect relationships. The type of research rarely gives us the complete answer, but it can clearly point us in the right direction when we are looking to solve a more complex puzzle.

Naturalistic Observation

Naturalistic observation is yet another way to investigate how people interact within social groups. As with other forms of nonexperimental research, this does not involve manipulating the research subjects. In naturalistic observation, the researcher simply observes behavior in the natural environment without affecting the situation. An example of this type of research may be a researcher of bullying behavior who follows a subject during a few days in a normal high school environment. The researcher will make every effort not to influence what goes on, so will only record what is witnessed.

Hawthorne Effect
Also referred to as the "reactivity effect." A psychological phenomenon that produces improved behavior or performance as a result of increased attention from others.

Again, as the variables are not consciously manipulated, this is considered nonexperimental research. The researcher cannot report on anything other than what is observed, and no generalizable conclusions can be drawn from this research. Another drawback of naturalistic observation research is the Observer, or **Hawthorne effect**. The Hawthorne effect, was so named due to an experiment conducted in a Hawthorne Works electric factory outside of Chicago in the 1920s to 1950s that sought to

Kaspars Grinvalds/Shutterstock.com

explore whether changes in work environment conditions would create positive changes in worker productivity (Mayo, 1949). The actual result of the study showed that increases in work productivity were caused more by the presence of interested observers than by the changes in environmental conditions. This behavior is seen in a variety of real-world settings. For example, students might work harder if there is an important visitor in the classroom. Employees tend to work harder when the boss is watching them work.

Survey Research

Nearly all of us have encountered survey research at one time or another. Many of us have called the phone number or visited the web address on the back of a restaurant receipt and answered questions about food quality and customer service; this is survey research. Survey research is one of the most common methods of investigating research questions because it is relatively easy to carry out and analyze. Questions on a survey may be presented as multiple choice, utilize a **Likert-type scale**, or be open ended.

Although survey research is common, there are also some drawbacks to using it. The fast food receipt example above showcases one of those drawbacks: the customers who choose to participate in the survey are likely to either be very happy or very unhappy with their experience at the restaurant, and so the results may not represent the real opinions of *all* customers. It is probably more common for a customer to have an "average" experience at a fast food restaurant, but if nothing went badly, customers are unlikely to be interested in completing a survey. This is considered a **self-selection bias** and must be taken into consideration when trying to determine whether results are generalizable.

Another possible problem with surveys has to deal with the manner in which questions are phrased. For example, if a question on a survey asked about an individual's belief regarding abortion, the answer given may be influenced by whether the phrases used are "pro-life" and "pro-abortion" or "anti-abortion" and "pro-choice."

Archival Research

Archival research uses already existing data to try to answer research questions. For example, researchers at the University of Chicago conduct the General Social Survey (GSS) every other year. The results of the hundreds of questions asked in the GSS are kept in a large database that is made available to researchers who want to try to draw conclusions by analyzing different pieces of data. In this type of research, the data collection has already been done, and the researcher's job is to find relationships between the variables that are available. Because of the wide array of questions asked in the GSS, it is possible to use the database to study questions such as does the number of hours worked in the last week correlate to the number of alcoholic drinks consumed in the last week? Or, does an individual's religion (or lack of religious affiliation) predict where he or she lives in the United States?

Likert-Type Scale
A fixed choice response format scale designed to measure intensity of attitudes or opinions; respondents may be offered a choice of five to seven or even nine precoded responses with the neutral point being neither agree nor disagree.

Self-Selection Bias
Results when survey respondents decide entirely for themselves whether or not they want to participate; the decision to participate is often determined by respondents' motivation (e.g., dissatisfied with a product or service).

The GSS is not the only archival data available to researchers. In fact, hundreds upon thousands of data sets exist for research use, including the US Census, the FBI's Uniform Crime Report and National Incident Based Reporting System databases, and the Center for Disease Control's Interactive Database Systems. The existence of these data sets is very helpful to researchers, and archival research is a very commonly used tool.

Although archival research is a very useful method of answering questions, we are limited by what was originally recorded; this is called **selective deposit**. Essentially, we are at the mercy of what the person or persons left for others to access. Selective deposit occurs when biases influence whether information is recorded, or deposited in an archival record, or whether a record is made at all. Older records are especially at risk for being missing or incomplete.

Selective Deposit
Occurs when biases influence what information is recorded or deposited in an archival record.

Meta-Analysis

Meta-analytical studies utilize statistical methods for comparing and contrasting multiple investigations simultaneously. Data are combined in order to identify patterns among these studies, discover sources of disagreement, and discuss and interpret interesting or unique relationships. The purpose of a meta-analysis is to help average across the results of multiple studies to find a general assumption. One such investigation (Weaver, 2014) compared the credentials of high school teachers from all 50 states plus the District of Columbia utilizing standardized test to validate candidates' content knowledge. Weaver found that new high school psychology instructors were ill-prepared to teach psychology, per American Psychological Association (APA) standards, which reflects psychology's meager presence in the schools. Through his meta-analysis, Weaver combined relevant results from multiple studies to draw general conclusions about preparedness of secondary education graduates to teach psychology at the high school level.

Institutional Research Board
Usually referred to as an "IRB." A committee established to review and approve research involving human (or animal) subjects; its purpose is to ensure the research is ethical.

Ethical Considerations

Anyone who engages in psychological research is embarking upon a path that requires both responsibility and accountability. First and foremost, conducting psychological research involves ensuring that the investigation itself is ethical, meaning that it does not cause harm to participants. Some of the components of ethical research include submitting a research proposal to an **Institutional Review Board** for approval, obtaining a signed **informed consent** from participants, making it known to participants that they may end their participation without reproach, and to debriefing participants at the end of the investigation.

Although these requirements may seem to be common sense, attention to ethical research guidelines began to appear only within the past 50 years or so. There are several examples of why such ethical guidelines are necessary, and two of the most famous (or infamous) are Philip Zimbardo's Stanford Prison Experiment (Haney, Banks, & Zimbardo, 1973) and Stanley Milgram's (1974) studies of obedience.

Although both studies are detailed in other later chapters, the investigators clearly caused undue harm to their subjects. One major violation seen in both studies was placing undue emotional stress on participants. Based on research ethics established by the APA (2010), neither of these studies would be ethical to replicate.

Informed Consent
A document received by research participants before the study begins. Participants are made aware of the study procedures, including any potential harm they might experience, so they can decide whether or not to participate.

THINKING CRITICALLY

A newspaper headline reads, "Heavy Drinking in College Leads to Increased Aggression."

Questions:
1. What claims are being made from this headline? Why is it misleading?
2. Why would it be unethical to design this study using the experimental method?
3. Can you predict the results of this study using the correlational method? Determine if this would be a positive or negative relationship?
4. What other variables could affect drinking or aggressive behavior?

Research and Its Application to Social Psychology

Research is a core activity in social psychology. Whether social psychologists' focus is on basic or applied research, the topics are concerned with the interaction of people and how they behave in the presence of others. Research in social psychology, whether theory-driven or practical, gives us the ability to better understand psychological processes and how relationships with others are affected by the social context in which people find themselves.

Rawpixel/Shutterstock.com

References

American Psychological Association. (2003, amended 2010). *Ethical principles of psychologists and code of conduct.* Washington, DC: Author.

DiNatale, S. (2015, August 14). More than 100 sent to drug treatment in Gloucester police program. *Globe Correspondent.* Retrieved from https://www.bostonglobe.com/metro/2015/08/14/gloucester-police-have-sent-more-than-for-drug-treatment/9dTb8pLEx9h9oln2ykRIKO/story.html

Festinger, L. (1957). *A theory of cognitive dissonance.* Evanston, IL: Row, Peterson.

Haney, C., Banks, W. C., & Zimbardo, P. G. (1973). Interpersonal dynamics in a simulated prison. *International Journal of Criminology and Penology, 1,* 69–97.

Mayo, E. (1949) *Hawthorne and the Western Electric Company: The social problems of an industrial civilization.* London, UK: Routledge.

Milgram, S. (1974). *Obedience to authority: An experimental view.* New York, NY: Harper Collins.

Park, A. (2013, September 9). First national anti-smoking TV ads help 200,000 smokers to quit. *Time,* 11 paragraphs. Retrieved from http://healthland.time.com/2013/09/09/first-national-anti-smoking-tv-ads-help-200000-smokers-to-quit/

Smith, R. A., & Davis, S. F. (2013). *Psychologist as detective: An introduction to conducting research in psychology.* Upper Saddle River, NJ: Pearson/Prentice Hall.

Stanovich, K. (2010). *How to think straight about psychology* (9th ed.). Boston, MA: Pearson.

Weaver, K. A. (2014). Credentialing high school psychology teachers. *American Psychologist, 69*(6), 612–619. doi:10.1037/a0036574

Chapter Three
Social Cognition: A World of Beliefs

Dr. Drew A. Curtis

Angelo State University

Learning Objectives

- Define social cognition
- Differentiate types of thinking
- Explain the role of beliefs within thinking
- Discuss paradoxical features of thinking
- Examine the impact of expectations on behavior
- Analyze the process of forming impressions
- Describe aspects of nonverbal behavior
- List common emotions recognized cross-culturally
- Explain aspects of deception and detection accuracy
- Identify the process of attributions
- Recognize human error in thinking and biases

Chapter Outline

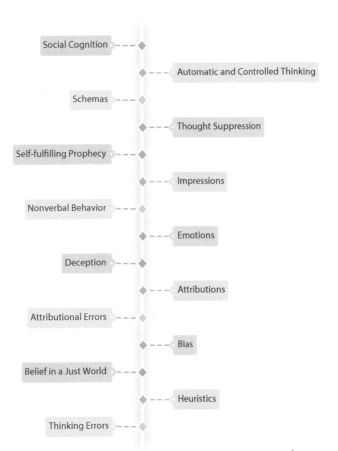

Social Cognition

Automatic and Controlled Thinking

Schemas

Thought Suppression

Self-fulfilling Prophecy

Impressions

Nonverbal Behavior

Emotions

Deception

Attributions

Attributional Errors

Bias

Belief in a Just World

Heuristics

Thinking Errors

Social Cognition

Who is ready to play a game? You? Let's try it! I want you to do your best to not think about something. I want you to try your hardest to not think about the pinky-toe that is on your left foot. Do it! Do not think about it! Do not think about the pinky-toe that is on your left foot. Pause right now and try your hardest to not think about the pinky-toe on your left foot. Well? Were you successful? Were you able to not, at all, think about the pinky-toe on your left foot? I am guessing you thought about it at least once. We will revisit why you thought about your pinky-toe, in more detail, later.

Before reading this chapter, you were most likely not even aware of your pinky-toe. It is also highly likely you will not be thinking of your toe shortly after reading this chapter. This demonstrates facets of thinking that are crucial to understanding social cognition. The power of our thinking is immense. The thoughts we have may shape our experiences and influence our behaviors and emotions. Every time we think about how we think, also called **metacognition**, it is amazing to consider how something that we do so frequently yields so much power within our lives. Thus, **social cognition** is how thinking about our social world and understanding it influences situations and our behaviors.

Social world.

Metacognition
Thinking about thinking.

Social Cognition
Thinking processes related to social contexts.

Automatic Thinking
Quick, reflexive, and effortless thinking.

The Power of Thoughts: Thinking and Beliefs

Automatic Thinking

Before the pinky-toe activity, much of your thinking was on auto-pilot or you were engaging in **automatic thinking**. Automatic thinking is the quick, nondeliberate, reflexive, and seemingly minimal effort thinking that we engage most of the time. Judith Beck (2011), a prominent psychology professor and therapist, considers automatic thoughts as the words or pictures that go through our minds and are the most readily available. This type of thinking is one method of how many people think about themselves and their social world. Given that we engage in a variety social situations in our daily lives, there are multiple opportunities to interpret those situations and how they become interpreted often indicates the automatic thoughts we possess. Essentially, we understand a large percentage of our social world with influence from our automatic thoughts. Further, these thoughts are evidence of how we understand our social world.

Automatic thinking can be an efficient means for thinking and often has innocuous effects. The fact that this type of thinking involves minimal effort means that it may serve you well in a variety of social situations. For example, late at night you are entering your car in a store parking lot and a man quickly moves into your vision from behind your car, you might automatically think that this is dangerous and get in your car quickly. If the man were a threat, then it would benefit you to quickly process that information as a threat. There are numerous situations where our automatic thinking may help us avoid harm and serve us well. However, the downside of efficiency in thinking is human error. For example, had the man been a helpful pedestrian who was quickly trying to get your attention to let you know that you left some of your groceries in the shopping cart, then the automatic thought of danger would have been an error and not have served you well. Let's consider another aspect of how automatic thinking may be potentially harmful or erroneous.

I am a failure! I can do nothing right. Every time that I try to study for class, things come up or something draws my attention away from reading. It seems pointless. I try studying for hours, I go to class, and I even like the lectures. However, somehow, it all doesn't matter. When I do read, I notice that everyone else is reading so much faster than me. I am a slow reader. I take so much time to read one page while every other student is two pages ahead of me. I am a failure. I should just quit school and find something else to do. I will never amount to anything anyway.

Hopefully, you do not think of yourself as a failure. However, a number of people do. These automatic thoughts stem from beliefs that people already hold, which begin to develop at a very early age and persist throughout the life-span. Beck (2011) refers to these beliefs as **core beliefs**. These beliefs are the foundational deep-rooted beliefs that you hold. In fact, as babies, we are like little scientists trying to figure out ourselves and our world. Specifically, we are even interested in discerning our social world. As babies, we have preferences for people compared to inanimate objects (Gopnick, Meltzoff, & Kuhl, 2001). As we live and experience countless social situations, those experiences get processed, organized, and become the basis for our beliefs.

Core Beliefs
Foundational beliefs developed at an early age and persist.

Schemas

The organization of information about ourselves and our social world is referred to as a **schema**. Our schemas are the consolidation of experiences and the way we interpreted those experiences from infancy (Piaget, 1954). Thus, social schemas are the beliefs we have about ourselves and others within social contexts.

Schema
Organization of information about one's self and social world.

Piaget asserted that schemas are largely developed through the processes of assimilation and accommodation. As early as being little scientists, we test the world and look for consistencies. Information that is consistent with our experiences become solidified beliefs and information not consistent becomes rejected. Consider tossing a pen up into the air. What would happen? You are using your schema when you answer this question. If you think that the pen would fall down to the ground, then you are relying on a schema built around the concept of gravity. You learned about gravity from an early age. Gravity became apparent when you began to walk and you fell. Think back to riding a

Peter Bernik/Shutterstock.com

bicycle. If you fell down after taking the training wheels off or while performing a stunt, then you began to solidify the concept of gravity, which Isaac Newton knew all too well.

Our schemas offer us a sense of consistency, completeness, and resolution about how our social world works. Gestalt and existential psychologists refer to this as our need for completeness, consistency, and closure (Baumesiter, 1991; Perls, Hefferline, & Goodman, 1951). We like things to be wrapped up in a nice bow. Let me demonstrate this need. I would like you to sing along to a classic song, which you can do in your head or out loud. Ready? Row, row, row your boat, gently down the stream, merrily, merrily, merrily, merrily, life is but a . . . .

Did you do it? Did you finish the end? You probably did because it would irk you a bit not to complete it. This demonstrates our need for completeness and closure. You cannot let the song end as "life is but a." No, you must complete it with, "life is but a dream." It feels unsettling to sing the song and not finish it with these lyrics. Similar to completing the lyric of the song, you yearn for your social world to be complete and resolved.

This human need for completeness can even be found in the television show called *Big Bang Theory*. One of the characters, Amy, attempts to reduce another character's, Sheldon, need for completeness and closure through a series of tasks. She erases a game of tic-tac-toe before Sheldon completes it and wins. Amy has Sheldon sing the Star Spangled Banner and ends the song before he can sing the final lyric, brave. Amy even asks Sheldon to make a wish and blow out his birthday candles but keeps him from blowing out the final candle. To see this need for closure and attempts to stop it, please check out the following Youtube clip: https://www.youtube.com/watch?v=Vm1-szIev3c.

In an effort to achieve complete and resolved beliefs, we will use experiences that confirm our schemas or may have to rework our schemas (i.e., assimilation and accommodation). However, our beliefs may become so crystallized that they do not change even when information is contrary to the belief (Anderson, 2007). This concept is referred to as **belief perseverance**.

Belief Perseverance
The continuation of a belief even when presented with contrary evidence.

Think back to the example above about being a failure. Let's say that this person has a grade point average of a 4.0. Now, many of us would think that this person's thinking of being a failure is ludicrous, given that there is evidence that the person is not a failure. A person who holds a rigid belief of being a failure would dismiss this evidence and look for other evidence to confirm his or her thinking. Therefore, rather than assuming other people are not meticulously reading and comprehending the material, this person thinks that he or she is a slow reader when compared to others. Thus, the power of our social schemas is weighty when considering how it influences our social behaviors. Our schemas are so deeply rooted that not only do beliefs persevere in the face of evidence that suggests otherwise, but information is also sought out to confirm the existing beliefs we have.

Faulty beliefs may develop from a number of influential sources. Let's consider deception. How can you tell when someone is lying to you? What is the first thing you think of? When people lie, do they tend to look away, or even look in a particular direction, say to the left? This is one of the more commonly held beliefs about deceptive behavior, which is also not a reliable indicator of deception. Across a variety of cultures, one of the most salient beliefs about deceptive behavior was that people look away when they are lying (Global Deception Research Team, 2006). However, research has indicated that eye gaze aversion is not a reliable indicator of deception (Vrij, 2008). Beliefs like these may be developed through cultural creations of the liar stereotype and even perpetuated within literature or media (Global Deception Research Team, 2006; Vrij, 2008). Even professionals have been shown to hold a number of these inaccurate beliefs (Curtis, 2015; Curtis & Hart, 2015).

Our beliefs shape our social world and our social world influences our beliefs. These schemas serve as the foundation for much of our thinking. However, through intentional thinking we may evaluate our schemas and consider how they might influence us.

Controlled Thinking

The intentional, deliberate, and effortful thinking is referred to as **controlled thinking**. This type of thinking is the thinking you used at the beginning of the chapter when you were asked to try your hardest to not think about your pinky-toe on your left foot. The moment that you intentionally switched your thought process was when you shifted from automatic thinking to controlled thinking.

Controlled thinking is often executed when confronted with making decisions that seem to have significant consequences. Deciding whether or not to take a certain job, what university to attend, what academic major to pursue, where to live, or what car to purchase are all decisions that may activate the controlled thinking process. By doing so, you are able to suspend information and give consideration to a variety of potential actions and their outcomes. Controlled thinking allows for you to plan, organize, and make informed and well thought-out decisions.

The thought of your pinky-toe even when you were asked to try your hardest to not think of it demonstrates a concept referred to as the paradoxical effects of **thought suppression**. Wegner, Schneider, Carter, and White (1987) were the pioneer researchers who studied this effect. Instead of using a pinky-toe, Wegner and colleagues illustrated these effects through asking participants to not think of a white bear. In their experiment, they randomly assigned participants to one of two conditions, a suppression or expression condition. In both conditions, participants were asked to read a set of instructions and report on their thoughts. Participants in the suppression condition were asked to verbalize their thoughts and to try not to think of a white bear. The participants were instructed to ring a bell each time they thought of a white bear. After being told to not think of a white bear, they were asked to try to think of a white bear. The expression condition did the same thing but in reverse order. The findings revealed that intentional thought suppression led to fixation on the thought. Further, when informed to express their thought, participants thought more about the white bear after being informed to not think about the white bear compared to the condition that was informed to initially express thoughts about a white bear. This phenomenon is referred to as the paradoxical effects of thought suppression because as we exert more effort to actively not think of something, we end up thinking about it more, thus, the paradox or irony.

How would this phenomenon be embedded in other aspects of social psychology? When you read about discrimination and prejudices in a later chapter, you may want to remember how actively not thinking about a prejudice attitude may lead to more prejudiced thoughts. Specifically, if you try hard to not think about any negative attitudes you hold toward another person, you may find yourself thinking those thoughts for a longer duration.

Controlled Thinking
Intentional, deliberate, and effortful thinking.

Thought Suppression
The process of actively not thinking about something that leads to thinking about it.

Eric Isselee/Shutterstock.com

Interaction of Automatic and Controlled Thinking

Much of our thinking, as stated earlier, is automatic. However, these automatic thoughts come from those beliefs developed from an early age or from changing beliefs we have, through controlled thinking. However, we have seen how controlled thinking can potentially bring out negative consequences when trying to actively suppress thinking. Thus, one of the ways to avoid the ironic effects of thought suppression would be to utilize an approach from Acceptance and Commitment Therapy (Hayes, Follette, & Linehan, 2004; Hayes, Wilson, Gifford, Follette, & Strosahl, 1996). Essentially, the idea is to not actively try to avoid thinking about something but rather briefly acknowledge your thought and let it pass. For example, if someone experiences an embarrassing situation and wants to not think of how embarrassed they are, then they may perseverate on the thought and continue to feel embarrassed. However, if someone acknowledges that they felt embarrassed without trying to actively not think about being embarrassed, then the embarrassment will pass. The automatic thought becomes a controlled thought, and without trying to suppress the thought, the thought becomes automatic again. This process can be illustrated in Figure 3.1.

This process can be useful for a variety of situations. Let's consider anxiety. Generalized anxiety disorders, only one of a number of anxiety disorders, are found in approximately 2.9% of the US population. Further, about 11.2% of the US population experience panic attacks (American Psychiatric Association [APA], 2013). One of the most common social responses we have with people who experience anxiety or panic attacks is to tell them "just calm down" or "relax." However, when we do this, though we often mean no harm, we tend to participate in heightening anxiety for the individual. The individual who experiences anxiety now actively tries to not be anxious. As we discussed earlier, the ironic effects of doing this type of thinking is that we think about it more. So, when someone tries to not be anxious, they often experience more anxiety because they cannot stop feeling anxious.

Along with this idea of acceptance or acknowledging the thought and letting it pass, there are a variety of other approaches that have been considered and deemed effective strategies for indirect means of thought suppression (Wegner, 2011). One method, focused distraction, involves actively thinking of some other thought or object. So, rather than trying to not think about your pinky-toe, you might try to think about a relaxing day by the water with a cold beverage.

Once again, there are a variety of situations where understanding these ironic effects of thought suppression may promote beneficial outcomes. These situations range from addictions to emotion regulation. So, when you may feel panic or find yourself constantly ruminating on whether you should have the cheeseburger or the salad, you may want to heed advice from the Beatles and just let it be.

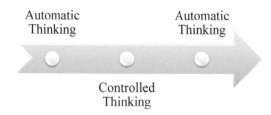

Figure 3.1.   Process of automatic and controlled thinking.

When Expecting It Makes It Happen: Self-Fulfilling Prophecy

Our thoughts, as stated before, are very powerful. Let's examine another aspect of thinking and how it can influence a situation. To do this I would like you to think of a time when you might have been at a party or some social gathering where you met a number of new people. At this function a friend or someone close to you told you something about someone that you would meet at the event, prior to meeting that person, who we will name Hugh. Let's say you were told, "Watch out for Hugh. You will not like him. He is arrogant, always seeking attention, and is just a jerk." So, before you meet Hugh, what do you think? You probably would assume Hugh would be a jerk. When you meet Hugh, due to your expectation, you avoid smiling and quickly say hello without shaking his hands. Due to not being greeted in a friendly manner, Hugh rolls his eyes and says some rude comment. Now, you think, "he really is a jerk."

This demonstrates what is called a **self-fulfilling prophecy**. A self-fulfilling prophecy is the social process of having a preconceived expectation, from a schema, that influences a situation in such a way to confirm that expectation. In other words, this phenomenon is when we think something about someone and our thoughts affect our behavior, which in turn affects the person's behavior, leading to validate what we initially thought of that person. Figure 3.2 shows this process.

This phenomenon was initially discussed in the writing of Robert Merton (1948). Merton (2010) discussed how the power of belief and expectation could influence our behavior and the behavior of others. Later, this idea was investigated by Rosenthal and Jacobson (1968) in their classic study, which explored the impact of teachers' expectations on student achievement. The researchers were concerned with expectancy effects. Simply, how do our beliefs affect our social world. They administered a test with public school elementary students. Then, they informed the teachers that based on the test they discovered that some students were "growth spurters." However, there was not a real testing instrument

Self-Fulfilling Prophecy
The social process of an expectation influencing an other's behavior and confirming the expectation.

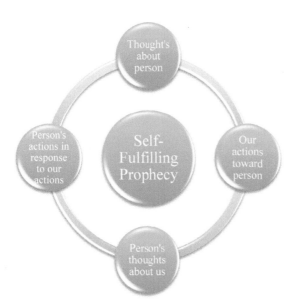

Figure 3.2. The steps involved in the self-fulfilling prophecy.

THINKING CRITICALLY

Think of a similar social function in which your friend tells you about someone you will meet. For sake of childhood nostalgia, let's call this person Mickey Mouse. Your friend tells you that you will meet Mickey Mouse at the social event and that he is "a riot of fun, extremely friendly, and everyone loves him." When Mickey comes through the door, your predetermined ideas about Mickey influence your behavior. Now, describe Mickey's response to you when you warmly welcome Mickey with a smile and a hug versus when you are negative and rolling your eyes at Mickey.

Through the self-fulfilling prophecy, you probably noted that when Mickey is greeted with such pleasantness, then he would extend an equally warm responsive greeting. On the other hand, if Mickey was greeted with an eye roll and unwelcoming demeanor, then he probably would match your greeting and offer an unkind greeting. Thus, his behavior has now confirmed what you initially thought of Mickey.

used to determine this and the students that were deemed "growth spurters" were randomly selected. Rosenthal and Jacobson found, at the end of the school year, that the students who were labeled as "spurters" revealed significantly higher intelligent quotient (IQ) scores compared to other students. The self-fulfilling prophecy, termed the Pygmalion effect by Rosenthal and Jacobson, has been well corroborated over 25 years of subsequent research (Rosenthal, 1995).

The self-fulfilling prophecy does not always have to lead to a negative outcome. In fact, it could work the other way and lead to a positive interaction. To illustrate this, let's turn to the Thinking Critically exercise located at the top of this page.

The power of thinking and beliefs influences our social world. Our mere expectation of social situations has the clout to shape it into a pleasant experience or a daunting one. Recent research has found that the influence of parental beliefs about their children's use of substances is related to their children's actual use (Lamb & Crano, 2014). A national sample of 3,131 parents and adolescent children were recruited for the study. The study implemented a survey that was used at two time periods, one year apart. During each time, children were asked about their use of marijuana during the past 12 months and parents were asked to report on how many times they thought their child used marijuana in the past 12 months. The results revealed children who reported not using marijuana initially and whose parents believed that they were using marijuana had used more marijuana when they were asked during the second time period.

Before you believe something to be true about your child, or someone else, you may want to ask yourself if you would like it to become true. Shift from automatic thinking to controlled thinking when you attend the next social gathering and consider your beliefs about a person before meeting that person, as it could change your whole interaction.

Worth 1000 Words: Forming Impressions

Now that you have thought exhaustively about thinking, consider some of these firsts. Deliberate on the reasons you may dress up for an interview. On a first date, what are the reasons that you put on your best outfit, give your hair some extra attention, spray some nice smelling cologne/perfume, and pop in a few mints? Well, your answer is probably that you might want a second date, assuming all goes well. The idea behind the reasons we do all these things is because we want to make a good impression. With this in mind, it is unfortunate that there are inaccuracies to **first impressions** formed (DePaulo, Hoover, Webb, Kenny, & Oliver, 1987). First impressions are the thoughts and attitudes that people form about others based on limited information and an initial encounter.

Our social world is one in which we encounter a number of new people throughout our day and these are opportunities to make impressions, good or bad. Impressions matter. It can feel stressful to make good first impressions because of the consequences of not doing so. A bad impression may lead to the end of a relationship before it begins or it may lead to not getting the job we wanted. What establishes a good first impression often depends on situational factors. For example, when forming impressions women who smile are perceived as having more warmth compared to men who smile (Hack, 2014). The cues for first impressions may be based on situational and context factors.

The college classroom is one social situation that often presents recurring occasions for impressions. As students on the first day of classes, you typically are sizing up each professor. You might think, "this will be a fun class" or "that teacher was awesome!" Unfortunately, it might be the case that you think, "this is going to be a long class and semester" or "I need to drop this class right away." These thoughts stem from your first impressions of your teachers. In fact, you may establish an impression of teachers as quickly as six seconds (Ambady & Rosenthal, 1993).

Plenty of literature has suggested that first impressions on the first day of class are extremely important (Ambady & Rosenthal, 1993; Anderson, Mcguire, & Cory, 2011; Buchert, Laws, Apperson, & Bregman, 2008; McKeachie & Svinicki, 2006). One particular study found that first impressions of teachers may trump teacher reputations (Buchert et al., 2008). For example, interacting with your teachers on the first day of class may put to death any poor ratings from a web page that is designed for students to rate professors. These reasons are sufficient for many teachers to invest in their first impression on the first day. Rather than the classic roll call, as seen in *Ferris Bueller's Day Off* (Hughes & Jacobson, 2006), or solely reviewing the syllabus, some professors seek to use the first day of class to foster positive first impressions (Curtis & Gray, 2012; Curtis & Cordell-McNulty, 2015).

Another social situation that often involves first impressions is dating. Dating situations call people to attend to other cues. Evolutionary psychology has suggested that men and women look for different components for reproductive success, in which males often seek short-term strategies and females seek long-term strategies (Buss, 1994). Males tend to focus more on aspects of appearance, whereas females place an emphasis on acquiring resources and relational commitment (Buss, 1989). Thus, when making first impressions on a first date each person strives to promote the qualities that the other is looking for. Often, this is done with some degree of deception, namely exaggeration. For example, a man may wear his most expensive outfit, pay for dinner at an expensive restaurant, and may even flash emblems representing high financial gains. Women, on the other hand, may exaggerate physical appearances through clothing, make-up,

First Impressions
Thoughts and attitudes about others based on an initial encounter.

or any other means. However, it has been found that these strategies for exaggerating first impressions may actually be viewed with more suspicion (Cowan, Curtis, & Hart, 2010; Curtis, Cowan, & Hart, 2010).

So, do you only get one shot? If you do not smile and put your best foot forward, are you doomed? Are you able to recover from a wrong first impression? Possibly. Mann and Ferguson (2015) conducted seven experiments and their results corroborated the notion that first impressions can be undone. Their results indicated that the mechanism by which to undo first impressions is through reinterpreting the knowledge that led to the first impression. In one of these experiments, participants were provided with a story about a person who breaks into a house and damages property. Then, participants in the experimental condition were informed that the person who committed the acts did so to save children in the house, whereas the control condition was given more information that the character also threw rocks at the house. Thus, when participants reinterpreted the behavior for a good cause (i.e., saving children), the negative first impression was undone and the character was viewed more positively.

Evaluating Others

The greatest cliché in telling others that you are studying psychology is the response, "are you analyzing me" or some variation of that. It is such a clichéd response that many students of psychology have often offered witty methods for responding, such as "you could not pay me enough" or "I am off the clock." The truth of the matter is that, yes, you are analyzing them. As humans we analyze others. We evaluate people through forming impressions and observing their behavior. Remember, you were once a scientist in the crib. Now, you still remain a scientist, just without the crib.

As young as 42 minutes old, you were evaluating others and able to imitate their expressions (Gopnik, Meltzoff, & Kuhl, 2001). You learn how to imitate a faux pas, sticking out your tongue. Gopnik and colleagues discuss their research involving infants who imitated adults by sticking out their tongues. They suggested that infants must not only observe a facial expression but they must also associate that with an internal feeling in order to imitate. Facial expressions are a form of **nonverbal behavior**. Nonverbal behavior is the means of communication through facial expressions or other body language. As discussed in forming impressions, you make judgments about people based on nonverbal behavior before people say a word (Ambady & Rosenthal, 1993).

Nonverbal Behavior
Behavior used to communicate without the use of words.

People often pick up on these nonverbal behavioral cues more so than the actual content of what you say, when considering initial interactions. If you were to simultaneously shake your fist at somebody and say, "I hope you are well," chances are that the person would assume you were unfriendly because of the nonverbal fist shaking behavior. This is the reason that you may smile when you pass by people on the street or at a store; you want them to assume you are friendly or a nonthreat.

Emotion

Smiling is a nonverbal expression of an emotion. From early on, we learn a variety of other things about people; we learn about emotions. Paul Ekman and Walter Friesen (1971) discovered that people across cultures are able to identify six emotions. Ekman and Friesen studied Neolithic individuals from New Guinea.

Individuals were shown various photographs of emotional expressions and they were read a story that conveyed one of six emotions. Their findings indicated that people across cultures, who had little exposure to other cultural influences, were able to recognize these six emotional expressions. These six emotions are

- Happiness
- Sadness
- Anger
- Surprise
- Disgust
- Fear

Look at these six pictures and see if you can determine which picture matches which of these six emotional labels.

Shutterstock.com

Recognizing emotional expressions is one of the most crucial tools for us to understand our social world. It is a basic way of communicating. Even Disney's newer movie, *Inside Out*, depicts these states of emotion (Rivera & Docter, 2015). Given that there are thousands of variations of languages and dialects, one of the methods that we can use to communicate across cultures is through nonverbal behavior. Nonverbal behavior is the means of behavior that expresses emotions through facial expressions or other body language.

You do not need someone to tell you whether or not your food was tasty, just look at their face. Do they express a smile, revealing happiness or do they wrinkle their nose, showing that they were disgusted? We wear our emotions, which allows us to communicate to others and for use to understand how others feel. However, through various learning channels, you suppress some emotional expressions and reveal others.

One of the most commonly accepted and encouraged emotional expressions is happiness (Lyubomrsky, 2001). We perpetuate the acceptability of this emotional expression over others by sayings such as "just do what makes you happy" or "choose what will bring you the greatest happiness" or "don't worry, be happy." We are less apt to reinforce negative effect, say fear. We rarely or never tell others "just do what makes you afraid" or "choose what will bring you the greatest fear" or "don't worry, be afraid." In turn, people learn to suppress some emotional expressions and reveal others. Specifically, it has been found that women in the United States are more likely to suppress anger expressions and express other emotions (Cox, Stabb, & Hulgus, 2000).

The acceptability of particular emotions is even witnessed in counseling sessions, where you might think people go to work through things and share emotions. In my experiences counseling, a majority of the people when asked how they were doing at the beginning of a session would often report that they were doing well, when they felt sad or some other emotion. People would express sadness through facial expressions but would force a smile or say "but it's nothing." Merely stating "you seem sad" was enough permission for the person to let out any genuine emotion, often eliciting more crying. Though many of these clients learned to suppress emotions, they still revealed emotions through **microexpressions**.

Microexpressions
Brief facial responses that are associated with various emotions.

Microexpressions are the physiological facial responses that are associated with various emotions. These expressions are the reflexive responses that reveal emotion prior to attempts at concealing an emotion (Ekman, 2009). Think about the times you may have been walking to some familiar place where you encountered people you knew. When seeing those people, did you smile when you may not have actually felt happy? What about at work? Have you gone to a job and entered with a smile even though you were not too excited to be there?

Deception

Deception
An intentional attempt to have someone else believe something you consider to be untrue.

There are a number of situations where you may suppress your emotional expressions and almost automatically express an acceptable emotional expression. On the other hand, there are instances where you intentionally suppress or express an emotion to have another person believe you are feeling a certain way. This would be considered an example of deception. **Deception** is defined as "a successful or unsuccessful deliberate attempt, without forewarning, to create in another a belief which the communicator considers to be untrue" (Vrij, 2008, p. 15).

As noted previously, people do not always convey an emotional expression that is congruent with how they feel. Thus, when you attempt to evaluate others, you often are faced with some

PathDoc/Shutterstock.com

barriers, deception being one of those. Simply, people lie. People lie approximately two times per day, to a variety of people (DePaulo, 2009; DePaulo & Bell, 1996).

Many studies have sought to unravel the various factors that lead to more successful rates of deception detection (Vrij, 2008). One avenue for detecting deception has been through the training and recognition of microexpressions (Paul Ekman Group, LLC, 2014). Attention to this route for detecting deception has gained so much attention that a television series, *Lie to Me*, began airing in January 2009, based on Ekman's work (Lie to Me, 2010). However, note that though the show is entertaining, merely watching this series will not make you a better lie detector (Levine, Serota, & Shulman, 2010).

Though people are relatively good at lying, they are not very good at detecting when someone is lying (Bond & DePaulo, 2006; Vrij, 2008). Moreover, analysis of 206 deception detection studies found that people are only slightly better than chance in detecting deception, around 54% accuracy (Bond & DePaulo, 2006). The reasons you may not be good at detecting deception are numerous. One of these reasons is that people hold a truth bias, in which you often assume most interactions are truthful (Vrij, 2008). Another reason is that people hold inaccurate beliefs about deceptive behavior (Forrest, Feldman, & Tyler, 2004; Global Deception Research Team, 2006).

You learn much from others through these channels of communication, unless they are actively seeking to conceal things from you. However, whether discerning emotion or the veracity of others' statements, you are constantly seeking information from others to navigate your social world. Another way that you evaluate your social context is through trying to explain the behavior of others.

Attributions

What is going on with this person? Why might he be homeless? Take a few minutes and write down your automatic thoughts, those first thoughts you had about why this person is homeless.

Well? This process you just undertook is the process of making **attributions**. Attribution theory was largely developed by Fritz Heider (1958) who posited that we seek to explain the reasons for others' behaviors. Further, our explanations of others' behaviors may be explained internally or externally. When you tried to explain why the man might be homeless, you were generating attributions. Maybe you thought the man is homeless because he is alcoholic, lazy, and depressed, does not care about life, has a mental disorder, or is financially inept.

If you thought any of these thoughts, then you would have formed what is known as **internal attributions**. These attributions essentially mean that when we try to explain why someone might be in their current situation, we think about personal aspects or their disposition that contributed to their situation. For example, witnessing someone get into an automobile accident may elicit these attributions. If you thought that they were irresponsible, careless, unaware, or bad drivers, then you made an internal attribution.

In revisiting the picture of the homeless man, maybe you had other thoughts. If you thought that the man had his house burned down, lost his job, or was recently divorced, then you produced **external attributions**. External attributions are explaining the causes of others' behaviors through favoring situational factors. Using the previous automobile accident example, you may have executed

Attributions
The process of explaining others' behaviors.

Internal Attributions
Explaining others' behaviors through dispositional factors.

External Attributions
Explaining others' behaviors through situational factors.

external attributions if you thought that the car accident was due to faulty tires, poor road conditions, or a piston that blew.

These attributions shape the way you interpret your social world. Would it matter to you if an automobile accident was due to a careless driver or due to a mechanical failure? Would it possibly change how you handled the situation or the person? You may incorrectly judge a situation based on making one particular attribution over the other.

Fundamental Attribution Error

The day was going as I had planned. I felt competent and in control of everything. As I noticed the amount of time I had before class started, I realized I would have to hurry to make it to class in time and catch my breath before lecturing. As I was running across campus and thinking, I got this, I approached the stairs to the building. As I tried an elegant James Bond type of jump up the stairs, I tripped and fell down. Embarrassment set in as people around me ceased walking toward their next class to catch a glance at the clumsy teacher. I was not so cool and smart now.

Have you ever been the one who watched someone like me fall down stairs? If so, you might have laughed and thought of those dispositional attributions. You may have thought that the person was clumsy, had two-left feet, was careless, unaware, or awkward. When you observe other people and try to explain their behavior, there is a tendency to explain others' behaviors through dispositional attributions more frequently than situational attributions, which is known as the **fundamental attribution error** (Ross, 1977).

Fundamental Attribution Error
Tendency to explain others' behaviors through disposition more frequently than situation.

We make these fundamental attribution errors often in our lives. Think of the times when you observe others and explain why they did something. It was because of who they are, right? Let's contemplate another situation where we might do this. Think of the people that you have caught lying. Why did they lie? You probably considered the reason they lied is because they are liars, have no consideration for others, are callous, or are just horrible people. The fundamental attribution has been discovered to even be a hindrance in detection deception (O'Sullivan, 2003). Dispositional attributions of trustworthiness were correlated with truthfulness. Thus, you would be less likely to detect deception if you make dispositional attributions about individuals regarding trustworthiness, as opposed to separating internal and external attributions of truthful behavior (O'Sullivan, 2003).

Actor-Observer Difference
Tendency to describe your own behavior through situation variables and others' behavior through dispositional variables.

Now, think back on the times you may have lied to someone. Why did you lie? Did you lie because you were trying to spare the person's feelings, protect a relationship, or avoid making the situation awkward and uncomfortable? If this is how you have thought about lying, then you engaged in the **actor-observer difference**. The actor-observer difference is the propensity to make fundamental attribution errors toward others and the tendency to describe your own behavior through external or situation variables (Jones & Nisbett, 1972). As an actor you tend to view your behavior through situational causes and as an observer you tend to understand actions based on dispositional causes. Simply, you assume others lie because they are liars and you lie due to situational, and maybe even beneficent, reasons.

Fundamental attribution errors and the actor-observer difference are forms of human error. The error is in the tendency to explain behavior in a manner that does not account for the social situational factors. Thus, to reduce this error, it might be wise to consider situational factors when assessing others' actions. When you catch someone tripping on stairs, you might want to consider that the steps could have been slippery as a likely possibility. Along with this type of error, there are a number of other contributors to human error.

Biases, Blindsides, and Blunders: Human Error

Imagine having a child that could not communicate with you. You have raised your child that you love unconditionally and have never been able to have your child reciprocate any words of love, compassion, or appreciation for you. Your child does not communicate with you because he or she has Autism Spectrum Disorder (ASD), requiring very substantial support. The marked features of ASD are deficits in social domains, with a range in severity, and coupled with repetitive and restricted behavioral patterns (APA, 2013).

Now, after years of your child being unable to talk with you, you discovered an approach that would open the door for your child to communicate with you. An approach that was designed to have nonspeaking children communicate through typing with the assistance. Wow! It seems like you would want to know how quickly you could do this, so that you could have your child tell you that he or she loves you for the first time.

This excitement turned out to be the reality for one family, the Wendrow family, who utilized the methods of facilitated communication for their daughter, Aislinn (Alexander, 2009). Facilitated communication was created with the intent to physically assist nonspeaking individuals so that they may communicate (Crossley, 1992). For the Wendrow family, all was well until one day, Aislinn had typed a message that indicated her father had sexually assaulted her, which led to confusion, interrogation, and turmoil (Alexander, 2009).

Facilitated communication had been previously scrutinized. A series of experiments revealed that individuals make attributions of behaviors when a person is not performing the behavior, implying that people may have incorrectly attributed responses made from facilitated communication to a nonspeaking individual rather than from the facilitated communicator (Wegner, Fuller, & Sparrow, 2003). In the case of Aislinn and her father, facilitated communication was put to the test again (Alexander, 2009). The facilitated communicator was asked to leave the courtroom when Aislinn was asked questions and return merely to facilitate communication. Through this process, Aislinn typed incoherent sequences of numbers and letters. Based on this test, all charges against Mr. Wendrow were dropped.

This case reveals the drastic consequences of human **biases** and error. A bias is a fixed belief that favors one perspective over others. In the case above, beliefs were initially biased in favor of believing that Aislinn could communicate, which was motivated by a strong desire to communicate with Aislinn. This bias was strong enough that testing whether or not Aislinn could actually communicate was not even a consideration. For Aislinn's parents, they had a deep drive to communicate with their daughter that they initially accepted facilitated communication as an effective means. As for the facilitated communicators, they too had a bias toward promoting a method that would allow nonspeaking individuals to communicate.

Biases
Fixed belief that favors one perspective over others.

Confirmation Bias

Confirmation Bias
Seeking information that verifies our existing beliefs.

Biases may often lead you astray and they introduce error into decision-making or thinking. Some errors due to biases you hold relate to belief perseverance or seeking to confirm preexisting beliefs. The **confirmation bias** is the tendency toward seeking information that verifies our existing beliefs or hypotheses and dismissal of information that may be contrary to these beliefs (Nickerson, 1998). The tendency for humans to engage in this bias has been documented and cautioned against by philosophers, researchers, and practitioners (O'Donohue, Lilienfeld, & Fowler, 2007; Nickerson, 1998).

Among many areas of literature, the confirmation bias has even been found within forensic settings. Kukucka and Kassin (2014) conducted a study investigating the confirmation bias within evaluating forensic evidence. They asked participants to read one of two summaries of a bank robbery based on an actual case. Then, based on which condition the participants were assigned, they were either provided with information that the defendant confessed to the crime or did not confess. Followed by the case description, participants were told to imagine they were a jury, were provided with evidence of a handwriting samples, and were asked to compare the samples. The researchers found that participants in the confession condition had judged the two handwriting samples as an actual match more so than participants in the nonconfession condition. Essentially, the researchers found that participants employed the confirmation bias by seeking to confirm the perpetrator's confession through affirming that the handwriting evidence was a match.

Hindsight Bias

Hindsight Bias
The tendency to view past events as determined and not consider the possibilities of other outcomes.

How often have you looked back on an event and said something to the effect of "oh well, it had to be that way and could have been no other way" or "I knew it would happen this way" and felt confident in the outcome of the event? This represents the **hindsight bias** (Fischhoff, 1975). People of a wide range of ages, across the life-span, engage in hindsight bias (Bernstein, Erdfelder, Meltzoff, Peria, & Loftus, 2011).

Generally, this bias is erroneous because when you look back at the events that unfolded, you think that they were bound and determined to occur that way and they could not have occurred any other way. In doing this, you overestimate the likelihood of the events happening one way versus others, which evidences the bias. It is quite possible that events could have turned out another way. Chances are, if they did, you would still think that it must have happened that way as well. This represents our tendency to not consider the possibilities of an outcome and conclude that the likelihood of the outcome was determined 100% due to the fact that that is the way it happened.

Consider the last time you got a job. Initially, you may have been uncertain and hopeful. You might have even been a little nervous or concerned that you would not be the best candidate for the job and that they would hire someone else. You might have waited by the phone or computer, desperately hoping for a message or call from the employer. Moving to the point after which you were informed that you got the job, you might have stated or thought that you knew it all along. You might have even more confidently asserted that you knew you would get the job all along, discounting the previous concerns and worries you had. So, what would have happened if you did not get the job? In looking back, would you think about the possibilities of not getting the job or would you then have used the hindsight bias to state that you knew you would not get the job?

This bias is based on what we knew to occur rather than the actual factors that contributed to its occurrence. Thus, the error lies in not accounting for the contributors of success or failure. Subsequently, future endeavors and decisions might be met with error because you do not learn from what occurred, rather you justified its occurrence.

Self-Serving Bias

Have you ever mastered a test or exam? Did you get an A or a high A? How did you feel afterward? Elated, euphoric, or ready to go out and celebrate your achievement because you worked hard and it paid off? Now, think about a time where you did not perform very well on a test, assignment, or major paper. Maybe you failed the exam or assignment. How did you feel afterward? Did you feel angry, upset, or ready to tell the world never to take a class from that instructor because she or he is a horrible teacher who assigns difficult or unrealistic assignments?

The inclination for you to assign credit for your own successes to your hard work or character and failures to external or situational causes is referred to as the **self-serving bias** (Miller & Ross, 1975). This bias leads to error because it does not properly account for successes and failures. Regarding test performance, you might have failed not because the teacher is merciless and out to get students but possibly due to a lack of studying or inefficient study behaviors. On the flipside, how many times have you attributed your success on a test or assignment to an instructor? After making a high A on an assignment, have you ever thought that it was merely reflective of how merciful and caring your teacher was? Your teacher would be very excited to hear you provide them with some credit of your success. However, factors contributing to success or failure might fall somewhere in between where we attribute the source. Your success in a classroom probably has influence from a variety of sources, including yourself, your teacher, and peers.

Self-Serving Bias
Accredit your own successes to dispositional factors and failure to situational factors.

Belief in a Just World

Along with biases of successes and failures, there is a tendency to believe that good things will happen to good people and bad things will happen to bad people. This belief is referred to as the **belief in a just world** (Lerner, 1980). This belief is perpetuated by the notion we discussed earlier that the world operates in an orderly, meaningful, and consistent manner. Essentially, the belief is that the world is consistently just and justice is delivered consistently.

When witnessing some crime or aggressive act toward others, you may later think that the person "will get what is coming to them" or "get what they deserve." On the other end of the belief in justice, you may think that someone who is a good person will also "get what they deserve" or "will be rewarded for their kindness." However, this belief is skewed and promotes error in thinking. Sometimes good things or positive states of affairs happen to people who commit crimes

Belief in a Just World
The tendency to believe that good things will happen to good people and bad things will happen to bad people.

enzoalessandra/Shutterstock.com

or are aggressive toward others. There are times when people commit crimes and get away with the crimes. On the other hand, misfortune occurs for those who engage in prosocial behaviors. There are times when you find individuals who provide a service to their country, state, or city will die while providing a service or helping others. These events are contrary to the belief in a just world.

The belief in a just world can also have detrimental effects on judgments. Schindler and Reinhard (2015) investigated the role of the belief in a just world with regard to deception detection accuracy. They found that the belief in a just world predicted deception detection accuracy, in that accuracy decreases when people hold a strong belief in a just world. Thus, you may erroneously judge others or situations when you hold pervasive beliefs about how the world operates, when those beliefs are biased in one direction without considering other variables.

Heuristics

Heuristics
Mental shortcuts used in decision-making.

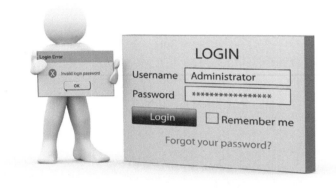

nasirkhan/Shutterstock.com

Computers often work in such a way that they are able to quickly process the information needed to achieve the desired goal or outcome. One way that computers do this is by using algorithms. Algorithms are typically a set of rules for a computer to use in problem-solving. Humans, on the other hand, process information at speeds slower than many computers. Thus, when we need to make judgments about people or information, we rely on mental shortcuts or **heuristics**. For example, a six-digit security password on a computer could be retrieved differently by computer and by human. Through an algorithm, a computer would be able to cycle through all possible number and letter combinations until it found the correct password. As humans, we could not fathom enduring such a task. We use heuristics and think of potential passwords, such as anniversary dates, birthdates, children's names, or names of beloved family pets.

In 1954, Paul Meehl published his work that essentially argued how mechanical methods (e.g., algorithms) of prediction outperform clinical methods (e.g., heuristics). In other words, predictions are more accurate when statistics are used over human thought or intuition. One of the reasons for these findings is that where human judgment is found, so is error. Mechanical methods do not introduce human error.

As you have read, humans possess biases, expectations, and beliefs that may influence decisions. This is apparent when considering passwords. Have you ever been locked out of a computer or website that required a password? In a world of many passwords, it can be difficult to remember them all. Thus, you may try a few variations of your pet's name and age (with special characters). Being locked out of a computer or your bank website reveals the downside of heuristics and memory. If the typical password you use does not work, then we see how heuristics introduce error. The benefit of the algorithm is that it will eventually, and quickly, process through all combinations until it has secured the password.

Representativeness Heuristic
Thoughts or decisions based on a typical example.

Heuristics are efficient given the right context but also lead to many potential errors. One heuristic that we use when we assume things are similar or using a typical example is the **representativeness heuristic** (Kahneman & Tversky,

1972). You use this heuristic often. For example, name out loud or think of the typical animals you would see at a zoo. You might have thought of a lion, tiger, or bear. These thoughts demonstrate representativeness heuristic. What about a liger? A liger is the offspring of a lion and a tiger. A liger may not have come to mind because it does not represent the typical case or typical animal found at the zoo. Thus, while you would have made correct judgments based on this heuristic, you could make error by not thinking about atypical cases.

You even use these biases when judging others' musical preferences (Lonsdale & North, 2012). Lonsdale and North randomly assigned participants to read one of two descriptions of people and subsequently judge how similar the person was to a typical fan of various music styles and how likely the person would be a fan of various music styles. They found significant correlations between participants' judgments of the person's likely musical taste with perceived similarity to the typical music fans. Thus, when we evaluate music genres, we think of what the typical fan might look like and other behaviors that represent that musical style.

Another common heuristic is the **availability heuristic** (Tversky & Kahneman, 1973). This heuristic is employed when your thinking or judgments are based on the first thing that comes to mind or the lack of effort by which something is brought into awareness. When you are asked to think about something or make a decision, you might notice that you become aware of some things quickly before considering other options. This is due to the notion that frequent events are more readily accessible than infrequent events (Tversky & Kahneman, 1973).

To illustrate your use of this heuristic, let's examine a study conducted by Tversky and Kahneman (1973). They asked participants to consider the letter R and if it is more likely to appear in the first position or third position of a word. Take a moment to think about this? Does the letter R occur more frequently at the beginning of a word or as the third letter of a word? Tversky and Kahneman found that most participants reported the letter to be more likely found at the beginning of words than as the third letter of words. However, the letter R occurs more frequently in the third position than in the first (Mayzner & Tresselt, 1965).

Availability Heuristic
Thoughts or decisions based on the how quickly something comes into awareness.

Thinking Errors and Cognitive Distortions

Thus far we have established how consequential thinking and beliefs can be in our social world. We have also noted how biases and other aspects of thinking may lead to error in judgments, decisions, or even how we understand social interactions. Our thinking, which flows from our schemas, may serve us well in a number of situations. However, there are times when we think erroneously about ourselves, our world, and our future. This is known as **thinking errors**, which are various ways in which people think that often lead to mistakes or a dismissal of other relevant information. A list of various thinking errors can be found on page 44 (Beck, 2011, pp.181–182).

These errors in thinking have been suggested to be the reason that many people will experience distress, dysfunction, or even lead to psychopathology (Beck, 2011; Ellis, 1973). In revisiting the example we discussed earlier in this chapter of the student who thought that he or she was a failure, we can examine the thinking and see how this student demonstrates thinking errors. The student may have adapted the thinking error of labeling, in that she or he adopted the label of a failure, even in light of the evidence that the student had a 4.0 GPA.

Thinking Errors
Various ways in which people think that often lead to mistakes.

Although some automatic thoughts are true, many are either untrue or have just a grain of truth. Typical mistakes in thinking include:

1. **All-or-nothing thinking** (also called black-and-white, polarized, or dichotomous thinking): You view a situation in only two categories instead of on a continuum.
   Example: "If I'm not a total success, I'm a failure."

2. **Catastrophizing** (also called fortune-telling): You predict the future negatively without considering other, more likely outcomes.
   Example: "I'll be so upset, I won't be able to function at all."

3. **Disqualifying or discounting the positive:** You unreasonably tell yourself that positive experiences, deeds, or qualities do not count.
   Example: "I did that project well, but that doesn't mean I'm competent; I just got lucky."

4. **Emotional reasoning:** You think something must be true because you "feel" (actually believe) it so strongly, ignoring or discounting evidence to the contrary.
   Example: "I know I do a lot of things okay at work, but I still feel like I'm a failure."

5. **Labeling:** You put a fixed, global label on yourself or others without considering that the evidence might more reasonably lead to a less disastrous conclusion.
   Example: "I'm a loser. He's no good."

6. **Magnification/minimization:** When you evaluate yourself, another person, or a situation, you unreasonably magnify the negative and/or minimize the positive.
   Example: "Getting a mediocre evaluation proves how inadequate I am. Getting high marks doesn't mean I'm smart."

7. **Mental filter** (also called selective abstraction): You pay undue attention to one negative detail instead of seeing the whole picture.
   Example: "Because I got one low rating on my evaluation [which also contained several high ratings] it means I'm doing a lousy job."

8. **Mind reading:** You believe you know what others are thinking, failing to consider other, more likely possibilities.
   Example: "He thinks that I don't know the first thing about this project."

9. **Overgeneralization:** You make a sweeping negative conclusion that goes far beyond the current situation.
   Example: "[Because I felt uncomfortable at the meeting] I don't have what it takes to make friends."

10. **Personalization:** You believe others are behaving negatively because of you, without considering more plausible explanations for their behavior.
    Example: "The repairman was curt to me because I did something wrong."

11. **"Should" and "must" statements** (also called imperatives): You have a precise, fixed idea of how you or others should behave, and you overestimate how bad it is that these expectations are not met.
    Example: "It's terrible that I made a mistake. I should always do my best."

12. **Tunnel vision:** You only see the negative aspects of a situation.
    Example: "My son's teacher can't do anything right. He's critical and insensitive and lousy at teaching."

Further, the student may have even engaged in catastrophizing by stating that because of her or his belief of being a failure, he or she will never amount to anything. The student is catastrophizing because he or she is making future negative predictions about his or her life based on not accurate outcomes. A 4.0 GPA and a perception that you read slower than others does not necessarily mean that you should quit school and it hardly guarantees that you will not amount to anything. On the contrary, maintaining a 4.0 GPA is usually evidence that you are performing quite well academically.

When we employ thinking errors, not only does it affect beliefs you hold regarding yourself but also affects beliefs you possess about others. You may misinterpret information on a first date if you were to engage in mind reading. You might think that your date is thinking that you are uninteresting because the conversation halted momentarily. The conversation could have halted due to your date taking time to appreciate other aspects of being with you or even to take a bite of food. However, if you assume that you know what he or she is thinking, then you could promote inaccurate thoughts, which may lead to a bad first date.

These thinking errors might even intersect with some of the biases we have already discussed. Let's look at catastrophizing. If you have ever started your day with some bad event, such as spilling coffee on yourself or sleeping past an alarm, then you might have subsequently engaged in catastrophizing. You possibly think, "oh, is this how my day will be" or "I should just go back to sleep and try again tomorrow." At the core of this thinking is that you believe that the day will continue to deteriorate, or making a future prediction that the day will get worse. With that, you may seek any event that is negative in your day and ignore or dismiss positive events. Thus, you may have a confirmation bias, that your day was destined to be bad.

Conclusion

Much of your life may be filled with poor decisions, bad judgments, and errors in thinking. This is fine, and it is a good indicator that you are human and not a machine. Our beliefs and biases offer us a means to navigate and understand our social world. These beliefs offer consistency, completeness, and meaning. It is not that these beliefs should be completely removed. The process of learning about our social world is the process of relearning, shaping, and rethinking (i.e., assimilation and accommodation) ourselves and our social world. In fact, the aim should not be to completely remove error, which would mean to not be human, rather consider the implicit error you possess, how it affects your social world, and attempts to reduce it.

One way to reduce human error is through controlled thinking. Beck (2011) discusses how individuals might evaluate their thinking and beliefs in an attempt to change thinking errors. Thus, when evaluating social contexts you may want to consider the vast social variables that influence the situation. Reflect on your potential thinking errors, biases, attribution errors, or expectations. Someone who appears rude might just be acting from some other situational influence or you might be personalizing the behavior.

Another means for reducing error is through the use of science or the scientific method. In Chapter 2, you have become familiar with this approach and research methods designed to ameliorate your thinking, predictions, and decision-making. The goal of science is to aid in reducing some of these potential human errors.

In fact, many people hold a number of false beliefs about psychology (Lilienfeld, 2010). Some of these misconceptions involve how we think about others, such as the misconception that opposites attract (McCutcheon, 1991). Through making predictions, testing hypotheses, and gathering measurable data, you can put aside inaccurate thoughts and rely on observable data. Science not only assists you in understanding your social world, it is used by health professionals as a safeguard when making decisions relevant to providing treatment and care (O'Donohue et al., 2007).

Beliefs you possess are one of the most powerful tools for understanding your social world. In the same breath, it is the tool that carries some error. The crux of social psychology is considering the social situational influences of human behavior. In this chapter, you may have noticed the thread of situational factors as they influence thinking and how thinking may neglect considering these variables. Thus, when thinking about your social world, keep in mind the situation.

Advanced Topics/Suggested Readings

As you may have gathered, social psychology involves understanding human behavior through the various situational factors that work together. Some of the concepts identified in this chapter were discussed at a foundational level and did not delve into the complexities or nuances of research pertaining to the phenomena. Thus, consider some of the following for a more in-depth look into some of the topics discussed in this chapter.

Digging Deeper in Deception

To explore the accuracy of lie detection, read Bond and DePaulo's (2006) article titled "Accuracy of deception judgments." After reading this article, reflect on people's claims of being good lie detectors and consider research that suggests some professionals are better at detecting deception.

If you would like a comprehensive book that discusses deception and its many aspect from numerous research articles, then turn your attention to Vrij's (2008) *Detecting Lies and Deceit: Pitfalls and Opportunities* (2nd ed.). Another comprehensive book pertaining to various aspects of deception is Paul Ekman's (2009) *Telling Lies: Clues to Deceit in the Marketplace, Politics, and Marriage.*

Making Attributions: Not as Simple as It Seems

The attributions that you make in life are not as simple as internal attributions made for others and internal attributions made for yourself. The situation matters for making attributions. One theory has been developed that explores the other mechanisms involved in making attributions. Kelley's covariation model (1967) delineates the process of attributions in more detail, accounting for factors including, consensus, distinctiveness, and consistency. The reference for the work is

Kelley, H. H. (1967). Attribution theory in social psychology. *Nebraska Symposium on Motivation, 15,* 192–238.

Putting It into Practice

If you are interested in examining how social psychology intersects and influences applied contexts, namely therapy, then you may want to read Judith Beck's (2011) *Cognitive Behavior Therapy, Basics and Beyond* (2nd ed.). The book is intended for practitioners and therapists who want to learn and implement the art and science of cognitive behavioral therapy. However, when you read the book, you will notice the use of social psychological concepts addressed in this chapter and psychotherapy approaches.

References

Alexander, B. (2009, December 2). Dark shadows loom over 'facilitated' talk: Opening minds or telling tales? Michigan family torn apart by abuse claims. *NBC News*. Retrieved from http://www.nbcnews.com/id/34212528/ns/health-mental_health/t/dark-shadows-loom-over-facilitated-talk/#.VbJhytHbKUk

Ambady, N., & Rosenthal, R. (1993). Half a minute: Predicting teacher evaluations from thin slices of nonverbal behavior and physical attractiveness. *Journal of Personality and Social Psychology, 64*(3), 431–441.

American Psychiatric Association. (2013). *Diagnostic and statistical manual of mental disorders* (5th ed.). Washington, DC: Author.

Anderson, C.A. (2007). Belief perseverance. In R. F. Baumeister & K. D. Vohs (Eds.), *Encyclopedia of social psychology* (pp. 109–110). Thousand Oaks, CA: Sage.

Anderson, D. M., Mcguire, F. A., & Cory, L. (2011). The first day: It happens only once. *Teaching in Higher Education, 16*, 293–303. doi:10.1080/13562517.2010.546526

Baumesiter, R. F. (1991). *Meanings of life*. New York, NY: Guilford Press.

Beck, J. S. (2011). *Cognitive behavior therapy, basics and beyond* (2nd ed.). New York, NY: Guilford Press.

Bernstein, D. M., Erdfelder, E., Meltzoff, A. N., Peria, W., & Loftus, G. R. (2011). Hindsight bias from 3 to 95 years of age. *Journal of Experimental Psychology: Learning, Memory, and Cognition, 37*, 378–391. doi:10.1037/a0021971

Bond, C. F., Jr., & DePaulo, B. M. (2006). Accuracy of deception judgments. *Personality & Social Psychology Review, 10*, 214–234. doi:10.1207/s15327957pspr1003_2

Buchert, S., Laws, E. L., Apperson, J. M., & Bregman, N. J. (2008). First impressions and professor reputation: Influence on student evaluations of instruction. *Social Psychology of Education, 11*(4), 397–408.

Buss, D. M. (1989). Sex differences in human mate preferences: Evolutionary hypotheses tested in 37 cultures. *Behavioral & Brain Sciences, 12*, 1–49.

Buss, D. M. (1994). The strategies of human mating. *American Scientist, 82*, 238–249.

Cowan, L. K., Curtis, D. A., & Hart, C. L. (2010, April). *Female suspicion as an adaptive process in mate evaluation.* Poster presented at the 56th Annual Conference of the Southwestern Psychological Association, Dallas, TX.

Cox, D. L., Stabb, S. D., & Hulgus, J. F. (2000). Anger and depression in girls and boys: A study of gender differences. *Psychology of Women Quarterly, 24*, 110–112. doi:10.1111/j.1471-6402.2000.tb01027.x

Crossley, R. (1992). Lending a hand: A personal account of the development of Facilitated Communication Training. *American Journal of Speech-Language Pathology, 1*, 15.

Curtis, D. A. (2015). Patient deception: Nursing students' beliefs and attitudes. *Nurse Educator. 40*(5), 254–257.

Curtis, D. A., & Cordell-McNulty, K. (2015, April). *Set the stage: The effectiveness of first day teaching demonstrations.* Talk presented at the 11th Annual Southwest Teachers of Psychology Conference, Wichita, KS.

Curtis, D.A., Cowan, L. K., & Hart, C. L. (2010, April). *Looking good and honest: Perception of believability of males in dating videos.* Poster presented at the 56th Annual Conference of the Southwestern Psychological Association, Dallas, TX.

Curtis, D. A., & Hart, C. L. (2015). Pinocchio's nose in therapy: Therapists' beliefs and attitudes toward client deception. *International Journal for the Advancement of Counselling*, doi:10.1007/s10447-015-9243-6

Curtis, D. A., & Gray, A. (2012, April). *Using psychology to teach psychology: First impressions on the first day.* Talk presented at the 8th Annual Southwest Teachers of Psychology Conference, Oklahoma City, OK.

DePaulo, B. M. (2009). *Behind the door of deceit: Understanding the biggest liars in our lives.* Lexington, KY: CreateSpace.

DePaulo, B. M., & Bell, K. L. (1996). Truth and investment: Lies are told to those who care. *Journal of Personality and Social Psychology, 71*, 703–716. doi:10.1037/0022-3514.71.4.703

DePaulo, B. M., Hoover, C. W., Webb, W., Kenny, D. A., & Oliver, P. V. (1987). Accuracy of Person Perception: Do people know what kinds of impressions they convey? *Journal of Personality & Social Psychology, 52*, 303–315.

Ekman, P. (2009). *Telling lies: Clues to deceit in the marketplace, politics, and marriage.* New York, NY: W. W. Norton & Company Inc.

Ekman, P., & Friesen, W. V. (1971). Constants across cultures in the face and emotion. *Journal of Personality and Social Psychology, 17*, 124–129. doi:10.1037/h0030377

Ellis, A. (1973). *Reason and emotion in psychotherapy*. Secaucus, NJ: L. Stuart.

Fischhoff, B. (1975). Hindsight is not equal to foresight: The effect of outcome knowledge on judgment under uncertainty. *Journal of Experimental Psychology: Human Perception and Performance, 3*, 387–396.

Forrest, J. A., Feldman, R. S., & Tyler, J. M. (2004). When accurate beliefs lead to better lie detection. *Journal of Applied Social Psychology, 34*, 764–780. doi:10.1111/j.1559-1816.2004.tb02569.x

Global Deception Research Team. (2006). A world of lies. *Journal of Cross-Cultural Psychology, 37*, 60–74. doi:10.1177/0022022105282295

Gopnik, A., Meltzoff, A., & Kuhl, P. (2001). *The scientist in the crib: What early learning tells us about the mind*. New York, NY: HarperCollins Publishers Inc.

Hack, T. (2014). Forming impressions: Effects of facial expression and gender stereotypes. *Psychological Reports, 114*, 557–571. doi:10.2466/07.17.PR0.114k17w6

Hayes, S. C., Follette, V. M., & Linehan, M. M. (2004). *Mindfulness and Acceptance: Expanding the Cognitive-Behavioral Tradition*. New York, NY: Guilford Press.

Hayes, S. C., Wilson, K. G., Gifford, E. V., Follette, V. M., & Strosahl, K. (1996). Experiential avoidance and behavioral disorders: A functional dimensional approach to diagnosis and treatment. *Journal of Consulting and Clinical Psychology, 64*, 1152–1168. doi:10.1037/0022-006X.64.6.1152

Heider, F. (1958). *The psychology of interpersonal relations*. Hoboken, NJ: John Wiley & Sons Inc.

Hughes, J., & Jacobson, T. (2006). *Ferris Bueller's day off*. Hollywood, CA: Paramount Pictures.

Jones, E. E., & Nisbett, R. E. (1972). The actor and the observer: Divergent perceptions of the causes of behavior. In E. E. Jones, D. E. Kanouse, H. H. Kelley, R. E. Nisbett, S. Valins, & B. Weiner (Eds.), *Attribution: Perceiving the causes of behavior* (pp. 79–94). Morristown, NJ: General Learning Press.

Kahneman, D., & Tversky, A. (1972). Subjective probability: A judgment of representativeness. *Cognitive Psychology, 3*, 430–454. doi:10.1016/0010-0285(72)90016-3

Kukucka, J., & Kassin, S. M. (2014). Do confessions taint perceptions of handwriting evidence? An empirical test of the forensic confirmation bias. *Law & Human Behavior (American Psychological Association), 38*, 256–270. doi:10.1037/lhb0000066

Lamb, C. S., & Crano, W. D. (2014). Parents' beliefs and children's marijuana use: Evidence for a self-fulfilling prophecy effect. *Addictive Behaviors, 39*, 127–132. doi:10.1016/j.addbeh.2013.09.009

Lerner, M. (1980). *The belief in a just world: A fundamental delusion*. New York, NY: Plenum Press.

Levine, T. R., Serota, K. B., & Shulman, H. C. (2010). The impact of Lie to Me on viewers' actual ability to detect deception. *Communication Research, 37*, 847–856. doi:10.1177/0093650210362686

Lie to Me. (n.d.). Fox Broadcasting Company website, Retrieved from http://www.fox.com/lietome/about/

Lilienfeld, S. O. (2010). Confronting psychological misconceptions in the classroom: Challenges and rewards. *APS Observer, 23*(17), 36–39.

Lonsdale, A. J., & North, A. C. (2012). Musical taste and the representativeness heuristic. *Psychology of Music, 40*, 131–142. doi:10.1177/0305735611425901

Lyubomrsky, S. (2001). Why are some people happier than others? The role of cognitive and motivational processes in well-being. *American Psychologist, 56*, 239–249. doi:10.1037/0003-066X.56.3.239

Mann, T. C., & Ferguson, M. J. (2015). Can we undo our first impressions? The role of reinterpretation in reversing implicit evaluations. *Journal of Personality and Social Psychology, 108*, 823–849. doi:10.1037/pspa0000021

Mayzner, M. S., & Tresselt, M. E. (1965). Tables of single-letter and bigram frequency counts for various word-length and letter-position combinations. *Psychonomic Monograph Supplements, 1*, 13–32.

McCutcheon, L. E. (1991). A new test of misconceptions about psychology. *Psychological Reports, 68*, 647–653.

McKeachie, W. J., & Svinicki, M. D. (2006). *McKeachie's teaching tips: Strategies, research, and theory for college and university teachers* (12th ed.) Boston, MA: Houghton Mifflin Company.

Meehl, P. E. (1954). *Clinical versus statistical prediction: A theoretical analysis and a review of the evidence*. Minneapolis: University of Minnesota Press. doi:10.1037/11281-000

Merton, R. (1948). The self-fulfilling prophecy. *Antioch Review, 8*, 193–210.

Merton, R. K. (2010). The self-fulfilling prophecy. *Antioch Review, 68*, 173–190.

Miller, D. T., & Ross, M. (1975). Self-serving biases in the attribution of causality: Fact or fiction? *Psychological Bulletin, 82*, 213–225. doi:10.1037/h0076486

Nickerson, R. S. (1998). Confirmation bias: A ubiquitous phenomenon in many guises. *Review of General Psychology, 2*, 175–220. doi:10.1037/1089-2680.2.2.175

O'Donohue, W. T., Lilienfeld, S. O., & Fowler, K. A. (2007). Science is an essential safeguard against human error. In S. O. Lilienfeld, W. T. O'Donohue, S. O. Lilienfeld, & W. T. O'Donohue (Eds.), *The great ideas of clinical science: 17 principles that every mental health professional should understand* (pp. 3–27). New York, NY: Routledge/Taylor & Francis Group.

O'Sullivan, M. (2003). The fundamental attribution error in detecting deception: The boy-who-cried-wolf effect. *Personality and Social Psychology Bulletin, 29*, 1316–1327. doi:10.1177/0146167203254610

Paul Ekman Group, LLC. (2014). *Paul Ekman Group.* Retrieved from http://www.paulekman.com/

Perls, F., Hefferline, R.F., & Goodman, P. (1951). Gestalt therapy: Excitement and growth in the human personality. New York, NY: Delta Book/Dell.

Piaget, J. (1954). *The construction of reality in the child.* New York, NY: Basic Books.

Rivera, J., & Docter, P. (2015). *Inside out* [Motion picture]. United States: Walt Disney Studios Motion Pictures.

Rosenthal, R. (1995). Critiquing Pygmalion: A 25-year perspective. *Current Directions in Psychological Science (Wiley-Blackwell), 4*, 171–172. doi:10.1111/1467-8721.ep10772607

Rosenthal, R., & Jacobson, L. (1968). *Pygmalion in the classroom: Teacher expectation and pupils' intellectual development.* New York, NY: Holt, Rinehart & Winston.

Ross, L. (1977). The intuitive psychologist and his shortcomings: Distortions in the attribution process. In Berkowitz (Ed.), *Advances in experimental social psychology* (Vol. 10, pp. 173–220). Orlando, FL: Academic Press.

Schindler, S., & Reinhard, M. (2015). Catching the liar as a matter of justice: Effects of belief in a just world on deception detection accuracy and the moderating role of mortality salience. *Personality and Individual Differences, 73*, 105–109. doi:10.1016/j.paid.2014.09.034

Tversky, A., & Kahneman, D. (1973). Availability: A heuristic for judging frequency and probability. *Cognitive Psychology, 5*, 207–232. doi:10.1016/0010-0285(73)90033-9

Wegner, D. M. (2011). Setting free the bears: Escape from thought suppression. *American Psychologist, 66*, 671–680. doi:10.1037/a0024985

Wegner, D. M., Fuller, V. A., & Sparrow, B. (2003). Clever hands: Uncontrolled intelligence in facilitated communication. *Journal of Personality and Social Psychology, 85*, 5–19. doi:10.1037/0022-3514.85.1.5

Wegner, D. M., Schneider, D. J., Carter, S. R., & White, T. L. (1987). Paradoxical effects of thought suppression. *Journal of Personality and Social Psychology, 53*, 5–13. doi:10.1037/0022-3514.53.1.5

Vrij, A. (2008). *Detecting lies and deceit: Pitfalls and opportunities* (2nd ed.). West Sussex, England: John Wiley & Sons Ltd.

Chapter Four
The Self

Dr. Steven J. Hoekstra
Kansas Wesleyan University

new photo/Shutterstock.com

Learning Objectives

- Define the self-reference effect and describe why it is important to social psychology
- Describe various components of the self-concept
- Explain how self-complexity and possible selves are related to goal setting
- Compare and contrast high and low self-monitors
- Discuss how culture affects self-definition
- List various methods of establishing and maintaining self-esteem
- Examine benefits of evaluating the self
- Discuss how ego depletion affects behavior and how self-control can be enhanced
- Describe ways that mortality salience affects behavior

Chapter Outline

Defining the Self

Evaluating the Self

Maintaining the Self

Establishing One's Identity

"Who am I? Can I conceal myself for evermore?
Pretend I'm not the man I was before?
And must my name until I die be no more than an alibi?
Must I lie?
How can I ever face my fellow man? How can I ever face myself again?
My soul belongs to God, I know. I made that bargain long ago
He gave me hope, when hope was gone; He gave me strength to journey on.
Who am I? Who am I? I'm Jean Valjean!
And so Javert, you see it's true, that man bears no more guilt than you!
Who am I? 24601!" (*Les Miserables*, 2012)

Just like Jean Valjean in *Les Miserables*, a major question we all have is, "Who am I?" We want to know ourselves, and act in accordance with that truth in us. Knowing yourself is the major crisis of adolescence according to Erikson's developmental model (Erikson & Erikson, 1997). We differentiate ourselves from our parents, and in young adulthood strive to establish ourselves in the "real world." So, the self is important to individual psychology. But, why talk about how we think about ourselves in a "social" psychology book?

Identity
An internalized aspect of the self-definition used to shape behavior and feelings about the self.

The answer is that our self is the center of our social-cognitive world. As infants, we define all of existence through our own perceptions (infant egocentrism; Piaget, 1983), and even as we gain the ability to take the perspective of others, our self and its values and emotions are the center of our known universe (adolescent egocentrism; Elkind, 1985). As this sense of self develops and becomes internalized and habitual, the degree to which it defines us becomes our **identity**.

Blend Images/Shutterstock.com

Throughout our life, our self is our basis of comparison, our richest source of information, and our most detailed schema. Whenever we need to make a decision, our best benchmark and standard is our personal set of beliefs and experiences, a process known as the **self-reference effect** (Rogers, Kuiper, & Kierker, 1977). We evaluate others and make predictions about how they will act and what they think based on how we look at ourselves and how we might act and what we think. Our perspectives and experiences provide a lens through which we understand the world.

Self-Reference Effect
The tendency to efficiently process information relevant to the self and to use the self as a basis or standard for judging the world.

Self-Concept
How you define yourself.

Defining the Self

So how do we answer the question of, "Who am I?" A simple way is to just make a list. Kuhn and McPartland (1954) developed a measure of the **self-concept** called the 20-Statements Test, where participants simply number a page from 1 to 20 and try to complete the sentence "I am _____" or "I am a(n) _____."

Exercise: Take a moment and try this. Write down as many answers as readily come to mind. If you can't get 20, that's ok.

As you look at your list, you will learn a lot about not only yourself but also various components of the self-concept, or the **self-schema** (Markus, 1977).

Kuhn (1960) found, when looking across lots of people's lists, that there were common trends in the sorts of things people put down. Some people include *physical characteristics*, like gender or race. Some include various roles they play. These could be *sociological roles*, social groups like your major, your clique, or being a resident of your home state, or *interpersonal attributes*, the roles you have to other people, like a wife, father, child, or student. Some people put items related to interests and activities, what they enjoy doing, like painter, soccer player, or musician. Some people write deeper things, like their *internalized beliefs* (their attitudes, religion, political affiliation), their *self-determination*, **self-efficacy**, or *existential aspects* like their degree of self-love or their sense of uniqueness. Lastly, self-concept includes *self-awareness*. This is one's knowledge of your self-structure. Some people find a list like this easy to generate, others do not because they just don't think about it much.

Because all this self-concept data is stored cognitively as a schema, like any other schema we find, it is generally easier to process and assimilate aspects of the world that are related to the self, which is another aspect of the self-reference effect (Symons & Johnson, 1997). Self-relevant information is easier to learn and remember, and information that can't be easily related to the self-schema is often forgotten or distorted to make it fit (see the previous chapter). This is why your professors often suggest the study strategy of generating a personal example. If you can tie an unfamiliar concept to a personal experience, you make it more memorable.

Now, as you look at your list, how many of the 20 statements were you able to complete? The number of items you completed is related to not only your self-awareness but also your **self-complexity** (Linville, 1985). People who are high in self-complexity have a rich and diverse list of different aspects to themselves. They have multiple roles, skills, talents, and interests. People who are lower in self-complexity have a shorter list of things that make up their identities, not necessarily because of a lack of awareness, but because they just have fewer roles or a less diverse self-concept. They define themselves by a short list of things or aspects. We'll come back to this later, but can you think of some advantages of being high in self-complexity? What about being low?

Possible Selves

On your list, did you include just things you currently are, or did you include what you'd like to be in the future? If you didn't include any future things, generate a list like that now. Where do you see yourself in five years? Ten years? Twenty-five years? Your answer to this is what Markus and Nurius (1986) called your **possible selves**. Possible selves are visions of different hypothetical futures, hypothetical yous, and how you might turn out with different sorts of choices. These selves are

Self-Schema
The cognitive mechanism for processing self-relevant information.

Self-Efficacy
Feeling that you are capable.

Self-Complexity
Having a self-concept with multiple, diverse roles and interests.

Possible Selves
Different hypothetical future you.

Alexyz3d/Shutterstock.com

affected to some extent by your self-complexity, somewhat by your background experiences, and a lot by your various goals, hopes, and dreams.

It turns out that your possible selves can actually in some ways guide and shape your future. Oyserman and Markus (1990) did an exploration of possible selves, comparing delinquent and nondelinquent youth. The adolescents were asked to describe three possible selves: hoped for selves, expected selves, and feared selves. The less-delinquent youth were more likely to mention school success, jobs, and other achievement goals as being within reach, whereas the more delinquent youth mentioned school less, and possible selves included more depression, drug use, and crime. The point of this discussion is to ask yourself, "What am I capable of? Which outcomes are most likely?" It's easy to see how the realm of possibility can direct the sorts of goals and challenges you give yourself. Which youths would be most motivated to try to finish high school? Or go to college?

The existence of multiple possible selves means that at some level the self-concept is always evolving. Each choice you make shifts your path. Markus and Kunda (1986) call this the **working self-concept**. The working self-concept is a moment-to-moment, day-by-day, malleable version of the self. In essence, although the self-concept gives you your identity, the self adjusts and accommodates to new information or experiences. As skills develop, as you get feedback, and as you modify goals, the schema adjusts to take the new information into account to move you toward that future.

Working Self-Concept
The part of the self-schema that is currently activated.

Self-Awareness

But how aware are you of your self-concept, really? It turns out, it varies a lot from person to person and situation to situation. **Self-awareness theory** (Duval & Wicklund, 1972) suggests that sometimes individuals are chronically high or low in self-awareness, sort of like a personality trait. For most of us, however, we lack the cognitive capacity to continuously ruminate on oneself. Even if we have a certain level of self-knowledge, the demands of everyday life are such that aspects of ourselves only become salient when our attention is drawn to them. Interestingly, this can be relatively simple to do.

Self-Awareness Theory
You behave more consistently with your self-concept when it is salient.

Being aware of oneself can have both good and bad consequences. Self-awareness is good in that we are more likely to behave in accordance with our values and attitudes when we are reminded of them (Carver, 1975). This could be as blunt as having potential hypocritical behavior being pointed out by a friend, or as simple as seeing oneself in a mirror. When we are made aware of ourselves or are accountable for our actions, we are reminded of both our internal norms and societal norms and expectations and tend to behave in accordance with them. When self-awareness is low, as in times of **deindividuation** (Diener, Fraser, Beaman, & Kelem, 1976), we are either more likely to do things that are against social norms (like rioting behavior, or KKK members engaging in hate crimes when wearing hoods) or more likely to conform to the group (such as during military training, or when wearing a job or school uniform).

One way that self-awareness can be trait-like is in a trait known as **self-monitoring** (Snyder, 1980). Self-monitoring addresses an individual's tendency to adapt personal behavior to situational demands. High self-monitors are aware of themselves and how they come across, so they tend to be social chameleons, showing different facets of themselves in different social situations

Deindividuation
The tendency, when anonymous, to conform to group behavior and be less responsible to social norms.

Self-Monitoring
The trait related to how adaptable one is to show different aspects of oneself in different situations.

and accommodating to the expectations and needs of the situation they are in (Goffman, 1959). In a sense, they read situations well, identify the demands, and present a relevant mask or persona to suit that situation. They adjust their **self-presentation** (Schlenker, 1980) to suit the circumstances. Low self-monitors tend to be much more consistent across situations. The result is that high self-monitors often are socially successful and tend to have large numbers of acquaintances, while low self-monitors have a short list of close friends and tend to engage in longer term romantic partnerships.

Too much self-awareness can interfere with normal social activity. For example, one theory on chronically shy or social phobic individuals is that they experience interference from negative self-thoughts and hypothetical internal examples of social rejection (Bruch, 1996). This interference, in turn, results in the **self-fulfilling prophesy** of social awkwardness and conversational struggles. Additionally, rumination can serve not just as a distraction from present interactions but also as a way to perpetuate feelings of depression and anxiety (Nolen-Hoeksema, Wisco, & Lyubomirsky, 2008). A similar concept is self-consciousness (Fenigstein, Scheier, & Buss, 1975). There are two types: **private self-consciousness** and **public self-consciousness**. Someone high on private self-consciousness tends to be preoccupied with thinking about what's going on in their own head, their thoughts and feelings. People high on public self-consciousness are preoccupied with how they appear to others. Both forms of self-consciousness are positively correlated with shyness and social anxiety. So, one has to find the appropriate balance where one is aware enough of oneself to adjust to the social demands of the situation while at the same time not be so self-focused that it pulls attention inward and disrupts one's social flow.

Culture and the Self

Part of the self is influenced by one's culture. Tajfel and Turner (1979) argue that people internalize their various roles and group memberships, identify with the characteristics of those groups, and use that to define their self-concept, a theory known as **social identity theory.** Belonging to meaningful, important groups allows us to be meaningful and important by inclusion, and these groups also provide a guide for what sorts of behaviors are expected and acceptable, in the form of social norms.

It has been argued that cultures differ on a number of dimensions (Hofstede, 1991). The individualism/collectivism dimension is one of the most heavily studied (Hofstede, Hofstede, & Minkov, 2010). **Individualistic cultures** are characterized by personal goals and decisions, personal well-being, mobility, and distance from extended family. **Collectivist cultures** typically are more likely to define individuals as members of their group or family, be concerned with honor, have decisions (for example, jobs or marriage partners) made for children by family elders, more often live close to or with extended family, and be less geographically mobile.

Markus and Kitayama (1998) apply these concepts to the self in what they call the independent and interdependent selves. People with an **independent self** define their self-concept as separate from others. There is a need for being unique (Park, 2012) and making one's own decisions, and one's value is defined by personal success. People with an **interdependent self,** however, define

XiXinXing/Shutterstock.com

Self-Presentation
The desire to strategically control your public image.

Self-Fulfilling Prophesy
The tendency of people to behave in ways that confirm others' expectations of them.

Private Self-Consciousness
An awareness of your own thoughts and concerns.

Public Self-Consciousness
An awareness of how you appear to others.

Social Identity Theory
Defining yourself in terms of the social groups to which you belong.

Individualistic Cultures
Cultures that value the self, personal achievement, independence.

Collectivistic Cultures
Cultures that value group membership, honor, extended family, subservience to and success of the group.

Independent Self
Self-concept that is unique and separate from others.

Interdependent Self
Self-concept that is defined as related to and intertwined with others.

Self-Esteem
Sense of self-worth or self-value, feeling good about yourself.

themselves by the social groups or units of which they are a part. Their sense of success comes from the success of their group; their worth comes from their family honor. Their roles in relation to others drive their self-concept.

Evaluating the Self

Although it is important to consider how we *think* about ourselves, our self-concept, it is also important to consider how we *feel* about ourselves, our self-evaluation, or **self-esteem**.

One way to measure our self-evaluation is by figuring out if it is high or low, our *level* of self-esteem. This could be done on a general level, how happy you are about yourself generally (Rosenberg, 1979), or about a particular domain or area, such as how you feel about your body image (Franzoi & Shields, 1984). Level of self-esteem, despite the measure's tendency toward a **ceiling effect,** has shown to be a very sensitive measure in terms of being related to a host of other things. A recent PsychInfo search on "self-esteem" generated over 32,000 hits. People with high levels of self-esteem tend to have many psychological benefits, including general life satisfaction (Kong, Ding, & Zhao, 2015) and relationship and work satisfaction (Erol & Orth, 2014; Kuster, Orth, & Meier, 2013).

B Calkins/Shutterstock.com

Ceiling Effect
Restricted range in measurement where the scores cluster at the top of the allowable responses.

Social Comparison
Judging one's value in relation to the performance of others.

But, it is also important to think of self-esteem not just as a stable *trait*, but as a *state*. That is, sometimes self-esteem serves a barometric function, reacting moment-to-moment to feedback and other environmental experiences. Kernis (1993, 2005) discusses this as *stability* of self-esteem, which he measured with frequent assessments of current self-esteem. He found that while stable high and stable low self-esteem individuals behave as typical highs and lows, unstable highs (that is, those who are generally high but occasionally dip toward low) tend to react strongly, angrily, and defensively when confronted with negative feedback and unstable lows (that is, those who usually are low but have occasional times of a self-esteem boost) tend to be more "clingy" or anxious for social approval. Furthermore, overall, individuals with unstable self-esteem appear to be less intrinsically motivated and tend to respond more strongly, positively or negatively, to feedback, particularly feedback related to social acceptance. So although level of self-esteem is the traditional measure, the potential effects of self-esteem stability should not be overlooked.

Sources of Self-Esteem

Everett Collection/Shutterstock.com

Where does self-esteem come from? How do we get it? How do we truly evaluate ourselves? There are several possible theories, which we will now explore in turn.

One way we can evaluate ourselves is through **social comparison** (Festinger, 1954). The idea here is that if a person was stranded on a desert island, they would have no idea whether they were good at something or not, because they would have nobody with whom to compare themselves. In other words, if I'm better at something than the person next to me, I can feel good about myself, and if I'm not as good as the next person, I can beat myself up about it.

Now, I can also use social comparison strategically. If I need or want to feel better about myself, I can engage in **downward social comparison**, purposely selecting someone for whom I am superior (or even better, derogate someone to make sure that I am superior—we'll come back to this in the prejudice chapter), so that I can make myself feel better by comparison. Sometimes, we engage in **upward social comparison**. Of course, if we select a comparison other who is too superior to us, we will just depress ourselves, but if we pick someone like us but just a little better, we can use that as motivation or to help us set challenging but achievable goals. "Keeping up with the Jones'" is an example of this phenomenon, wanting to be like people we perceive to be successful others.

Bem (1965) proposed an alternate model, **self-perception theory**. Bem argued that we can use the same attributional mechanism we use to form impressions of others (see earlier chapter) to form impressions of ourselves. When we go into a new situation, we observe our own behaviors and make attributions for why we did what we just did. We can make an external attribution, but if there is no obvious external cause, we can perform an internal attribution, and form or judge the value of our self-concept in that domain.

Another alternative for self-evaluation is to internalize the evaluations of others (Cooley, 1902; Mead, 1934), a process known as **reflected appraisals.** We define ourselves to some degree through a **looking glass self** (Cooley, 1902), seeing ourselves as others see us. But others are showing us who we are by how they act toward us; they also show us what they think about who we are, whether they approve or disapprove of our identity. Therefore, when people (especially people who are close to us or whose opinions we value) express praise or disappointment, that translates into high and low self-esteem.

So far, we've talked about self-evaluation from comparing ourselves to others, perceiving ourselves, and perceiving others' perceptions of ourselves. An additional option is **self-discrepancy theory** (Higgins, 1989), where we compare our current selves with the possible selves that we perceive we or other people want us to be. (Confused yet? ☺) In self-discrepancy, we compare our *actual self* (that is, our current self-perception) to our *ideal self* (like our hoped-for possible self, what we *want* to be) and our *ought self* (our perception of what our significant others, parents, and friends think we *should* be). The closer our actual is to the other two, the higher our self-esteem should be. The greater the distance between actual and ought selves, the more depression we should experience, and the lower our self-esteem, because we are failing to achieve what is expected of us and we are letting others down. The greater the distance between actual and ideal selves, the more anger and frustration we should experience, and the lower our self-esteem. In this case, we are being prevented from achieving what is our due, or from becoming self-actualized, which should result in aggression according to the **frustration-aggression hypothesis** (Dollard, Miller, Doob, Mowrer, & Sears, 1939, see later chapter). Basically, if we don't live up to expectations, for ourselves or internalized expectations from others, we feel bad. The more we are who we want to or think we should be, the more success we feel and the higher we evaluate ourselves.

Downward Social Comparison
Comparing oneself to someone less fortunate.

Upward Social Comparison
Comparing oneself to someone better.

Self-Perception
Defining yourself through making observations of your own behavior.

Reflected Appraisal
Defining our value based on how highly others evaluate us.

Tiplyashina Evgeniya/Shutterstock.com

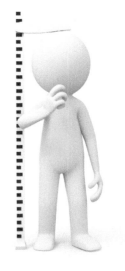

Jane0606/Shutterstock.com

Looking Glass Self
Defining our value based on our perceptions of what others think of us.

Self-Discrepancy
Identifying differences between various models of self.

Frustration-Aggression Hypothesis
The tendency of people who are frustrated to turn more aggressive.

Self-Assessment
The motivation to measure oneself accurately.

Self-Enhancement
The motivation to raise self-esteem, to feel good about oneself.

Self-Verification
The motivation to confirm beliefs you hold about yourself.

Purposes of Self-Evaluation

What purpose does self-evaluation have? Why do we do it? Sedikides (1993) describes three possible motivations: self-assessment, self-enhancement, and self-verification. In **self-assessment**, the goal is to have accurate information about oneself. For example, a person could run. They think they run pretty fast. But how fast? So they time themselves. Now they know how fast they can run 500 meters. But is that pretty fast? They don't know unless they have some access to average speeds for that distance, along with maybe a standard deviation or slow and record fast speeds. A valedictorian in a small high school graduating class may not be the top of the class when they go to college and have stiffer competition. The star high school athlete may or may not start when they are recruited for the college team.

Another purpose of self-evaluation is to feel good about oneself, **self-enhancement** (Taylor, 1989). If we can strengthen our self-esteem, or maintain high self-esteem we can be happy and have a sense of well-being or success. Below we will discuss several ways through which we can boost our level of self-esteem, or keep it at a high level.

But some people have low self-esteem, and don't seem to be all that motivated to try to boost it. Why aren't those people engaging in self-enhancement? One possible reason is because they are choosing to emphasize a different self-goal, that of **self-verification** (Swann, 1983). Self-verification is when the desire is to confirm information about the self-concept, to check the accuracy of self-assessment. Someone with low self-esteem may have a partner who tells them they are stupid or ugly. This may not be making them happier, but it may be confirming a self-belief. Sometimes it may be better to be right than to feel good (Swann, 1997).

Albert Bandura (1997) discussed another use of self-evaluation, self-efficacy, the sense of being capable of something. As we discussed earlier, this is a component of the self-concept. Like with self-esteem, self-efficacy can be global/general ("I am a capable person.") or domain-specific ("I am good at math."). By evaluating our performance, we can build a sense of whether success at a given task is likely or unlikely. The more likely success is, that is, the higher one's self-efficacy, the better we feel about ourselves, the more likely we are to take on challenges in that area, and the less stress we will feel about future performance in that area. If we combine self-efficacy with social comparison, we can doubly feel good because we are not only good at something but also good at something that many people are not.

Maintaining the Self

How do we maintain our self-concept? How do we balance the competing needs for self-verification and self-enhancement? How does our self-evaluation react to positive and negative feedback, or prepare for it occurring in the future?

We mentioned earlier using self-perception (Bem, 1965) to form aspects of self-concept. Miller and Ross (1975) carried strategic attributional patterns one step further in their concept of the **self-serving bias**. Recall that with the fundamental attribution error (Jones, 1979), we tend to prefer making internal, dispositional attributions of others' behavior. Jones and Nisbett (1971) expanded on this with the **actor-observer effect,** where people tend to make internal attributions when they are the observer of others' behavior, but tend to make external attributions of their own behavior, particularly when such behavior is less than socially desirable. Miller and Ross carried this one step further, by showing that high self-esteem people strategically use the actor-observer effect to meet self-enhancement motivations. Specifically, they argue that high self-esteem people maintain high self-esteem by generating external attributions for failures, but internal attributions for success. For example, someone could say, "I earned an A on the exam because I am a smart person" but say, "I got a D on that exam because there was too much material on the test" or "my teacher hates me." It turns out that low self-esteem people can meet their self-verification needs by using a similar but opposite pattern. They say, "I got an A because I got lucky" or "I studied extra hard for this test," while saying, "I got a D because I'm stupid" (low self-concept) or "I'm a bad test-taker" (low self-efficacy).

Self-Serving Bias
An attribution pattern that favors self-enhancement goals.

Actor-Observer Effect
To blame others' behaviors on their personality, but one's own behavior on circumstances.

People can also use social identity processes to maintain self-esteem. If one can glean a self-concept from one's group membership, one can gain a good self-esteem from being a member of a successful group. Cialdini and colleagues (1976) defined this as **basking in reflected glory**. They found that students were more likely to wear school colors on the Monday following a sports victory than on the Monday following a loss. In other words, again, we want to internalize success ("We won") and external-ize failure ("The team lost," i.e., not me). We accept our group membership when it is to our advantage to do so, when it brings us credit, and distance ourselves inasmuch as is possible when the group reflects poorly on us.

Basking in Reflected Glory
Improving self-worth by pointing out group membership when one's group is successful.

Alicke (1985) argues that we strategically boost our self-esteem by rating ourselves highly on socially desirable characteristics, otherwise known as the **better than average effect**. For example, we mentioned earlier that global self-esteem measurement suffers from a ceiling effect. People are much more likely to score perfect high scores than perfect low scores. In fact, self-esteem usually has to be divided into high and low not by the midpoint of the scale, but by a median split (50% higher, 50% lower) of the obtained scores. In my experience, if I use a 7-point scale to measure self-esteem, I get about 5–10% of people averaging a 7 across the 10 items, and the median is typically about a 5.5. It is rare to have someone score less than a 3, unless they are also scoring highly on measures of clinical depression. It is like how Garrison Keillor of the Prairie Home Companion radio show describes the residents of Lake Woebegon, "Where the women are strong, the men are good-looking, and all the children are above-average." If the world is populated with more downward social comparisons than upward social comparisons, you can feel pretty good about yourself.

Better than Average Effect
The tendency to score yourself as above average, especially on socially desirable characteristics.

One phenomenon that I have seen with increasing frequency as I advanced through school was the **imposter syndrome** (Kolligian & Sternberg, 1991). This is when talented people with low self-esteem, unstable high self-esteem, or moderately low self-efficacy are faced with what they perceive to be upward social

Imposter Syndrome
To feel like you are unworthy and fake.

comparison. For example, if someone performs well in college, but perhaps not the best, and then goes to graduate school, but is accepted by some and rejected by others (which is, incidentally, a common experience), they find themselves in a classroom full of fellow graduate students. However, their sense of self is weaker. So they feel like an imposter, like a fake, someone who doesn't belong. They are surrounded by "smart people," and they think, "I'm not as smart as they are, and it's only a matter of time until I make a mistake and they find out that I don't belong here." Interestingly, this strategy leads to high performance, but no change in self-esteem. Because they don't want to be found out, imposters work really hard to learn what they need to, to maintain the façade. In doing so, they actually are successful. However, because they attribute the cause of their success to hard work more than ability, their unstable specific attribution means they don't accept personal credit (and the resulting esteem boost) from their success. They just think they got lucky this time, but will be discovered soon enough, and the cycle continues.

Defensive Pessimism
To expect to fail, so that you don't feel as bad if you actually do fail.

A related concept is that of **defensive pessimism** (Norem & Cantor, 1986). A person with low self-esteem expects negative feedback and tries to boost self-protection by not setting their hopes too high ("This is going to be hard, and I'm probably going to fail."). But, because they expect a challenge, they prepare extra well. So, when it comes time for the performance, they end up avoiding the negative consequence and are pleasantly surprised by the positive feedback. Like with the imposter syndrome, the downside to this, unfortunately, is that they tend to attribute this success to temporary causes ("I only did well because I studied hard this time. I'll probably fail next time."), which perpetuates the cycle.

igor-stevanovic/Shutterstock.com

Another way that people can protect the self-concept is by **self-handicapping** (Berglas & Jones, 1978). Self-handicapping is when one prepares for potentially negative feed-

Self-Handicapping
To make excuses in advance of potential negative feedback.

back by providing an external attribution in advance. This protects from negative reflected appraisals. For example, a student comes in to an exam, and on the way in tells the professor, "I hope I do well on this. I didn't get to study as much as I wanted to because they were understaffed at both of my jobs the past week so they increased my hours and I didn't have a lot of time to study. I will do my best, though." Self-handicapping has a double bonus in the self-protection department because if the student does poorly, the evaluator has a handy external attribution and so is less likely to do the fundamental attribution error. But if the student performs well, the professor can enhance the internal attribution, "Look at them and how well they did even on top of working two jobs and not studying. They must really be smart!" One downside to self-handicapping is that the excuse is often real, that the person did not study as much as he or she should have, which increases the likelihood of failure.

Self-complexity can protect the self from the effects of negative feedback by serving as a buffer (Linville, 1987; Rafaeli-Mor & Steinberg, 2002) or compensation (Greenberg & Pyszczynski, 1985). People low in self-complexity have sort of put "all their eggs in one basket." If they receive negative feedback in that domain or role, they are cast adrift. They have no choice but to feel badly because they have been criticized at the core. However, if someone has high self-complexity, they have a diverse self-concept. This allows them to be more resilient against criticism because they can choose to deemphasize the low-performing domain and emphasize talents in other areas ("I may have done poorly on the algebra test, but I'm really good at art and I like that! I just don't like math, I guess."). The only time this isn't really a functional strategy is if the underperforming domain is not able to be devalued because of its value for the larger society (for example, education), which leads to depression or disengagement (Downey, 2008).

Maintaining a Positive Mindset—Current Areas of Research

There have been several mechanisms and traits that have been proposed for how we can keep a positive outlook. One perspective that has received a lot of research attention in recent years is **terror management theory** (Rosenblatt, Greenberg, Solomon, Pyszczynski, & Lyon, 1989; Greenberg et al., 1990). The basic premise is that we have a perpetual unconscious existential fear of death. Death is unknown and is guaranteed to occur at some point. So, we have a chronic level of anxiety about our mortality. We deal with this by buying into cultural worldviews (religion, politics, etc.) to find a sense of meaning and purpose for this life, and reasons to not fear a next. What researchers have shown is that reminding people of their own mortality creates anxiety, but that people are capable of reducing this anxiety by tapping into cultural values in their self-concept, and emphasizing

kornpoj/Shutterstock.com

social identities by rewarding people who reflect those cultural values and punishing those who are perceived as deviant. These effects seem to be particularly enhanced for people with high self-esteem.

Another area of research recently is trying to understand mechanisms of **self-regulation** or **ego depletion** (Baumeister, Bratslavsky, Muraven, & Tice, 1998), related to self-control. The argument is that our ability to stay focused, make decisions, exercise restraint, etc. uses a finite fuel of the self. In other words, concentration and thinking take effort, and we only have so much effort each day that we are able to spend. The more we have to exercise self-control, the more of that resource we burn and the harder it is to exercise it later. For example, people are more prone to engage in road rage at the end of the day on the way home than early in the day on their way to work (Denson, 2009). Stress causes us to have more difficulty disciplining children, or more prone to eating take-out for supper. Thankfully, with a good night's sleep, ego strength appears to recharge for the coming day. There are interesting implications for self-regulation theory in the area of addictions, weight control, delinquency, stress management, and domestic violence.

Self-determination theory (Ryan & Deci, 2000) provides another area of research with a lot of potential benefits to self and society. This theory of

9nong/Shutterstock.com

Terror Management Theory
When reminded of one's own mortality, people's tendency to conform to dominant cultural worldviews as an esteem buffer.

Self-Regulation
Controlling one's thoughts, feelings, and behaviors to achieve goals.

Ego Depletion
Self-control resources dwindle over time as they become overused.

Self-Determination
The motivation to have well-being and personal success.

Self-Compassion
A forgiveness of one's own failures or shortcomings.

motivation argues that we have an innate desire to be healthy, happy, and effective. People cross-culturally have three core needs (competence, autonomy, and relatedness) which, if met, lead to personal and interpersonal thriving, and if not met, lead to passivity and alienation. Competence is the need to feel successful or effective (White, 1959). Autonomy is the need to be able to make choices in your own best interest (deCharms, 1968). Relatedness comes out of attachment theory (Hazan & Shaver, 1987), and is the idea that people need to feel secure, loved, and loving in their relationships with others (Baumeister & Leary, 1995). These three needs translate into our intrinsic motivations, life goals, and overall well-being, and have been shown to have implications in education, health, organizations, environment, sports, interpersonal relationships, and therapy.

An additional approach to come out of the positive psychology movement is the trait of **self-compassion** (Neff, Kirkpatrick, & Rude, 2007). Billed as the new alternative to the study of self-esteem, self-compassion is a trait where you are kind and understanding toward oneself, see failures as something that is normal and common to everybody, and maintain an objective view of painful experience. Self-compassion has been shown to protect against ego threat and to enhance well-being. It serves as a buffer to stress and provides psychology with an outward-focused, less emotionally volatile aspect to psychological health. In essence, if you are able to accept your personal flaws and mistakes and not obsess over negative feedback, you are able to stay emotionally stable and appreciative of life. It too has shown benefits in motivation, school, health, jobs, and social services.

THINKING CRITICALLY

1. Looking at your list from the 20-Statements exercise, analyze it more closely. How has it changed, if at all, in the past 6 months? How much of it was shaped by your parents? Your friends? Are there aspects you'd like to add, or eliminate? What might you try in order to accomplish that? How might you enhance your degree of self-complexity? Or self-efficacy?

2. Ask five other people from different backgrounds to generate a list of five possible selves each. "Imagine yourself eight years from now. Describe who you are and what you are doing." Complete the exercise yourself as well. Examine the answers. What similarities and differences do you see between lists, and how might you explain them?

3. Susan is a successful physics major with a 3.70 grade point average. She is also on the volleyball team and works part-time as a server at a local restaurant to help pay her way through school. Mid-semester she gets her Calculus test back and she scored a C+. How does she react, and what does she do in response? Explain using concepts from the chapter.

4. Blake is on Facebook and sees several of his friends posting about a recent school shooting. Blake has never experienced anything like that, but he can imagine what it would be like. On his way to class, he sees some fellow students teasing that weird girl who dresses differently and is always off by herself. What does he probably do?

   a.   Step between them and defend the girl

   b.   Join in on picking on her

   c.   Walk on by and try to forget about it

   Explain your answer, using theories and concepts from the chapter.

Conclusion

As we have seen in the last few pages, the self is a rich, diverse, and fascinating area of study for social psychologists. Understanding the self and how it works can be applied to both individual and interpersonal aspects of psychology, and used at home, school, work, recreation, and innumerable other settings. See the Thinking Critically Box on page 62 to reflect on concepts covered in this chapter.

Advanced Topics and Additional Readings

Barlett, C., Harris, R. J., Smith, S., & Bonds-Raake, J. (2005). Action figures and men. *Sex Roles, 53*(11–12), 877–885. doi:10.1007/s11199-005-8304-4

Baumeister, R. F., & Tierney, J. (2011). *Willpower: Rediscovering the greatest human strength.* New York, NY: Penguin Press.

Burke, B. L., Martens, A., & Faucher, E. H. (2010). Two decades of terror management theory: A meta-analysis of mortality salience research. *Personality and Social Psychology Review, 12*(2), 155–195. doi:10.1177/1088868309352321

Cozzarelli, C., & Karafa, J. A. (1998). Cultural estrangement and terror management theory. *Personality and Social Psychology Bulletin, 24*(3), 253–267. doi:10.1177/0146167298243003

Foster, J. D., Kernis, M. H., & Goldman, B. M. (2007). Linking adult attachment to self-esteem stability. *Self and Identity, 6*(1), 64–73. doi:10.1080/15298860600832139

Matsumoto, D. (1999). Culture and self: An empirical assessment of Markus and Kitayama's theory of independent and interdependent self-construals. *Asian Journal of Social Psychology, 2,* 289–310.

Sirois, F. M. (2014). Procrastination and stress: Exploring the role of self-compassion. *Self and Identity, 13*(2), 128–145. doi:10.1080/15298868.2013.763404

Vaughan, J., Zeigler-Hill, V., & Arnau, R. C. (2014). Self-esteem instability and humor styles: Does the stability of self-esteem influence how people use humor? *Journal of Social Psychology, 154*(4), 299–310.

References

Alicke, M. D. (1985). Global self-evaluation as determined by the desirability and controllability of trait adjectives. *Journal of Personality and Social Psychology, 49*(6), 1621–1630. doi:10.1037/0022-3514.49.6.1621

Allott, N. (Executive Producer), & Hooper, T. (Director). (2012). *Les miserables* [Motion picture]. United States: Universal Pictures.

Bandura, A. (1997). *Self-efficacy: The exercise of control.* New York, NY: Freeman.

Baumeister, R. F., Bratslavsky, E., Muraven, M., & Tice, D. M. (1998). Ego depletion: Is the active self a limited resource? *Journal of Personality and Social Psychology, 74*(5), 1252–1265. doi:10.1037/0022-3514.74.5.1252

Baumeister, R. F., & Leary, M. R. (1995). The need to belong: Desire for interpersonal attachments as a fundamental human motivation. *Psychological Bulletin, 117,* 497–529. doi:10.1037/0033-2909.117.3.497

Bem, D. J. (1965). An experimental analysis of self-persuasion. *Journal of Experimental Social Psychology, 1*(3), 199–218. doi:10.1016/0022-1031(65)90026-0

Berglas, S., & Jones, E. E. (1978). Drug choice as a self-handicapping strategy in response to noncontingent success. *Journal of Personality and Social Psychology, 36*(4), 405–417. doi:10.1037/0022-3514.36.4.405

Bruch, M. A. (1996). Cognitive interference and social interaction: The case of shyness and nonassertiveness. In I. G. Sarason, G. R. Pierce, & B. R. Sarason (Eds.), *Cognitive interference: Theories, methods, and findings* (pp. 211–229). Hillsdale, NJ: Erlbaum.

Carver, C. S. (1975). Physical aggression as a function of objective self-awareness and attitudes toward punishment. *Journal of Experimental Social Psychology, 11*(6), 510–519. doi:10.1016/0022-1031(75)90002-5

Cialdini, R. B., Borden, R. J., Thorne, A., Walker, M. R., Freeman, S., & Sloan, L. R. (1976). Basking in reflected glory: Three (football) field studies. *Journal of Personality and Social Psychology, 34*(3), 366–375. doi:10.1037/0022-3514.34.3.366

Cooley, C. H. (1902). *Human nature and the social order*. New York, NY: Scribner.

deCharms, R.(1968). *Personal causation: The internal affective determinants of behavior*. New York, NY: Academic Press.

Denson, T. F. (2009). Angry rumination and the self-regulation of aggression. In J. P. Forgas, R. F. Baumeister, & D. M. Tice (Eds.), *Psychology of self-regulation: Cognitive, affective, and motivational processes* (pp. 233–248). New York, NY: Psychology Press.

Diener, E., Fraser, S. C., Beaman, A. L., & Kelem, R. T. (1976). Effects of deindividuation variables on stealing among Halloween trick-or-treaters. *Journal of Personality and Social Psychology, 33*(2), 178–183. doi:10.1037/0022-3514.33.2.178

Dollard, J., Miller, N. E., Doob, L. W., Mowrer, O. H., & Sears, R .R. (1939). *Frustration and aggression*. New Haven, CT: Yale University Press.

Downey, D. B. (2008). Black/White differences in school performance: The oppositional culture explanation. *Annual Review of Sociology, 34*, 107–126. doi:10.1146/annurev.soc.34.040507.134635

Duval, T. S., & Wicklund, R. A. (1972). *A theory of objective self-awareness*. New York, NY: Academic Press.

Elkind, D. (1985). Egocentrism redux. *Developmental Review, 5*, 218–226. doi:10.1016/0273-2297(85)90010-3

Erikson, E. H., & Erikson, J. M. (1997). *The life cycle completed*. New York, NY: Norton.

Erol, R. Y., & Orth, U. (2014). Development of self-esteem and relationship satisfaction in couples: Two longitudinal studies. *Developmental Psychology, 50*(9), 2291–2303. doi:10.1037/a0037370

Fenigstein, A., Scheier, M. F., & Buss, A. H. (1975). Public and private self-consciousness: Assessment and theory. *Journal of Consulting and Clinical Psychology, 43*, 522–527. doi:10.1037/h0076760

Festinger, L. (1954). A theory of social comparison processes. *Human Relations, 7*(2), 117–140.

Franzoi, S. L., & Shields, S. A. (1984). The Body-Esteem Scale: Multidimensional structure and sex differences in a college population. *Journal of Personality Assessment, 48*, 173–178.

Goffman, E. (1959). *The presentation of self in everyday life*. New York, NY: Doubleday.

Greenberg, J., & Pyzsczynski, T. (1985). Compensatory self-inflation: A response to the threat to self-regard of public failure. *Journal of Personality and Social Psychology, 49*(1), 273–280. doi:10.1037/0022-3514.49.1.273

Greenberg, J., Pyszczynski, T., Solomon, S., Rosenblatt, A., Veeder, M., Kirkland, S., & Lyon, D. (1990). Evidence for terror management theory II: The effects of mortality salience on reactions to those who threaten or bolster the cultural worldview. *Journal of Personality and Social Psychology, 58*(2), 308–318. doi:10.1037/0022-3514.58.2.308

Hazan, C., & Shaver, P. (1987). Romantic love conceptualized as an attachment process. *Journal of Personality and Social Psychology, 52*(3), 511–524. doi:10.1037/0022-3514.52.3.511

Higgins, E. T. (1989). Self-discrepancy theory: What patterns of self-beliefs cause people to suffer? In L. Berkowitz (Ed.), *Advances in experimental social psychology* (Vol. 22, pp. 93–136). New York, NY: Academic Press.

Hofstede, G. (1991). *Cultures and organizations: Software of the mind*. London, England: McGraw-Hill.

Hofstede, G., Hofstede, G. J., & Minkov, M. (2010). *Cultures and organizations: Software of the mind, revised and expanded* (3rd ed.). New York, NY: McGraw-Hill.

Jones, E. E. (1979). The rocky road from acts to dispositions. *American Psychologist, 34*, 107–117. doi:10.1037/0003-066X.34.2.107

Jones, E. E., & Nisbett, R. E. (1971). *The actor and the observer: Divergent perceptions of the causes of behavior*. New York, NY: General Learning Press.

Kernis, M. H. (1993). The roles of stability and level of self-esteem in psychological functioning. In R. F. Baumeister (Ed.), *Self-esteem: The puzzle of low self-regard* (pp. 167–182). New York, NY: Springer.

Kernis, M. H. (2005). Measuring self-esteem in context: The importance of stability of self-esteem in psychological functioning. *Journal of Personality, 73*(6), 1569–1605. doi:10.1111/j.1467-6494.2005.00359.x

Kolligian, J., Jr., & Sternberg, R. J. (1991). Perceived fraudulence in young adults: Is there an "Imposter Syndrome"? *Journal of Personality Assessment, 56*(2), 308–326.

Kong, F., Ding, K., & Zhao, J. (2015). The relationships among gratitude, self-esteem, social support and life satisfaction among undergraduate students. *Journal of Happiness Studies, 16*(2), 477–489. doi:10.1007/s10902-014-9519-2

Kuhn, M. H. (1960). Self-attitudes by age, sex and professional training. *Sociological Quarterly, 1,* 39–56. doi:10.1111/j.1533-8525.1960.tb01459.x

Kuhn, M. H., & McPartland, T. S. (1954). An empirical investigation of self-attitudes. *American Sociological Review, 19*(1), 68–76. doi:10.2307/2088175

Kuster, F., Orth, U., & Meier, L. L. (2013). High self-esteem prospectively predicts better work conditions and outcomes. *Social Psychological and Personality Science, 4*(6), 668–675. doi:10.1177/1948550613479806

Linville, P. W. (1985). Self-complexity and affective extremity: Don't put all your eggs in one cognitive basket. *Social Cognition, 3,* 94–120. doi:10.1521/soco.1985.3.1.94

Linville, P. W. (1987). Self-complexity as a cognitive buffer against stress-related illness and depression. *Journal of Personality and Social Psychology, 52*(4), 663–676. doi:10.1037/0022-3514.52.4.663

Markus, H. (1977). Self-schemata and processing information about the self. *Journal of Personality and Social Psychology, 35,* 63–78. doi:10.1037/0022-3514.35.2.63

Markus, H. R., & Kitayama, S. (1998). The cultural psychology of personality. *Journal of Cross-Cultural Psychology, 29*(1), 63–87. doi:10.1177/0022022198291004

Markus, H., & Kunda, Z. (1986). Stability and malleability of the self-concept. *Journal of Personality and Social Psychology, 51*(4), 858–866. doi:10.1037/0022-3514.51.4.858

Markus, H., & Nurius, P. (1986). Possible selves. *American Psychologist, 41*(9), 954–969. doi:10.1037/0003-066X.41.9.954

Mead, G. H. (1934). *Mind, self, and society.* Chicago, IL: University of Chicago Press.

Miller, D. T., & Ross, M. (1975). Self-serving biases in the attribution of causality: Fact or fiction? *Psychological Bulletin, 82,* 213–225. doi:10.1037/h0076486

Neff, K. D., Kirkpatrick, K. L., & Rude, S.S. (2007). Self-compassion and adaptive psychological functioning. *Journal of Research in Personality, 41*(1), 139–154. doi:10.1016/j.jrp.2006.03.004

Nolen-Hoeksema, S., Wisco, B. E., & Lyubomirsky, S. (2008). Rethinking rumination. *Perspectives on Psychological Science, 3,* 400–424. doi:10.1111/j.1745-6924.2008.00088.x

Norem, J. K., & Cantor, N. (1986). Defensive pessimism: Harnessing anxiety as motivation. *Journal of Personality and Social Psychology, 51*(6), 1208–1217. doi:10.1037/0022-3514.51.6.1208

Oyserman, D., & Markus, H. R. (1990). Possible selves and delinquency. *Journal of Personality and Social Psychology, 59*(1), 112–125. doi:10.1037/0022-3514.59.1.112

Park, H. S. (2012). Culture, need for uniqueness, and the false consensus effect. *Journal of Social, Evolutionary, and Cultural Psychology, 6*(1), 82–92. doi:10.1037/h0099223

Piaget, J. (1983). Piaget's theory. In W. Kessen (Ed.), *Handbook of child psychology: Volume I. Theoretical models of human development* (pp. 103–128). New York, NY: Wiley.

Rafaeli-Mor, E., & Steinberg, J. (2002). Self-complexity and well-being: A review and research synthesis. *Personality and Social Psychology Review, 6*(1), 31–58.

Rogers, T. B., Kuiper, N. A., & Kierker, W. S. (1977). Self-reference and the encoding of personal information. *Journal of Personality and Social Psychology, 35,* 677–688. doi:10.1037/0022-3514.35.9.677

Rosenberg, M. (1979). *Conceiving the self.* New York, NY: Basic Books.

Rosenblatt, A., Greenberg, J., Solomon, S., Pyszczynski, T., & Lyon, D. (1989). Evidence for terror management theory: I. The effects of mortality salience on reactions to those who violate or uphold cultural values. *Journal of Personality and Social Psychology, 57*(4), 681–690. doi:10.1037/0022-3514.57.4.681

Ryan, R. M., & Deci, E. L. (2000). Self-determination theory and the facilitation of intrinsic motivation, social development, and well-being. *American Psychologist, 55*(1), 68–78. doi:10.1037/0003-066X.55.1.68

Schlenker, B. R. (1980). *Impression management: The self-concept, social identity, and interpersonal relations.* Monterey, CA: Brooks/Cole.

Sedikides, C. (1993). Assessment, enhancement, and verification determinants of the self-evaluation process. *Journal of Personality and Social Psychology, 65,* 317–338. doi:10.1037/0022-3514.65.2.317

Snyder, M. (1980). The many me's of the self-monitor. *Psychology Today, 13,* 33–40.

Swann, W. B., Jr. (1983). Self-verification: Binging social reality into harmony with the self. In J. Suls & A. G. Greenwald (Eds.), *Social psychological perspectives on the self* (Vol. 2, pp. 33–66). Hillsdale, NJ: Erlbaum.

Swann, W. B., Jr. (1997). The trouble with change: Self-verification and allegiance to the self. *Psychological Science, 8,* 177–180.

Symons, C. S., & Johnson, B. T. (1997). The self-reference effect in memory: A meta-analysis. *Psychological Bulletin, 123*(3), 371–394. doi:10.1037/0033-2909.121.3.371

Tajfel, H., & Turner, J. C. (1979). An integrative theory of intergroup conflict. In W. G. Austin & S. Worchel (Eds.), *The social psychology of intergroup relations* (pp. 33–47). Monterey, CA: Brooks/Cole.

Taylor, S. E. (1989). *Positive illusions: Creative self-deceptions and the healthy mind.* New York, NY: Basic Books.

White, R. W. (1959). Motivation reconsidered: The concept of competence. *Psychological Review, 66,* 297–333. doi:10.1037/h0040934

Chapter Five
Gender

Darin Challacombe and Christopher Kiker-Beury

Fort Hays State University—Washburn University

Learning Objectives

- Define gender, gender differences, and gender relations
- Outline what are gender roles and how they have impacted society and culture
- Describe the history and current theories on sexuality
- Discuss heterosexism and homophobia

Chapter Outline

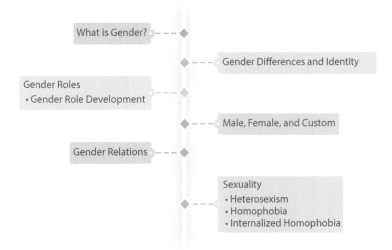

What is Gender?

Gender Differences and Identity

Gender Roles
• Gender Role Development

Male, Female, and Custom

Gender Relations

Sexuality
• Heterosexism
• Homophobia
• Internalized Homophobia

Halloween night, 2013, I drove to a downtown bar to pick up a friend who needed a ride. My friend got in the car and, sheepishly, asked if we could talk. I listened as my friend told me that, although being born a male, my friend felt like a girl since childhood. I had never had anyone tell me something like this before. I was not sure how to act in this situation, but I told my friend that I cared about him and would continue to be supportive.

It has been nearly two years since that night. In that time, my friend, "Summer," began taking hormones, legally changed her name, and officially became transsexual. Summer is a good friend whom I care about deeply. It took a while to transition pronouns from "he" to "she," and, even to this day, I sometimes will think of Summer by her former name. To me, Summer is more woman than most women. She has gone against seemingly insurmountable odds and challenges to match her outward appearance with her inward feelings. She may not be as public as Caitlyn Jenner, but Summer is one of my heroes.

What Is Gender?

To understand gender, you need to first understand sex. **Sex** is the presence of physical or biological aspects that make someone male, female, or intersex. For the most part, these are usually present at birth. **Gender**, on the other hand, describes culture or society's views, behaviors, and attitudes on what makes a person male or female (American Psychological Association, 2011).

How does this work? My friend Summer could be considered intersex because she still has the male reproductive organ but also has breasts; however, Summer's gender is female; she looks and acts like a female. If she did not tell you she was transgender, you would likely have no idea. In a few months when Summer undergoes an operation, both her sex and gender will be female.

Gender Differences and Identity

In the movie *Anchorman*, Will Farrell's character states that women's brains are not as big as men's brains. Most people know this statement is incorrect, hence why some people find it is so funny. There are physical differences between males and females, but do these physical differences manifest in psychological functioning? Are women smarter than men, on average? Are men more aggressive than women?

Since the beginnings of psychology, researchers have examined gender differences (Shields, 1975). Most people believe females and males have considerable differences. However, after reviewing 46 meta-analyses (or summaries of the results of multiple studies), Hyde (2005) developed the **gender similarities hypothesis**. The gender similarities hypothesis states males and females are psychologically similar in *most* instances—just not all. Hyde's theory is based on statistical reports showing only minor differences between the two sexes.

According to Hyde (2014), most gender differences are trivial or insignificant. For example, you would probably imagine girls have a better grasp of

---

Sex

Sex is the physical or biological presence of male, female, or intersex aspects like genitalia, chromosomes, or internal reproductive organs.

Hollygraphic/Shutterstock.com

Gender

Gender describes culture or society's views, behaviors, and attitudes on what makes a person a male or a female.

Gender Similarities Hypothesis

Gender Similarities Hypothesis states men and women are similar in most psychological areas (Hyde, 2005).

language during elementary school. Although research does suggest this is true, the difference is very small (Hyde, 2014). Girls are better at inhibitory control (e.g., saying no) and paying attention than their male counterparts (Else-Quest, Hyde, Goldsmith, & Van Hulle, 2006).

What about sex and sexual contact? Isn't there a *big* difference between females and males in the field of sex? According to Petersen and Hyde (2010), the answer is no. There are some moderate differences, like males masturbate and view pornography more than females, but these differences would not be considered major.

Researchers have discovered differences between females and males regarding their actual attitudes and expressions of love and sex (Harrison & Shortall, 2011). Females generally are more emotionally expressive than males; females also are able to interpret or understand emotional expression better than their male counterparts. Males tend to place a greater emphasis on sexual intimacy than women, whereas women tend to be more romantic.

Virginity loss is also something females and males view differently (Eriksson & Humphreys, 2014). Carpenter (2002, 2005) outlined three reasons for an adolescent to lose his or her virginity: gift, stigma, and process. Females tend to focus on virginity as a *gift*, and often females see their first intimate partner as a long-term partner. Males often see their virginity as either a *stigma* (e.g., virginity is something negative) or a *process* (e.g., rite of passage). Movies such as *Superbad* or *40-Year Old Virgin* propagate both the stigma and process views.

As with most gender differences, these are all generalities. Females may tend to be more romantic, but there are some males who are romantic and sensitive. When you start believing you must act a certain way because you are a certain gender, then you start going into the area of gender roles.

Gender Roles

My friends think I am strange, but I have always liked ironing. Not ironing in general, just ironing my clothes. To me, there is a certain satisfaction that comes when I know the shirt or pants I wear look pressed and neat. I don't see anything strange about a male ironing, but I have friends that look at me funny because of it. Why? Gender roles.

Since you were a child, you have probably heard people refer to some things as a woman's job (e.g., doing dishes, sewing, babysitting) versus things that are men's jobs (e.g., fixing cars, carpentry, boxing). These are the stereotypes of **gender roles**—there is no reason why a male cannot sew or babysit (or iron, for that matter), but, unfortunately, society has a tendency to consider this behavior as "odd."

Why do my friends think that I am strange because I like to iron? It is because ironing, sewing, housework, and other domestic tasks are often considered feminine tasks. Of course, American society also used to view childrearing as a female's job, yet men are getting more and more involved in this task. My brother, a high school teacher, spent his summer vacation taking care of his son (my nephew) so that my sister-in-law could work during the day.

Gender Roles
Gender roles describe how society views acceptable behavior for male and female individuals.

Ho Yeow Hui/Shutterstock.com

Masculine	Androgynous	Feminine
Ambitious		Affection
Leader		Sensitive
Dominant		Submissive
Athletic		Shy

Figure 5.1.   Visual representation of gender roles as proposed by Bem.

I frequently get the opportunity to travel with my job. When I fly, I find it interesting to see male flight attendants. If you look at an advertisement for an airline, it will likely feature a female flight attendant serving a beverage or smiling at a customer (Chen, Lee, Yu, & Shen, 2014). How do you think a male flight attendant feels when even the marketing department for their airline is showing their position as more feminine? In reality, most flight attendants' main job is passenger safety.

In her research, Bem (1981a) believed individuals use a schema (or an automatic mental process) to categorize an individual's traits into feminine, masculine, and gender-neutral categories. In a way, people tend to view certain gender roles on a continuum with the two ends being masculine and feminine. Bem (1974) proposed gender roles could be viewed on this continuum with the addition of a middle point: androgynous (see Figure 5.1).

Society dictates the views on what makes a trait masculine or feminine (Bem, 1981a). The traits listed under the feminine and masculine categories (Figure 5.1) were American society's perspective 30 or 40 years ago (Bem, 1974). As such, these gender roles influenced not only how society viewed both women and men but also the importance of women and men. For example, it has only been less than 150 years that women have been able to vote.

Though there are still societies and organizations with marginalized views toward women, much of society has evolved and uplifted women to a higher position than in the past. Even with this relatively higher position, women are still not equal to men. According to the Center for American Progress, women make up 50.8 percent of the US population; yet, women significantly lag behind men in positions of leadership (Warner, 2014). Unfortunately, the **glass ceiling** is still present in today's societies (Carnes & Radojevich-Kelley, 2011).

A few decades ago, there was a significant disparity between females' and males' college graduation rates. Recently, more females are completing both undergraduate and graduate degrees. However, traditional gender role beliefs tend to impact female/male wage disparities: Women who held traditional gender roles tended to make less money than those with more modern views or men (Judge & Livingston, 2008).

Perhaps you have heard jokes about the Women's National Basketball Association (WNBA) or women carpenters. People who tell these jokes help reinforce negative gender roles regarding women in a way that is similar to the view males should not be flight attendants (Chen et al., 2014). To Bem (1974) and others, these views are inaccurate and should be changed. An

Glass Ceiling

Glass ceiling describes the fact that women technically have the ability to be equal with men in employment settings. However, they are not given the opportunity or are not actually equal in pay with men.

Jacob Lund/Shutterstock.com

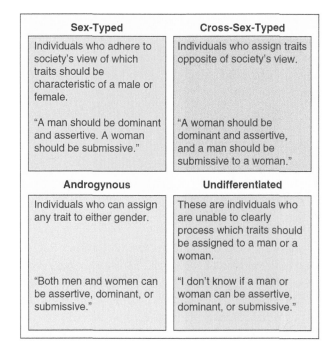

Figure 5.2.   Gender role clustering as proposed by Bem.

individual's assigned gender at birth does not determine whether they will behave in more "masculine" or "feminine" characteristics.

The Bem Sex-Role Inventory (BSRI; Bem, 1974) is a tool used to identify sex-typed individuals—individuals who hold strong views about what traits are feminine and masculine (Bem, 1981b). Our society continues to hold strong, rigid beliefs on gender roles, thinking in terms of black or white. However, there is more of a grey area when it comes to gender roles. Bem (1981a) identified four categories of gender role clustering: sex-typed, cross-sex-typed, androgynous, and undifferentiated (Figure 5.2).

If you take the BSRI, you view lists of traits considered to be masculine, feminine, or neutral (e.g., friendly, sincere, adaptable) and rank to what extent the trait describes you (Bem, 1981b). Being a man and having masculine traits may be what is typical for you, or you might be opposite and have more feminine traits. Instead of letting society dictate how you should act based on your gender, just be yourself, whether that is masculine, feminine, or androgynous. If you want to see where you fit on gender roles, you can take the BSRI online at http://garote.bdmonkeys.net/bsri.html.

Gender Role Development

Where do we get our views on gender roles? Most of these views come from our parents. Media, books, television, and movies can shape a child's view on what is appropriate for gender. Women were generally portrayed as stay-at-home care-givers during the early days of television (Martinez-Sheperd, 2006). Shows like *Leave It to Beaver* or *The Dick Van Dyke Show* portray the main female character as focused mostly on domestic matters. Fortunately, these stereotypes have shifted; popular shows like *Modern Family*, *Breaking Bad*, and *Grey's Anatomy* all feature women in the workplace.

Television programming and movies continue to mirror or shape societal views. Hentges and Case (2012) found that three large children's television-oriented networks had more programming featuring male characters over female characters; however, they did not find a big difference between these female versus male characters' authority roles—females were portrayed in authority about the same amount as males (Hentges & Case, 2012). In fact, the 2013 movie "Frozen" features a female princess as a very strong authority figure.

Even though religion is not entirely to blame, some religions helped promote gender role-specific views. In fact, many religions still adhere to latent **misogynistic** viewpoints. For instance, the Catholic Church still does not allow women to serve in roles as priests (Sinlao, 2013). Islam, another one of the world's largest religions, has very strict rules regarding women and their subservient role to men (Jones-Pauly, 2011).

Gender role development begins at an early age with some parents choosing specific colors for male and female children. Baby girls tend to be dressed in pink while baby boys tend to be dressed in blue. In addition, many baby girls are put in dresses and get ribbons added to their hair. Parents often continue with ingraining this gender-role development by steering boys away from dolls and girls away from guns or aggressive items. This also manifests in the types of chores children are given to complete. Even extracurricular activities also tend to be designated for certain genders, such dance for girls or sports for boys. However, there are many popular male dancers or female athletes.

There is nothing illegal with a parent giving their child certain toys or using certain colors. However, it would seem that society will eventually move toward using gender-neutral items on a more regular basis. Target (2015) has already started removing gender-suggestive signs and colors from certain areas where it is not necessary, such as bedding and toys. This movement and others like it serve to reestablish societal norms surrounding gender that can cause conflict. Much of this conflict is occurring because of a lack of understanding or a stubborn hold of traditional gender roles. However, society seems to be moving in the right direction with regard to gender roles.

Male, Female, and Custom

Previously in this chapter, we reviewed the differences between males and females—specifically, what makes a person a male or female. Being born a certain gender at birth does not necessarily mean a person will identify with that same gender: A boy at birth could identify more as a girl, or vice versa. **Gender identity** is how a person self-identifies: male, female, or other. With my friend Summer, she always had felt she was a female. According to the *Diagnostic and Statistical Manual of Mental Disorders* (DSM-5; American Psychiatric Association, 2013), Summer may have **gender identity disorder** (GID).

Imagine you identify as transgender and you have to fill out a form where you identify your gender. What do you choose? Companies like Facebook have begun to make this decision much easier by allowing individuals to be more specific on their gender (Oremus, 2014). There

Misogyny
Misogyny is the dislike or hatred of females.

Gender Identity
Gender identity is how a person chooses to describe who they are, be it male or female or other.

Gender Identity Disorder
Gender identity disorder is the formalized diagnosis for an individual who suffers discontentment with their birth-assigned sex.

LoloStock/Shutterstock.com

are over 50 choices available in Facebook, including **Bigender**, **Cisgender**, **Gender Fluid**, and **Intersex**.

An acquaintance of mine, "Kyle," is self-described as **agender**, or someone genderless. Kyle uses the pronoun "it" instead of "he" or "she" to describe itself. Kyle is not confined to dress in traditional feminine or masculine clothing—Kyle dresses comfortably. Kyle is often the target of ridicule or shame as Kyle lives in a conservative state. Fortunately, Kyle lives in a society that is changing for the better.

Facebook and other companies have taken progressive steps toward recognizing other gender identities. However, research has demonstrated there are still strong prejudices against transgender individuals (Hill & Willoughby, 2005; Tebbe, Moradi, & Ege, 2014). In order to better understand these prejudices, psychologists Hill and Willoughby developed the Genderism and Transphobia Scale (GTS). The GTS attempts to tease out individuals' latent attitudes regarding these matters. The following are some of the questions on the GTS:

> 3. *If I found out that my best friend was changing their sex, I would freak out.*
> 5. *If a friend wanted to have his penis removed in order to become a woman, I would openly support him.*
> 7. *Men who cross-dress for sexual pleasure disgust me.*
> 14. *Children should play with toys appropriate to their own sex.*
> 16. *I would avoid talking to a woman if I knew she had a surgically created penis and testicles.*
> 18. *If I found out that my lover was the other sex, I would get violent.*
> 22. *If a man wearing makeup and a dress, who also spoke in a high voice, approached my child, I would use physical force to stop him.*
> 23. *Individuals should be allowed to express their gender freely.*
> 30. *It is morally wrong for a woman to present herself as a man in public.*
> *(Hill & Willoughby, 2005, p. 543)*

Many prejudicial attitudes come from being taught negative or inaccurate views as a child. Fortunately, people who grow up associated with a transgender individual or are taught factual information about transgender individuals will likely have more positive views toward transgender individuals later in life. In fact, researchers have found individuals who have had a positive interaction with a transgender individual generally have lower scores on the GTS than those who have not (Hill & Willoughby, 2005). Tebbe et al. (2014) reflect these findings and posit some of this prejudice may be found in the out-group biases (see the chapter on this topic).

When Summer told me that she was transgender, I was a little taken aback. She was the first individual I had known for a while who was able to open up and express to me something this personal about herself. I am glad she felt comfortable enough to do that, and I remain very supportive of her. As I said before, she is my hero.

Gender Relations

So far, we have discussed the idea of gender and what it means. Gender can be the sex of an individual based on biology, or it can be how an individual feels, regardless of biology. We also discussed the differences (or similarities) between males and females, gender roles, and gender variations. There are

Bigender

Bigender describes an individual who either simultaneously or abruptly between both male and female (Kirkova, 2015).

Cisgender

Cisgender describes an individual who internal perception of their gender matches their biological or physical elements (Steinmetz, 2014).

Gender Fluid

Gender fluid describes a person who does not feel confined to being on one end of the gender spectrum or the other, but, rather, can vacillate between ends (Gray, 2015).

Intersex

Intersex describes an individual who was born with the biological or physical aspects that do not appear to fit the typical physical characteristics of female or male (Intersex Society of North America, 2008).

Agender

Agender is an individual who describes themselves as genderless.

Gender Relations
Gender relations describes the interactions between males and female, including communication, attitudes, and behaviors.

many variations in the way people can express their sex or gender, and it is important to remember that we may all express ourselves in different ways. What we have not yet discussed is **gender relations**—the interactions between females and males—or sexuality (Kerr & Multon, 2015).

One of my first experiences at falling in love was when I was in 10th grade. Her name was Jenny, and from the moment I saw her, I wanted to get to know her better. As an awkward teen, I was shy and could not get up enough nerve to say hi to her. About halfway through my 10th-grade year, we were both at a school event and I asked her to dance. My palms were sweaty as we line danced with the rest of the school. Even though I always considered this unrequited love (since we never dated or even kissed), I remember how my attraction for her influenced me. I changed the way I dressed to impress her. I acted in the school play to get her attention. I even tried out for the school basketball team.

When someone is in love, they often do some unusual things. For instance, Kerr and Multon (2015) found that gifted female college students often spent considerable time helping their boyfriends with their homework or doing domestic stuff around the boyfriends' residences. If these women spent more time helping their partners, they would likely have considerably less time to focus on their education. In addition, women who married or had children were less likely to be successful compared to men with children as well as single women with no children.

Think back to when you were 8 or 9 years old. Were you thinking about love or boys/girls at this time? Although some of us did, I know I did not focus on love. I was a kid. I joked with my friends about "coodies" when they would interact with a girl. Interestingly, Musto (2014) found that pre-teen coed athletes on the same team did not experience the gender biases often seen in other age groups. That is, the boys on the team did not make fun of the girls because they were girls—the boys functioned as a team with the girls.

So, when do these changes take place from seeing someone as a friend or teammate to seeing them as potential for something more? Puberty. It is during this period in a youth's life when they begin to have sexual desires, as well as changes in physical development (Salerno, Tosto, & Antony, 2015). This change is manifested in all aspects of the youth—from their communication to their friendships or relationships.

During puberty, it is clear we start to get sexual desires. In fact, Baams, Dubas, Overbeek, and van Aken (2014) found that the timing of puberty actually affected the sexual behavior of the youth. Youth who physically developed faster or sooner than their peers were more likely to engage in earlier sexual behavior than their peers who developed on the average scale. Additionally, these early-developing youth were more likely to engage in riskier sexual behavior, like sex without a condom or use of alcohol or drugs before or during sex.

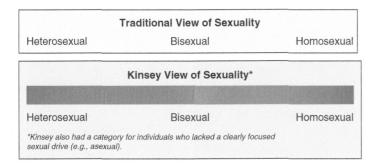

Figure 5.3.

Sexuality

In this chapter, we have focused on gender. So far, we have neglected an important aspect of gender: sexuality. Sexuality is basically who likes who and why. In Chapter 11, you will learn about Alfred Kinsey, a significant pioneer in understanding sexuality (Weinrich, 2014). Earlier researchers viewed sexuality as falling on one of three distinct points (e.g., heterosexuality, homosexuality, and bisexuality). However, Kinsey viewed sexuality as more of a continuum, falling somewhere along a 7-point scale. These two different views of sexuality are depicted in Figure 5.3. You can find more on Kinsey and the sexual continuum in Chapter 11.

Although Kinsey advanced society's views on sexuality, Wienrich (2014) pointed out that Kinsey's scale is often misunderstood. Nowadays, many researchers think that sexuality is on a scale—people can vacillate between ends. That is, a person is not necessarily straight or gay, but can be at various levels of these extremes. In the same way some people view gender as black or white, others view sexuality on either extreme. However, sexuality can be viewed in more of a grey area since it exists along a continuum.

Heterosexism

In Chapter 10, you will learn about prejudice. You will learn that, even though significant progress has been made, there is still a significant amount of prejudice in society. People often have prejudice against people that are different from them. In addition, an individual's prejudice sometimes goes unnoticed even to themselves.

Walls (2008) focused on the prejudices against gays and lesbians. As you can imagine, there are places in the United States where two men or two women can walk down the street holding hands. However, there are other places where this is not advised—people may be upset with this public display of affection, and some may even resort to violence, hostility, or in some cases death. This unnecessary hostility is due to heterosexism.

Heterosexism is loosely defined as a system of beliefs in favor of heterosexual relationships as being normative and more superior compared to homosexual relationships (Walls, 2008). These beliefs often serve to stigmatize and discriminate against any nonheterosexual form of behavior. For example, the U.S. Supreme Court just ruled that gays and lesbians have the right to get married. After this decision, many people protested against the decision. Those protesting could be considered to be expressing heterosexism.

Heterosexism
Heterosexism describes behavior by heterosexual individuals that marginalizes or is contrary to homosexual expression.

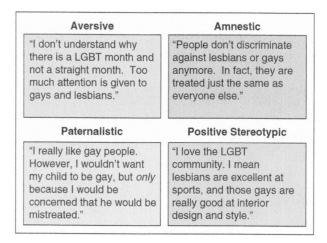

Figure 5.4.   Four types of heterosexism

Walls (2008) extended theories of modern prejudice to include prejudice against gays and lesbians, which consists of increasing multiple dimensions of heterosexism. He created a four-part classification system for heterosexism. He even created a scale to help identity the specific types of heterosexism. Specifically, he identified four heterosexism expressions: aversive, amnestic, paternalistic, and positive stereotypic.

The Multidimensional Heterosexism Inventory is an instrument developed by Walls (2008) to help capture the four types of heterosexism, as presented in Figure 5.4. Aversive heterosexism is the most hostile of the four types of heterosexism, but is strategically noninflammatory. An individual who scores higher on amnestic heterosexism is likely to believe heterosexism no longer exists today. Individuals who score higher on paternalistic heterosexism are likely to have friends who are gay or lesbian, but they would express concern about having a gay or lesbian child. In order to not appear heterosexist, they may say they do not want a gay or lesbian child only because they do not want their child to grow up to face unfair social realities. Finally, an individual who scores higher on positive stereotypic heterosexism is likely to reinforce positive stereotypes about gays or lesbians and may not even be aware they are being heterosexist since the attitudes are positive. However, even positive stereotypes serve to marginalize individuals and can even elicit negative reactions from those with a heteronormative viewpoint (Walls, 2008).

Kiker-Beury and Hockett (2015) found that students who scored higher on positive stereotypic heterosexism were less likely to report learning about LGB issues in the classroom, perhaps because they were unaware of their heterosexist beliefs and thus did not think they needed to learn about LGB issues. In addition, students who scored higher on amnestic heterosexism were less likely to learn about ongoing training and education, and students who scored higher on paternalistic heterosexism were less likely to learn about LGB psychosocial issues. Conversely, clinical psychology and social work graduate students who were associated with lesbian, gay, or bisexual (LGB) individuals, along with those who were more actively involved in training, were more open to learning about LGB issues. Thus, it may be that our own heterosexism must be addressed in order to be open and willing to learn more about LGB issues.

Homophobia

Homophobia is the disapproval and fear of homosexual behavior (Bucher, 2014). Homophobia is not as hostile as heterosexism and is different because homophobic individuals actually have no level of acceptance to the behavior due to their fear. Individuals with enough fear tend to avoid what they are afraid of, whether that is to block it out physically and/or mentally. Others learn they must face their fears in order to overcome them, thus breaking free of homophobic attitudes.

Like many of you, I grew up going to church on a regular basis. Several times, I heard a minister talk about why homosexual behavior was bad—actually condoning homophobia. This homophobia can then be taught to others, and they may grow up falsely learning to fear homosexual behavior. When I was old enough to understand homophobia, my views changed completely, and I realized that the minister was wrong to condone homophobia.

In Bucher's (2014) research, he looked at the relationships between fathers of gay sons and sons of gay fathers. He found that both sets displayed elements of homophobia, but fathers of gay sons were more homophobic than sons of gay fathers. Interestingly, Bucher also found that even though the sets did display homophobic tendencies, the love of the fathers for the sons or sons for the fathers was stronger than the homophobia.

Internalized Homophobia

I grew up in a small, conservative town with one openly gay male and people often made fun of him behind his back or avoided him. I have feminine characteristics, so I was made fun of in my younger years for being "girly" or "gay." In addition, I often heard the minister of my church preach that being gay was wrong. As a result, I tried to act more masculine and reject the image of being gay. It took me a while to finally come out because I had internalized the homophobia and heterosexism I grew up around. In other words, as I saw others express hatred toward gay people, I began to express that same hatred toward myself as a gay person. As a result, I became depressed and my self-esteem was not very high. I finally moved to a bigger city and I was able to meet other gay people and hear similar stories. This newfound support system helped me to open up and accept myself for who I am. As a result, my depression lifted and my self-esteem has grown significantly.

Many individuals who identify as gay or lesbian internalize forms of prejudice they have experienced due to living in a homophobic and heterosexist society. Internalized homophobia is when an individual who identifies as gay or lesbian directs society's negative attitudes toward themselves, resulting in poor self-esteem and a devaluation of the self. In addition, internalized homophobia may lead to substance abuse, eating disorders, suicide, and difficulty with intimacy or commitment. Conversely, individuals who are involved in the gay community have healthy and satisfying relationships, disclose their sexuality in their personal and work lives, and are less likely to develop internalized homophobia due to developing a healthy adjustment to their own sexuality (Williamson, 2000).

THINKING CRITICALLY

Think about your gender, race, ethnicity, and sexual orientation. Are any of these aspects that you chose yourself? Now, think about what you would consider the opposite for each and describe how your life would be different. Would it be different if you were born differently?

Many in society still hold views that sexuality is something chosen or taught. These views are extrapolated into rigid opinions about rights for LGB and other individuals. Imagine the roles were reversed and not being LGB was the minority. How would you feel in this instance?

References

American Psychiatric Association. (2013). *Diagnostic and statistical manual of mental disorders* (5th ed.). Washington, DC: Author.

American Psychological Association. (2011). Guidelines for psychological practice with lesbian, gay, and bisexual clients. *American Psychologist, 67*(1), 10–42.

Baams, L., Dubas, J. S., Overbeek, G., & van Aken, M. A. G. (2014). Transitions in body and behavior: A meta-analytic study on the relationship between pubertal development and adolescent sexual behavior. *Journal of Adolescent Health, 56*(6), 586–598. doi:10.1016/j.jadohealth.2014.11.019

Bem, S. J. (1974). The measurement of psychological androgyny. *Journal of Consulting and Clinical Psychology, 42*(2), 155–162.

Bem, S. L. (1981a). The BSRI and gender schema theory: A reply to Spence and Helmreich. *Psychological Review, 88*, 369–371. Retrieved from http://doi.org/c8pnbt

Bem, S. L. (1981b). Gender schema theory: A cognitive account of sex typing. *Psychological Review, 88*, 354–364. Retrieved from http://doi.org/bc94r5

Bucher, J. (2014). "But he can't be gay": The relationship between masculinity and homophobia in father-son relationships. *The Journal of Men's Studies, 22*(3). doi:10.3149/jms.2203.222

Carnes, W. J., & Radojevich-Kelley, N. (2011). The effects of the glass ceiling on women in the workplace: Where are they and where are they going? *Review of Management Innovation and Creativity, 4*(10), 70–79.

Carpenter, L. M. (2002). Gender and the meaning and experience of virginity loss in the contemporary United States. *Gender and Society, 16*, 345–365. doi:10.1177/0891243202016003005

Carpenter, L. M. (2005). *Virginity lost: An intimate portrait of first sexual experiences*. New York: New York University Press.

Chen, Y. C., Lee, C. S., Yu, T. H., & Shen, J. Y. (2014). Effects of gender role and family support on work adjustment among male flight attendants in Taiwan. *Social Behavior and Personality, 42*(3), 453–463.

Else-Quest, N. M., Hyde, J. S., Goldsmith, H. H., & Van Hulle, C. (2006). Gender differences in temperament: A meta-analysis. *Psychological Bulletin, 132*(1), 33–72.

Eriksson, J., & Humphreys, T. P. (2014). Development of the virginity beliefs scale. *Journal of Sex Research, 51*(1), 107–120. doi:10.1080/00224499.2012.724475

Gray, E. (2015, June 17). Ruby Rose breaks down what it means to be gender fluid. *Huffington Post*. Retrieved from http://www.huffingtonpost.com/2015/06/17/ruby-rose-gender-fluid-video-interview_n_7603186.html

Harrison, M. A., & Shortall, J. C. (2011). Women and men in love: Who really feels it and says it first? *The Journal of Social Psychology, 151*(6), 727–736.

Hentges, B., & Case, K. (2012). Gender representations on Disney Channel, Cartoon Network, and Nickelodean broadcasts in the United States. *Journal of Children and Media, 7*(3), 319–333.

Hill, D. B., & Willoughby, B. L. B. (2005). The development and validation of the genderism and transphobia scale. *Sex Roles, 53*(7). doi:10.1007/s11199-005-7140-x

Hyde, J. S. (2005). The gender similarities hypothesis. *American Psychologist, 60*(6), 581–592.

Hyde, J. S. (2014). Gender similarities and differences. *Annual Review of Psychology, 65,* 373–398.

Intersex Society of North America. (2008). What is intersex? Retrieved from http://www.isna.org/faq/what_is_intersex

Jones-Pauly, C. (2011). *Women under Islam: Gender, justice, and the politics of Islamic law.* London, England: I. B. Tauris.

Judge, T. A., & Livingston, B. A. (2008). Is the gap more than gender? A longitudinal analysis of gender, gender role orientation, and earnings. *Journal of Applied Psychology, 93*(5), 994–1012.

Kerr, B. A., & Multon, K. D. (2015). The development of gender identity, gender roles, and gender relations in gifted students. *Journal of Counseling and Development, 93*(2), 183–191. doi:10.1002/j.1556-6676.2015.00194.x

Kiker-Beury, C., & Hockett, J. M. (2015). *Learning through Heterosexism: Prejudice and Learning about Lesbian, Gay, and Bisexual Issues in Clinical Classrooms.* Manuscript submitted for publication.

Kirkova, D. (2015). 'I've got no control on whether I'm going to be Layton or Layla': Bi-gender teenager lives life as a man and a woman . . . wearing baggy jeans or revealing dresses. DailyMail. Retrieved from http://www.dailymail.co.uk/femail/article-2919585/Bi-gender-teenager-lives-life-man-woman.html#ixzz3fzoQ6vtW

Martinez-Sheperd, I. (2006). *Portrayals of women in prime time reality TV programs* (Masters thesis). Retrospective theses and dissertations. Retrieved from http://lib.dr.iastate.edu/cgi/viewcontent.cgi?article=2395&context=rtd

Musto, M. (2014). Athletes in the pool, girls and boys on deck: The contextual construction of gender in coed youth swimming. *Gender and Society, 28*(3), 359–380.

Oremus, W. (2014, February 13). Here are all the different genders you can be on Facebook. *Slate.* Retrieved from http://www.slate.com/blogs/future_tense/2014/02/13/facebook_custom_gender_options_here_are_all_56_custom_options.html

Petersen, J. L., & Hyde, J. S. (2010). A meta-analytic review of research on gender differences in sexuality: 1993 to 2007. *Psychological Bulletin, 136*(1), 21–38.

Salerno, A., Tosto, M., & Antony, S. D. (2015). Adolescent sexual and emotional development: The role of romantic relationships. *Procedia—Social and Behavioral Sciences, 174,* 932–938. doi:10.1016/j.sbspro.2015.01.714,

Shields, S. (1975). Functionalism, Darwinism, and the psychology of women. *American Psychologist, 30*(7), 739–754.

Sinlao, J. J. (2013). "To the ends of the earth": Catholic women religious in nineteenth-century San Francisco. *U.S. Catholic Historian, 31*(2), 25–49.

Steinmetz, K. (2014, December 23). This is what 'cisgender' means. *Time.* Retrieved from http://time.com/3636430/cisgender-definition/

Target. (2015, August 18). What's in store: Moving away from gender-based signs. *A Bullseye View.* Retrieved from https://corporate.target.com/article/2015/08/gender-based-signs-corporate

Tebbe, E. A., Moradi, B., & Ege, E. (2014). Revised and abbreviated forms of the genderism and transphobia scale: Tools for assessing anti-trans prejudice. *Journal of Counseling Psychology, 61*(4), 581–592.

Walls, N. E. (2008). Toward a multidimensional understanding of heterosexism: The changing nature of prejudice. *Journal of Homosexuality, 55*(1), 20–70.

Warner, J. (2014, March 7). The women's leadership gap: Women's leadership by the numbers. *Center for American Progress.* Retrieved from https://cdn.americanprogress.org/wp-content/uploads/2014/03/WomenLeadership.pdf

Weinrich, J. D. (2014). Notes on the Kinsey scale. *Journal of Bisexuality, 14*(3), 333–340.

Williamson, I. R. (2000). Internalized homophobia and health issues affecting lesbians and gay men. *Health Education Research, 15*(1), 97–108.

Chapter Six
Attitudes and Persuasion

Chelsea A. Schnabelrauch Arndt

Kansas State University

Learning Objectives

- Define attitudes
- Identify ways that attitudes are measured
- Explain how attitudes are formed
- Understand how attitudes change
- Define persuasion
- Explain factors that influence persuasion
- Understand how researchers experimentally study attitude change

Chapter Outline

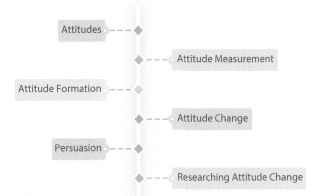

Attitudes

Attitude Measurement

Attitude Formation

Attitude Change

Persuasion

Researching Attitude Change

Attitudes

Have you ever heard the song "My Favorite Things"? It is quite possibly the most popular song from the musical *The Sound of Music* (Wise, 1965). In the song, the main character, Maria, makes a list of some of her favorite things that she thinks about whenever she needs to be cheered up. Maria sings about how she likes kittens' whiskers, sleigh bells, apple strudels, warm wool mittens, and numerous other sights, sounds, and objects. You may be familiar with this song, and perhaps you've wondered what things *you* would include in a song about *your* favorite things. How would you decide what to include in the song? I'm sure that coming up with things that you like and dislike is relatively easy to do, but have you ever wondered *how* you came to like certain things and dislike other things?

The things that we like and dislike can be considered things that we have attitudes about. Our **attitudes** are thus the evaluative feelings that we have toward people, places, objects, and ideas. The concept of attitudes has been around a very long time and is a central idea in Social Psychology (Allport, 1935, 1954). Attitudes are so important to Social Psychologists because they influence how we think and behave. Because attitudes can be indicative of thought and predictive of behavior, attitudes are very heavily studied in Social Psychology. In this chapter, we will dig deeper into what attitudes are and explore how some attitudes differ from other attitudes. We will then learn some of the ways that researchers measure attitudes, how attitudes are formed, and how attitudes change.

Positive, Negative, and Neutral Attitudes

Attitudes can be positive or negative. **Positive attitudes** are attitudes that we have that are favorable. The things that Maria sings about in the song "My Favorite Things" are all things that she has a positive attitude toward. Think about foods, movies, activities, places, and people that you enjoy. These are all things that you have a positive attitude about. I love *The Sound of Music* (Wise, 1965) musical; thus, I have a positive attitude toward it. I enjoy the songs, characters, and the plot. You may have a similar positive attitude toward *The Sound of Music*. You, like me, may enjoy watching it and listening to the music.

Attitudes can also, of course, be *unfavorable*. These are called **negative attitudes**. Any foods, movies, sports, and places that you dislike are things that you have a negative attitude toward. Perhaps you *don't* like *The Sound of Music* (Wise, 1965); if you don't enjoy watching it, or listening to the songs, you may have a negative attitude toward it.

Attitudes toward certain people, places, objects, etc. can of course be neutral or nonexistent. Perhaps you have never seen *The Sound of Music* (Wise, 1965) and thus can't say for sure whether you like or dislike it. You therefore wouldn't really have an attitude toward it. Or perhaps you have seen *The Sound of Music* but feel very neutral about it. Saying that you have a **neutral attitude** toward something means that your attitude is neither favorable nor unfavorable toward it.

Attitude Strength

We certainly like some things and people more than others. Not only can our attitudes toward people, places, and things be favorable or unfavorable, our attitudes can also vary in strength. When you think about foods that you like, you can probably list some foods that you like more than others. Conversely, I'm sure you can think of foods that you *dis*like more than others. Your attitudes toward

Attitudes
The evaluative feelings that an individual has toward people, places, objects, and ideas that influence how that individual thinks and behaves.

Positive Attitudes
Favorable attitudes toward people, places, objects, and things.

Negative Attitudes
Unfavorable attitudes toward people, places, objects, and things.

Neutral Attitudes
Attitudes that are neither favorable nor unfavorable toward people, places, objects, and things.

some things may be stronger than your attitudes toward other things. You may have a positive attitude toward *The Sound of Music* (Wise, 1965), but the strength of that positive attitude may not be as strong as my positive attitude toward the movie. The strength of our attitudes is how we determine what people, places, activities, and things we like more or less than other things. Making a list of your favorite things implies that among all of the things that you like, there are certain things that you like most.

Valery Sidelnykov/Shutterstock.com

Explicit and Implicit Attitudes

Explicit attitudes are attitudes that are most often deliberately formed and easily measured. Explicit attitudes are often formed through **conscious attitude formation**, which is the process of forming an attitude in which the individual is consciously aware that he/she is forming an attitude. When you are cognizant that something you see, hear, or experience is influencing the development of your attitude toward someone or something, you are experiencing conscious attitude formation. Conscious attitude formation may occur when you see an advertisement for a product and are aware that it influences how you feel toward that product or company, or when a person you are talking to says or does something that you know affects the way that you feel about them. Sometimes, you might not only be aware that you are forming an attitude, but you might actually make a deliberate effort to do so! Interviewers, for example, deliberately form attitudes about prospective job applicants that they meet with. They are not only aware that they are forming an attitude, but they make a conscious effort to do so in order to determine if the applicant is right for the position.

In contrast to explicit attitudes, **implicit attitudes** are attitudes that an individual may not consciously realize that he/she has. These attitudes may be involuntarily formed and may be difficult to measure. The involuntary formation of attitudes is called **unconscious attitude formation**. Such attitudes are formed without the individual's awareness that he/she is forming an attitude. In such instances that you unconsciously form an attitude toward a person or thing, you aren't likely to be aware that you even have an attitude toward that person or thing.

Sometimes we unconsciously form attitudes about things simply because we are familiar with them and have been exposed to them often. This is called **mere exposure** (Zajonc, 1968). Just seeing a person, object, or some other thing often makes you more likely to form a positive attitude toward it. Of course, there are times that being exposed to someone or something often makes you form a negative attitude toward it. This is usually the case when the initial encounter with that object, person, or thing is a negative one. In these instances, initial negative attitudes are amplified in consequent encounters. Attitudes that are formed as a result of mere exposure are usually implicit attitudes, which you can recall are attitudes that an individual is not aware that he/she holds. Researchers Kunst-Wilson and Zajonc (1980) illustrated this by showing participants a series of polygon images. When participants were shown these images again mixed with other polygon images that they had not seen before, they rated the images

Explicit Attitudes
Attitudes that are deliberately formed and easily measured.

Conscious Attitude Formation
The process of forming an attitude in which an individual is consciously aware that he/she is forming an attitude.

Implicit Attitudes
Attitudes that an individual may not consciously realize that he/she has. Implicit attitudes may be involuntarily formed and difficult to measure.

Unconscious Attitude Formation
The involuntary process of forming an attitude in which the individual is not aware that he/she is forming an attitude.

Mere Exposure
An unconscious attitude formation in which individuals form a more favorable attitude toward something simply because it is familiar.

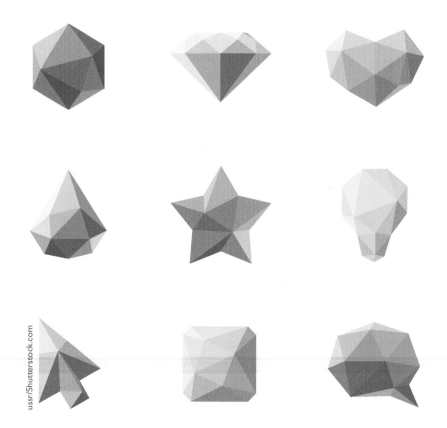

they had previously seen as more favorable than the other images, even though they did not remember which ones they had seen and which ones they had not.

Because implicit attitudes are generally more difficult to measure than explicit attitudes, researchers often have to measure implicit attitudes differently than they measure explicit attitudes. In the next section of this chapter, we will discuss some of the techniques that researchers employ to measure both explicit and implicit attitudes.

Attitude Measurement

As was mentioned earlier, attitudes are very important. Past research has found that our attitudes are often predictive of our intended behaviors (Ajzen & Fishbein, 1977). Social psychologists thus rely on attitudes as an indication of people's thoughts and intended behaviors. Many social psychologists incorporate attitudes into their research, but how exactly do they measure individuals' attitudes?

Explicit and Implicit Attitude Measurements

Explicit Attitude Measurement

A direct way to measure an individual's attitude.

If I want to find out what your attitude toward a movie, food, or place is, the easiest way for me to do so would be to ask you directly. This would be an example of an **explicit attitude measurement**. Explicit attitude measurements are a direct way to measure an individual's attitude. Sometimes, however, it isn't as easy as it sounds. People are sometimes reluctant to report their true attitudes toward someone or something because they are embarrassed or ashamed of their true attitudes. Thus, attitudes can sometimes be tricky and difficult to measure.

There are, of course, other ways that I could try to determine your true attitude. I might monitor your behavior to see what movies you watch, what food you eat, and what places you visit. Or, rather than asking you directly how you feel about a particular movie, food, or place, I could casually strike up a conversation about the topic in question and try to read your body language and facial expressions. These tactics are examples of **implicit attitude measurements**. Implicit attitude measurements assess individuals' attitudes indirectly and are particularly useful for determining implicit attitudes that individuals are not consciously aware that they hold.

Implicit Attitude Measurement
An indirect way to measure an individual's attitude that is particularly useful for measuring implicit attitudes.

There are a number of both explicit and implicit attitude measurements that are used by researchers in attempts to determine individuals' attitudes. In the following sections, we will talk about some specific ways that researchers measure individuals' attitudes. These measurement techniques vary in how easy they are to use, how accurately they measure attitudes, and how commonly they are utilized in research.

Self-Reports The most straightforward way that researchers measure attitudes is by using self-report techniques. On self-reports, researchers simply ask individuals their attitude toward something or someone. It is aptly called self-report because the individual is reporting things about him-/herself.

The most common way that researchers use self-report measures is by asking individuals to agree or disagree with opinion statements. Researchers may ask

individuals to respond to these statements with either a "yes" or a "no" answer, but more commonly researchers utilize Likert scales (Likert, 1932). Likert scales ask individuals to rate *how much* they agree or disagree with each opinion statement. For example, rather than just asking you to respond "yes" or "no" if you agree with the death penalty, I might ask you to rate *how much* you agree or disagree with the death penalty on a scale ranging from 1 to 5. Each number on a Likert scale represents a level of agreement or disagreement, as you can see in Figure 6.1.

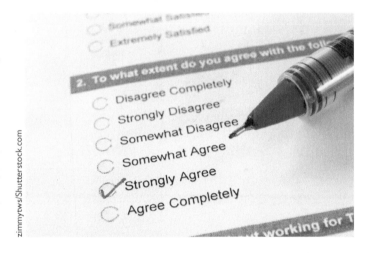

Attitude Likert scales do not have to be from 1 to 5. Researchers might use a −3 to +3 scale with 0 indicating a neutral attitude. You'll notice that a −3 to +3 scale has seven agreement/disagreement options for the respondent to select from. This is called a 7-point scale. Researchers often use 5-point and 7-point Likert scales, but an even number scale (i.e., a 4-point or 6-point scale) can be just as effective.

Researchers may just ask one question to gauge individuals' attitude toward someone or something, or they may use a series of questions. For example, rather than simply asking you to rate how much you agree or disagree with the death penalty, I may ask you multiple different questions that all relate to your attitude about it. In Figure 6.2, there are five sample questions that I might ask you to

1	2	3	4	5
Strongly disagree	Disagree	Neutral	Agree	Strongly agree

Figure 6.1. A Likert scale.

Figure 6.2.   Multiple Likert scale questions.

measure your attitude toward the death penalty. Note that individuals responding to these questions are asked the degree to which they agree or disagree with each statement.

As you can see, your responses to each of the questions above would give me an idea of your attitude toward the death penalty. Taken together, I can better determine whether you have a positive or negative attitude toward capital punishment than I could from just one question, or from one or more yes/no questions. Likert scales give more information than do yes/no questions and are therefore very useful in attitude research.

As you can imagine, self-report attitude measurements have quite a few benefits. Self-reports are fairly easy and relatively cheap to create and distribute. I could easily make an online survey or print out some paper surveys to gather people's attitudes toward some topic, issue, person, or thing. Asking individuals to directly report their attitudes using self-report methods is also presumably an accurate way of measuring individuals' attitudes. Sometimes, though, self-report measures are not always accurate because individuals may knowingly or unknowingly falsely report their attitudes. If individuals' true attitudes are socially undesirable, they may purposefully report a socially desirable attitude rather than their real attitude, even if they are aware that their responses are confidential. Likewise, people's attitudes may not necessarily be socially undesirable, but individuals may want to make a good impression on the researcher or report what attitudes they think the researcher wants them to report. These can all be reasons why individuals may report an opposite or skewed attitude from what they really feel. Controversial issues (such as abortion), sexual behavior, prejudice attitudes, and drug use (including smoking and alcohol) are often topics that individuals may be reluctant to report their true attitudes toward. Individuals may also be reluctant to truthfully report their attitudes toward dieting, certain religions, mental health issues, and other attitudes that may be embarrassing or unpopular.

Some ways that researchers get around this problem is by assuring individuals that their responses are anonymous or confidential. By allowing individuals to report their attitudes on a piece of paper that will not be immediately viewed or by responding with their attitudes on a computer, individuals feel less pressure to report socially desirable attitudes and are thus more likely to report their true attitudes. Another way that researchers sometimes encourage individuals to report their true attitudes is to trick individuals into thinking that the researcher has a way of knowing whether the individual is lying or not. This usually involves the researcher(s) hooking individuals up to a device and telling them that they are hooked up to a lie detector test. This technique has, for the most part, been demonstrated to work 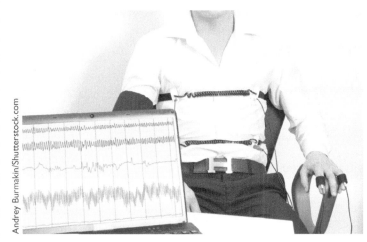 (Aguinis, Pierce, & Quigley, 1993). Specifically, individuals find it more undesirable to be caught lying than to report their true (though possibly unflattering) attitudes. However, this technique is very time consuming and somewhat controversial due to the necessary deception of and lying to participants.

Despite the various drawbacks of self-report measures, researchers overwhelmingly rely on explicit self-report measurements in order to identify individuals' attitudes. Overall, the benefits outweigh the costs, and direct self-report attitude measures are superior to the indirect attitude measurements that we will discuss next. In addition to self-report measurements being less expensive and time consuming, they also tend to be more accurate and precise. Self-report measurements, particularly Likert scales, are more precise and sensitive to the direction of a person's attitude (positive or negative), as well as the strength of the attitude. Though there are definitely certain attitudes in which individuals are inclined to lie about their attitudes, most attitudes that researchers are interested in measuring are not hot button issues; thus, self-report explicit attitude measurements are accurate most of the time.

Observing Behaviors Though less common, researchers sometimes measure people's attitudes by observing their behaviors. Because our attitudes influence our behaviors, it seems reasonable that a person's behavior would indicate his/her attitude. For example, if you really like chocolate, I could perhaps infer your attitude toward chocolate based on your behavior. If I see you eat some chocolate, I can assume that you probably have a positive attitude toward it. If I see you eating a *lot* of chocolate, it's probably safe for me to assume that you have a strong positive attitude toward it. Of course, it's not always safe

Andrey Burmakin/Shutterstock.com

Yuriy Rudyy/Shutterstock.com

to assume things. You may buy broccoli at the store not because you like it, but because you know it's good for you and need its nutrients. I would be wrong, then, in assuming that your behavior indicated your attitude toward broccoli. That's why observing people's behavior in order to determine their attitudes isn't always the best approach.

Observing individuals' behavior as a measurement of attitudes can be fairly easy to do; however, it can be very time consuming for researchers. Unless researchers have access to records that show how many individuals purchased a product or used a particular service, researchers have to collect their data themselves. This involves either observing individuals' behaviors in public ("people watching") or bringing participants into a lab one at a time or in small groups in order to observe their behaviors. Both of these options can require a lot of time and effort on behalf of the researcher to gather data. Furthermore, these techniques can be complicated if behaviors are ambiguous. Does taking a sample at a grocery store indicate that an individual likes a product, or does that person's facial expression after trying the sample indicate his/her attitude toward the sample? Since behaviors can sometimes be subjective, behavioral observation is not the most ideal technique to measure attitudes.

Physiological Responses Researchers also observe and measure people's physiological responses as an indication of their attitudes. One way to do this is to measure an individual's galvanic skin reflex. Essentially, galvanic skin reflex measures a person's amount of perspiration, or sweat, using electrodes. The idea is that people sweat when they are emotionally aroused, thus indicating an emotional response to someone or something. This measure, however, doesn't

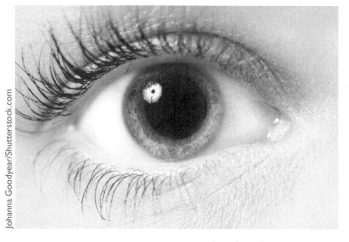

Johanna Goodyear/Shutterstock.com

tell researchers whether a person's attitude is positive or negative—the galvanic skin reflex only indicates the *strength* of an attitude.

Another way that researchers can measure individuals' attitudes using physiological responses is by measuring pupil dilation in the eye. The idea is that individuals' pupils dilate (gets larger) when they have a positive attitude toward something and constrict (gets smaller) when they have a negative attitude toward something. Using pupil dilation as a measure of individuals' attitudes is quite risky though; more research exists that discredits pupil dilation as an accurate measurement of attitudes than research exists that supports it (Woodmansee, 1970). Because pupil dilation is not considered to be a reliable and valid measure of attitudes, it is mostly avoided by researchers.

A last physiological measure that researchers sometimes use to measure individuals' attitudes is the measurement of facial muscle contractions. Specifically, using facial electromyography (EMG) technology, researchers can measure the electrical activity in major facial muscles used to express different emotions. These electrical activities allow researchers to detect facial expressions that may not be visible to the human eye. The muscles' electrical activity may be so subtle that the facial muscles do not visibly move, but the EMG technology can detect the changes in the muscles' electrical activity. More electrical activity in the facial muscles that are used to smile while viewing a person, place, or thing, for example, indicate a positive attitude toward that person, place, or thing. Conversely, more electrical activity in the muscles associated with sadness can indicate a negative attitude.

In addition to the mentioned drawbacks for each of the previously discussed physiological measures, physiological measurements are often time consuming and can be expensive. Not only do participants have to come into a laboratory one at a time, researchers also have to set up the equipment on each participant. As you might imagine, this can be quite laborious. Furthermore, equipment can malfunction. As a result, data may be lost, recorded incorrectly, or not recorded at all.

Projective Attitude Measures Projective attitude measures are yet another way that researchers measure people's attitudes. Projective measures are particularly useful when researchers want to measure implicit attitudes or attitudes that they suspect individuals will falsely report. You can think about projective attitude measures as self-report measurements in disguise. Researchers ask individuals questions in order to determine their attitudes; however, the questions asked do not directly address the attitudes of interest. Instead, researchers get responses from individuals that *indicate* their attitudes.

For example, if we wanted to assess a person's attitudes toward smoking, we may be concerned that some individuals may not report their true attitudes toward smoking. As smoking is widely recognized as an unhealthy habit, some individuals may be embarrassed or ashamed to report that they have a positive attitude toward the behavior. Rather than directly asking individuals to explicitly report their attitudes toward smoking, we might instead show them a picture of a person smoking and ask them to describe the person. We might ask them to describe the pictured person's personality or how successful they are. We might even ask individuals to make up a story about the pictured person. We can then use the responses that individuals give to help us determine each individual's attitude toward smoking. If an individual responds that the smoking individual in the picture is most likely rude, reckless, and unreliable, or the story that the individual tells about the pictured smoker is negative, we can infer that the individual has a negative attitude toward smoking. The idea is that individuals will project their own feelings and attitudes toward smoking into their descriptions and story (Proshansky, 1943). If we want to assess people's attitudes toward doctors, we might show individuals a picture of a doctor examining a patient and ask them what they think the patient is thinking and feeling. We can assume that what individuals say the patient is thinking and feeling represents their own thoughts and feelings toward doctors and doctor appointments.

Dmitry Melnikov/Shutterstock.com

Now, of course, asking individuals to ascribe personality characteristics to a pictured individual or tell a story about a picture are not fool-proof ways of assessing a person's attitude toward smoking. Just like all of the other attitude measurements we have previously discussed, projective measurements have their flaws. Because projective measurements are implicit attitude measurements and therefore are not directly measuring individuals' attitudes, we can't be certain that the conclusions we make based on a person's responses are accurate. We can only *infer* attitudes, but we can't be certain.

Like physiological response measures, an additional drawback of projective measurements is that they tend to be fairly time consuming for the researcher. Think about the projective attitude measurement techniques we discussed. Would you agree that showing individuals a picture and asking them to describe the person or tell a story about the person probably takes more time than simply asking individuals to rate their attitudes toward smoking and doctors on a series of Likert scales? Definitely! Though projective measurements can certainly be collected via paper or online, they tend to be more effective one-on-one. This is because when asked to tell a story or describe a picture, some people may be less motivated to write or type their responses. Researchers actively seek out ways to make participation as easy as possible for participants. Because participants may be more inclined to give more information verbally than in writing, projective attitude measurements are best if conducted in an in-person setting.

The Implicit Association Test (IAT)   Another implicit attitude measurement that researchers use is the Implicit Association Test (IAT; Greenwald, McGhee, & Schwartz, 1998). The IAT was developed to measure individuals' cognitive associations. Though there are many variations of the test, individuals are generally tasked with categorizing a series of words. Typically, individuals accomplish this by pressing one key on a computer if the displayed word belongs to one category and a different key if the displayed word belongs to the other category. For example, Greenwald and colleagues had participants decide whether words such as "daisy," "rose," "mosquito," and "cockroach" were flowers or insects. The idea is that the stronger an individual's association is between a displayed word and a category, the faster the individual's categorization response will be.

So how does this translate into measuring attitudes? Well, the categories in the IAT don't have to be flowers or insects; they can be directions of attitudes. For example, the categories could be "good" and "bad" or "acceptable" and "unacceptable." If an individual is tasked with assigning the word "cigarettes" to one of these categories, a person who has a very strong negative attitude toward cigarettes and smoking would be quick to categorize the word into the "bad" or "unacceptable" category. A person who has a positive attitude toward smoking and cigarettes may still categorize the word "cigarettes" into the "bad" or "unacceptable" category despite his/her true attitude toward smoking; however, he/she would categorize the word slower than would a person with a negative attitude toward smoking. This slower response time would thus indicate that the individual's *true* attitude toward smoking is not as negative as the person's who responded faster.

Because many prejudice attitudes are socially undesirable to express, most people who hold such attitudes are reluctant to express them on explicit self-report attitude measurements. Implicit attitude measurements are thus essential to accurately measure individuals' prejudice attitudes, and the IAT, in particular, is useful. You will learn more in depth about the IAT and how it is utilized in prejudice research in Chapter 10.

Like physiological and projective measurements, the IAT can be fairly time consuming for researchers. The IAT typically needs to be conducted using a computer program. Like the physiological measurements, the use of technology always introduces the possibility for technical problems and data failing to be recorded or lost completely. Furthermore, the use of computer programs limits the number of participants that can complete the IAT at the same time. This requires more time from researchers in order to collect data. Lastly, another downside to using the IAT as an attitude measurement is that the results again only *infer* people's attitudes.

Attitude Measurement Summary

Though each of these attitude measurement techniques has limitations, researchers overwhelmingly rely on explicit self-report measurements to measure attitudes. In addition to being less expensive and time consuming, explicit self-report measures tend to be more accurate and precise than indirect attitude measures because individuals can indicate both the direction and strength of their attitudes. Though implicit attitude measurements are often superior when individuals might be inclined to lie about their attitudes, most of the time researchers are not interested in measuring attitudes on sensitive topics.

Attitude Formation

Most psychologists agree that attitudes are almost exclusively learned. This means that you were not born with the attitudes that you have; rather, you *learned* them. We form attitudes based on information that we gather. Information can be gathered through our direct experiences or from indirect sources.

Direct Experiences

Our direct experiences are things that we encounter first-hand. When you try a new food, you are experiencing that food directly. Thus, any attitude you form about that food (whether you like it or dislike it) is formed as a result of the direct experience that you had with information (the flavor on your taste buds). There are two main ways that we form attitudes through direct experiences: operant and classical conditioning.

Operant Conditioning You may remember learning about operant conditioning in your general psychology course. Operant conditioning is the idea that learning occurs when an individual's behavior is either reinforced or punished (Skinner, 1953). Reinforcement is a desirable consequence of a behavior, and conversely punishment is an undesirable consequence of a behavior. Let's say that you go to an amusement park and ride the park's newest roller coaster. If that ride jerks you around so much and is so bumpy that you get sick afterward, the ride essentially just gave you a *punishment*, or an undesired outcome (assuming you didn't *want* to get sick). Because of that undesired outcome, or punishment, you are *less* likely to ride that roller coaster again. If, instead of getting sick, you get off the new ride and feel a sense of exhilaration and elation, you would have experienced *reinforcement*, or a desired outcome. Because of that desired outcome, you are more likely to ride that roller coaster again.

Operant conditioning can easily be applied to attitude formation. You form an attitude through operant conditioning when your experience with an event, person, or object is either reinforcing or punishing. Punishments (undesired outcomes) increase the likelihood that you will form a *negative* attitude toward someone or something, whereas

Ron Leishman/Shutterstock.com

reinforcements (desired outcomes) increase the likelihood that you will form a *positive* attitude toward the event or person/object you encountered. Getting sick as a consequence of riding a new roller coaster will not only make you less likely to ride that roller coaster again, it will also increase the likelihood that you will form a negative attitude toward the ride. If, instead of getting sick, you thoroughly enjoy the ride, you are more likely to form a positive attitude toward the ride. Think of the school subjects that you have a positive attitude toward (i.e., subjects you enjoy and like). Chances are you are doing/have done well in these subjects. Operant conditioning may be responsible for your attitude toward these subjects. You may indeed like these subjects *because of the reinforcements* you received (i.e., your good grades). Good grades are a positive, favorable reinforcement that increases your attitude toward those subjects in school.

Classical Conditioning If you are familiar with operant conditioning, you are hopefully also familiar with classical conditioning. Classical conditioning is the idea that through the repeated pairing of two events, something associated with one event can become associated with the second event, even if it was originally not associated with the second event to begin with. Classical conditioning is sometimes referred to as associative learning, because classical conditioning occurs when a favorable or unfavorable attitude toward one person or thing "transfers" to another person or thing due to the two being associated. Say, for example, that you just met a new person, and while conversing with that person, you start to develop a headache. That headache probably has nothing to do with the person you are talking to, but nonetheless, you might *associate* that person with your headache. This could lead to you forming a more negative attitude toward that person, since you have a negative attitude toward headaches. You're even more likely to associate that person with having a headache and consequently form a negative attitude toward that person if you frequently see this person and almost always develop a headache. You may likewise start to despise a product if the song used in the commercial is obnoxious to you. Because you repeatedly hear that song played in association with the product, you *learn* to associate the product with the annoying song, and consequently perceive the product negatively as well.

Imagine that you are watching a movie for the first time at a movie theater while enjoying some of your favorite movie theater snacks. The positive attitude that you form about the movie might in part be due to the association between the snacks and the movie. Of course, there might not be enough of your favorite movie snacks in the world to make you form a positive attitude about some movies! Classical conditioning is most influential on your attitude formation when the person or thing you are forming an attitude about is mostly neutral, meaning that you don't feel very strongly about it. The temperature of the movie theater, the snacks that you have, how annoying the other people are in the theater, and how tired you are will affect your attitude *more* toward a movie that is neither great nor terrible.

Researchers have previously demonstrated people's susceptibility to the influence of favorable and unfavorable associations when existing attitude are neutral or nonexistent. In 1957, researchers Staats and Staats presented participants visually with nonsense syllables such as "laj" and "wuh." Because these syllables were not actual words, they were unfamiliar to the participants and thus would not invoke any positive or negative reactions. Each nonsense syllable that participants saw was repeatedly paired with an auditory word that was favorable (i.e., sweet, gift), unfavorable (i.e., ugly, sad), or neutral (i.e., chair). Staats and Staats found that participants formed positive attitudes toward the nonsense syllables that were paired with favorable words, negative attitudes toward the nonsense syllables that were paired with unfavorable words, and neutral attitudes toward the nonsense syllables that were paired with neutral words.

Indirect Sources

Imagine that before you try a new food, your friend tries it first. If your friend reacts in such a way that suggests that he/she likes this new food, you might form a positive attitude toward it without having actually tried it yourself. Your friend might verbally tell you or nonverbally indicate that the food is good. Even if your friend isn't trying to communicate to you his/her attitude toward the food, you may pick up on your friend's facial expressions or behaviors (such as reaching for more) as he/she tries the food. Every indication that your friend either likes or dislikes the food is an indirect source of information that you can then use to form your own attitude toward the new food. It is considered an indirect source of information because you did not obtain information regarding the food first-hand, but rather from a second-hand source.

g-stockstudio/Shutterstock.com

Another indirect source of information that we often use to form attitudes is the media. Television, radio, music, movies, and advertisements are just some of the media outlets that influence what attitudes we form. Advertisements for products often indirectly influence our attitudes toward those products—and that's exactly the purpose! Advertisements are made for the sole purpose of exposing people to a product and providing information to promote it in the hopes that audiences will form positive attitudes toward the product and the company.

Observational (Social) Learning A way that we commonly form attitudes is called observational (or social) learning. One of the ways that we gather information to form attitudes indirectly is through observing and communicating with others and learning from *their* first-hand experiences. While in line for a new ride at an amusement park, you might observe another person getting off the ride and getting sick. Though you personally did not experience getting sick after the ride, you still gathered information about the ride. A friend indicating to you that a new food tastes very bad is also an example of observational, or social, learning. Your friend may verbally pass on this information, or you may

Artisticco/Shutterstock.com

observe his/her body language or facial expressions that indicate his/her dislike. Advertisers sometimes rely on this vicarious learning to influence individuals' attitudes about products. Commercials frequently depict favorable outcomes coming to those who use the product, or portray individuals raving about the product. This is an attempt to communicate and associate positive things with a product.

Forming Attitudes Using Multiple Sources of Information

It is often the case that our attitudes are formed as a result of a combination of information rather than just a single experience or information source. We weigh all the pieces of information that we have gathered in order to form an attitude. Of course, not all pieces of information are weighted the same. It is not unusual for information from our direct experiences to have more influence on our attitudes than indirect sources of information. Just because your friend told you that he/she liked a new food doesn't mean that you will form a positive attitude toward it if *you* didn't like it. In this instance, your own experience tasting the food is more powerful than your friend's indirect source of information. Sometimes, however, the opposite is true. Indirect sources of information are more powerful than our direct experiences. For example, we sometimes feel social pressure to have a certain attitude toward a person or thing, especially if everyone else seems to have the same attitude. As you will learn more about in Chapter 7, attitudes that are unanimously agreed upon by a group of people are more influential and persuasive than attitudes that are not.

Up until now, we have been discussing how multiple pieces of information influence our attitude formation as if we obtain these pieces of information simultaneously. This is, in fact, rarely the case. We usually do not wait until we have gathered multiple pieces of information before forming an attitude; it is more common that we obtain a single piece of information and form an attitude accordingly. Then, as we gather other pieces of information, we *alter* our original attitude. This brings us to the next topic of this chapter: attitude change.

Attitude Change
The process of an attitude becoming stronger, weaker, or opposite from what it previously was.

Attitude Change

Just because we form a positive attitude toward someone or something doesn't mean that our attitude will stay positive. Our attitudes are constantly changing: getting stronger, weaker, or completely reversing and becoming the opposite. **Attitude change** is thus the process of an attitude becoming stronger, weaker, or opposite from what it previously was.

Direct Experiences

Just as our direct experiences influence our formation of attitudes, information that we obtain after an attitude is already formed can cause an attitude to change. Have you ever gotten sick with the flu and found that after you got better you no longer like the food that you had eaten

i-m-a-g-e/Shutterstock.com

before you got sick? This is called taste aversion, which you may have learned about in an introductory Psychology course. Taste aversion is an example of how classical conditioning can change our attitudes. Classical conditioning is not the only way that attitudes can be changed, however. Our attitudes can be changed as a result of punishments and reinforcements that we receive (operant conditioning). For example, though you may originally form a positive attitude toward an amusement park ride because you experienced feelings of exhilaration and elation (a reinforcement) the first time you rode it, you may feel sick (a punishment) after riding the same ride years later.

Indirect Sources of Information

Information that we obtain indirectly through observing others' experiences or communicating with others about their experiences can also cause us to change our attitudes. Your attitude toward a restaurant's nightly special might change after you witness another customer discover a hair or bug in their food. You don't even have to personally witness this discovery in order for your attitude to be affected; even just hearing the story from another person can be enough to change your attitude toward the nightly special.

It is not uncommon for our communications with others to result in us changing our attitudes. This attitude change sometimes is, and sometimes is not, the goal of the communication. Sometimes, others purposefully communicate information to us in a deliberate attempt to change our attitudes, and sometimes we do the same to others.

Persuasion

Persuasion is an active attempt by an individual or group of individuals to change another's attitude. Our day-to-day lives are full of persuasion. In Western society, we are constantly bombarded by advertisers' attempts to change our attitudes, usually through the media. Every commercial, billboard, and magazine advertisement that you see is a persuasion attempt. Companies use these mediums in an attempt to persuade a lot of people all at once. Some persuasions that we encounter are less obvious than a big sign or loud commercial. Your friend recommending a movie, restaurant, or product to you is an example of persuasion.

Persuasion
An intentional attempt to change an individual's attitude.

Olivier Le Moal/Shutterstock.com

Anytime that you or any person shares information with another person with the intention to change their attitude toward a person, place, event, object, or issue, it is considered persuasion.

It is important to note that persuasion is not always synonymous with manipulation. You can attempt to change someone's attitude without manipulating them into doing so. Manipulation attempts can actually backfire; if it is apparent to us that someone is trying to manipulate us, we are inclined to reject the persuasion (Hass & Grady, 1975; Kiesler & Kiesler, 1964). Similarly, if we sense that someone's intent to persuade us is corrupt, we are less likely to be persuaded. Fortunately, it is likely that most of the persuasions we encounter have positive intentions. When you recommend something to your friends, your intention is [hopefully] to aid them, not steer them into destruction and misery.

Routes of Persuasion

Central Route of Persuasion
A persuasion attempt that seeks to persuade individuals by engaging them with the content information.

Peripheral Route of Persuasion
Persuasion attempts that do not engage individuals intellectually and take little to no effort to process.

Persuasion Cues
Anything used in a persuasion attempt that has nothing to do with the persuasion topic or object that is intended to persuade the individual.

When you are trying to change someone's attitude, there are essentially two ways that you can go about it. The most obvious way you might think of to persuade someone is to focus on the relevant information. If you attempt this route of persuasion, you are hoping that the person whose attitude you are trying to change will give thoughtful consideration to the information you presented. This type of persuasion is called a **central route of persuasion**. Persuasion that occurs as a result of a central route of persuasion is sometimes referred to as *thoughtful message processing*, because such persuasion relies on an individual's effortful processing about the message, or persuasion attempt.

Alternatively, you might attempt to change another person's attitude by using a **peripheral route of persuasion**. Peripheral routes of persuasion are persuasion attempts that do not engage individuals intellectually. Persuasion that occurs as a result of a central route of persuasion is sometimes referred to as *spontaneous message processing* because the persuasion took little to no effort to process and was done spontaneously without thought. Peripheral routes of persuasion are very popular in television and magazine advertisements and often utilize **persuasion cues**. Persuasion cues are anything used in a persuasion attempt that have nothing to do with the persuasion topic or object. A perfect example of a persuasion cue is anything that a salesperson uses to sell a product that has nothing to do with the product itself. Advertisers often rely on catchy jingles, attractive actors and actresses, humor, and other superficial ploys to persuade potential customers' attitudes toward the product being advertised. Advertisers hope that by using cues that do not require much thought or processing to catch viewers' attention, viewers will change their attitudes toward the product and company spontaneously based on these cues rather than the actual information or product itself. Similar to implicit attitude formation, individuals at the receiving end of peripheral routes of persuasion may not be fully aware that their attitudes were changed as a result.

So which is a more effective route of persuasion, a central or peripheral route? The answer is that it depends. When an individual cares about and is invested in a topic or issue, he/she will most likely attend to any information presented regarding the topic/issue (Cacioppo & Petty, 1980). Therefore, central routes of persuasion are most effective, since the individual is focusing and paying attention to the information presented. In contrast, when an individual does not care as much about a topic or issue or pays little attention to the persuasion attempt, peripheral routes of persuasion are more effective. See the Thinking Critically Box on page 97 for more details.

Persuasion Factors

Beyond the factors that determine how effective central and peripheral routes of persuasion are, there are certainly other factors that impact how successful a persuasion attempt is. Particularly, the source of the persuasion (who is doing the persuading), the message (what is being said in the persuasion attempt), and the audience (who is the source attempting to persuade) are all major factors that interact and determine how successful a persuasion attempt will be.

THINKING CRITICALLY

Imagine that you are a researcher investigating whether a central or peripheral route of persuasion is more effective. To do this, you have college students listen to a message that promotes the implementation of a senior comprehensive exam at their school. You tell some of the students that this policy will be enacted the following school year, which means the exam is something that they will have to take. You tell the other students that the exam policy won't begin for another 10 years. Which students do you think will be more persuaded by a central route of persuasion: the students who will be affected by the exam policy or the students who will not be?

The hypothetical study above is similar to an actual research study conducted by Petty, Cacioppo, and Goldman in 1981. In their study, students who were told that the senior exams would go into effect the next year were more persuaded by central routes of persuasion. Because these students were personally invested in the issue, they paid more attention to the message and were more persuaded by messages that made strong arguments. Students who believed that the senior exam policy would not be enacted for 10 years were not as invested in the issue and consequently paid less attention to the message content. These students were not influenced by the strength of the arguments made but were instead influenced by peripheral routes of persuasion, such as who the source of the message was.

Persuasion Source   The source of a persuasion attempt plays a very important role in the effectiveness of that persuasion. A source can be an individual person, a group of people, a company, or an institution. The main factors that influence how persuasive a source is are the source's:

- Credibility—sources that are more credible, respected, and trusted are generally more persuasive.
- Expertise—sources that are thought to have expertise in a topic are more persuasive *on that topic*.
- Familiarity—sources that are familiar to the audience are more persuasive.
- Similarity—sources that share similarity with the audience are more persuasive.
- Attractiveness—sources that are more physically attractive are more persuasive.

ostill/Shutterstock.com

We are more persuaded by an argument coming from a scientific journal than an argument coming from a blog post that we found online. This is because we see scientists as more credible and trustworthy than an unknown blogger. However, a source's expertise is also a factor. For example, a dentist and a marine biologist may be equally respected and trusted; however, if the persuasion topic regards the impact of oil drilling on marine life, the marine biologist will most likely be more persuasive. The dentist, though a respected and trusted source of information, is not an expert in marine biology, and thus will most likely be less persuasive. Overall, not only is the credibility of the source important but also the expertise of the source on the topic.

We are also generally more persuaded by individuals who we are familiar with and see ourselves as similar to. For example, our friends and family are usually more persuasive than sources that we don't know or differ from. This is why advertisements often use famous people to promote a product or company. Because we are familiar with celebrities, we are more persuaded by

Edyta Pawlowska/Shutterstock.com

them. Additionally, celebrities are often attractive, which further increases an advertisement's persuasiveness.

Advertisers often maximize as many of these source factors as they can when promoting a product. For example, a toothpaste commercial may portray a dentist (maximizing credibility and expertise), as well as a seemingly average mother (maximizing similarity) promoting the toothpaste. If that wasn't enough, chances are the dentist and the mother in the commercial are also both attractive! The way that advertisers maximize these persuasion source factors in order to change our product attitudes are examples of peripheral routes of persuasion and are discussed more in depth along with other compliance techniques in Chapter 7.

Persuasion Message Just as the source of persuasion is important, the message that the persuader is giving is important. Three persuasion message factors are particularly important:

- Comprehensibility—messages that are easily understood are more persuasive.
- Quantity—messages with more arguments tend to be more persuasive.
- Quality—messages with higher quality arguments are more persuasive.

It seems obvious, but we are more persuaded by messages that we understand than messages that we don't understand. You are unlikely to be persuaded by a message that is presented in a language that you do not speak. This also applies to the accessibility of the language being used; effective messages are presented at the cognitive level of the audience. For example, in chemistry and biology, there are typically longer, more complicated names for chemical compounds and animals than what nonchemists and nonbiologists use. For example, *sodium chloride* is the scientific name for table salt, and *Acinonyx jubatus* is the scientific name for a cheetah. If you did not know the scientific name for a cheetah and went to a lecture on the ethicality and danger of domesticating the *A. jubatus*, you might be very lost if the presenter never acknowledged that an *A. jubatus* is a cheetah. You would probably not be very persuaded by any of the arguments that the presenter gave for or against domesticating cheetahs. Your attitude toward the issue would most likely remain unchanged. It is thus important that persuasion attempts are comprehended by the audience intended for persuasion.

Another factor that influences the effectiveness of a persuasion message is the quality and quantity of the message. The more information that you are given, generally the more likely you are to change your attitude. Of course, quality is more valuable than quantity. At some point or another, we've all heard a very sound argument and a very weak argument. When someone puts forth an argument that you can't find any flaws with, you are more likely to be persuaded by that argument. Though the amount of information that you are given can be persuasive, the *quality* of that information matters more. You are more likely to be persuaded by one very good piece of information than by five weak pieces of information. You might be tempted to think that the recipe for a very persuasive message maximizes both quantity and quality of information; however, there is a delicate balance to strike with message quality. A large quantity of arguments (even if those arguments are high quality) can, in some cases, repel an audience due to the length of the message. For example, if a friend is trying to persuade you to go see a movie with her, you might get irritated with her if she goes on and on naming reason after reason why you should go with her. Your irritation might deter you from going even if the reasons your friend gave were all valid and high-quality arguments.

Other Persuasion Message Factors. In addition to the influence of a persuasion message's content, the way that a persuasion is presented and how often it is presented also influence how successful the persuasion will be.

- Presentation style—messages that are presented in a style that compliments the topic/issue and audience are more persuasive.
- Medium—messages delivered face-to-face tend to be more persuasive.
- Repetition—messages that are repeated tend to be more persuasive.

The style with which a persuasion is presented can sometimes be as important as the content of the message itself. If a message is presented in a humorous style, it may appeal to you more and be more persuasive. On the other hand, you may be turned off by a humorous message style presentation (perhaps if the topic is serious) and thus not be persuaded by it. Additionally, the confidence with which the message is presented makes a difference in its persuasiveness. Telling you that a toothpaste "will *potentially* make your teeth whiter and *might* make your breath smell better" will not be as persuasive as telling you that a toothpaste "will brighten your smile and enhance your kissability."

Additionally, the medium through which a persuasive message is delivered makes a difference in how effective it will be in changing individuals' attitudes. Persuasion messages can be delivered in a number of ways. Overall, research has found that face-to-face persuasions are the most effective (Katz & Lazarsfeld, 1955). Despite face-to-face persuasions being more effective than mass media advertisements, most companies choose to promote and market their products through television and radio commercials, billboards, magazine advertisements, and other forms of media. This is because the easiest way for advertisers to reach a large number of people quickly is through media outlets. Though research supports face-to-face persuasions as being the most effective way to change people's attitudes, a multitude of research does exist that supports the effectiveness of media persuasions (Chaiken & Eagly, 1976).

TAGSTOCK1/Shutterstock.com

How often a message is repeated is also important. Very seldom do we see commercials once. Though companies primarily repeat their commercials in order to save money on making new commercials, companies also repeat commercials to reap the benefits of repetition. Hearing an argument repeated increases the likelihood that you will change your attitude. Of course, too much repetition can have an opposite effect than intended on an audience's attitudes (Cacioppo & Petty, 1979). Imagine if every time a commercial break came on, you saw the exact same commercial over and over again. You would likely be annoyed and develop a negative attitude toward the advertisement (and consequently the product and company), even if your original attitude toward the advertisement was favorable.

Persuasion Audience In respect to the audience receiving the message, there are several factors that make a difference how successfully an audience will be persuaded by the message. In this section, we will focus on three of the main persuasion audience factors:

- Retention—messages that are forgotten are not persuasive.
- Attention—the amount of attention paid to messages influences how persuadable the audience will be.
- Knowledge and interest—audiences that have more knowledge and interest in the issue are less persuadable by messages that are false or counter to their current attitudes.

The longer that a persuasion message is remembered, the more likely individuals are to be persuaded by it. If you forget a message right after hearing, seeing, or reading it, how is it going to be effective? Likewise, if a person does not pay any attention to a persuasion attempt in the first place, he/she is unlikely to be persuaded due to the fact that he/she was oblivious to the persuasion attempt. If a person is paying at least some attention, however, the audience's *level* of attention makes a difference how the persuasion will be received. As previously mentioned, the *amount* of attention paid to a persuasion message can make a difference in how that persuasion message is received depending on the route of persuasion used. Central routes of persuasion are more effective when the audience is giving a lot of attention to the information, but peripheral routes of persuasion are typically more effective when the audience is giving very little attention to the persuasion attempt.

Audiences that have more knowledge and interest about the issue being discussed in a message are less likely to be persuaded by messages counter to their existing attitude. Knowledgeable individuals are more likely to be skeptical of a persuasion attempt and better equipped to make counterarguments to discredit the message. This makes sense. If you know a lot about cars, you are going to be less persuaded by a car salesman's pitch about all the features of a car that you have a negative attitude toward. The car salesman's persuasion attempt isn't going to have much of an effect on you because you already know the features and can point out the shortcomings of the car. Being knowledgeable and interested doesn't mean that you aren't persuadable, however. If you are knowledgeable and interested in a specific topic or issue and you hear or see a message that parallels your own current attitudes, you are *more* likely to agree with it and *more* likely to be persuaded by it.

dencg/Shutterstock.com

Researching Attitude Change

Since our attitudes are constantly changing, it should come as no surprise that researchers are just as interested in studying attitude change as they are interested in studying attitudes. As previously discussed, there are multiple factors that influence how effective a persuasion attempt is. The effectiveness of all of these factors has been established as a result of experimental research. Researchers who seek to investigate different aspects of attitude change utilize a variety of experimental research designs, many of which should be familiar to you from Chapter 2. There are three essential components that are always present in attitude change research: a persuasion manipulation, a postpersuasion manipulation attitude measurement, and a comparison attitude measurement.

Persuasion Manipulations

Persuasion manipulations are essentially the persuasion attempt that researchers are investigating the effectiveness of. Persuasion manipulations can be presented in a number of different formats: videos, written messages, face-to-face communication, etc.

Attitude Measurements

Participants' attitudes are measured utilizing one (or more) of the attitude measurement techniques described earlier in this chapter. As previously discussed, researchers most often use self-report measurements to assess participants' attitudes; however, behavioral observations, physiological response measures, projective attitude measures, and implicit association tests may also be utilized.

Postpersuasion Manipulation Attitude Measurements It is crucial to the theoretical nature of attitude change studies that researchers measure participants' attitudes following a persuasion attempt. As you will learn more about in the following sections, some attitudinal research designs utilize a control group, some utilize an attitude pretest, and some use both. What all of these designs have in common, however, is that they all include an attitude measurement following the persuasion manipulation.

Comparison Attitude Measurements

Pretest–Posttest Designs. In order to determine whether a persuasion manipulation actually changed participants' attitudes, an attitude measurement is needed to compare the postpersuasion manipulation attitude measurements to. Some researchers utilize a *pretest–posttest design* in order to accomplish this. In a pretest–posttest design, participants' attitudes are measured both before (pretest) and after (posttest) the persuasion manipulation. The pretest serves as a baseline measure of what participants' attitudes were before any attitude change occurred. By comparing participants' pretest attitudinal measures to their posttest attitudinal measures, researchers can determine how much participants' attitudes were changed (if at all) by the persuasion manipulation.

Posttest-Only Group Designs. Instead of using a pretest, researchers sometimes use a control group as an attitudinal comparison. In these designs, participants are randomly assigned to a control group or an experimental group. Participants in the experimental group are exposed to a persuasion manipulation, but participants in the control group are not. These designs are referred to as *posttest-only group designs*, because the attitudes of both the control group and the experimental group are only measured once—after the persuasion manipulation. In *posttest-only designs*, the control groups' attitudes serve as an attitudinal comparison. Since participants in the control group are not exposed to the persuasion manipulation, the idea is that if the experimental group's postmanipulation attitudes differ from the control group's attitudes, then the persuasion manipulation effectively changed the experimental group's attitudes.

Sometimes researchers use more than one experimental group as a means to determine the effectiveness of a persuasion manipulation. These groups may or may not include a control group. In these experiments, researchers have two (or more) experimental groups in which participants are randomly assigned to. Each experimental group is exposed to a persuasion manipulation, but the persuasion manipulations are different for each group. For example, if researchers want to determine how the length of a message affects a message's persuasiveness, they would expose one group of participants to a message of a certain length and expose another group to a message of similar content that is either longer or shorter in length. As you can see, the number of groups can certainly be increased in order to compare more than just two message lengths.

Pretest–Posttest Group Designs. The third type of experimental design that researchers use to empirically assess attitude change is a combination of pretest–posttest designs and posttest-only group designs. Due to the combinatory nature of this third design type, it is aptly called a *pretest–posttest group design*. In these experimental designs, participants are randomly assigned to a group. Regardless of the number of groups or whether a control group is present, the fundamental aspects of *pretest–posttest group designs* is that *all* groups receive both a pretest and a posttest attitude measure. Essentially, in these experimental designs, each group serves as an attitudinal comparison for the other groups, and additionally each group's pretest attitude measure serves as its own attitudinal comparison.

Conclusion

After reading this chapter, I hope that you are not only able to list a few of *your* favorite things, like Maria in *The Sound of Music* (Wise, 1965), but additionally reflect on how your attitude toward each of those things was originally formed and how your attitudes toward other things have changed and developed over time. Attitudes influence our day-to-day thoughts and behaviors, which is why social psychologists take a great interest in studying them. Because our attitudes are constantly changing, many social scientists also study attitude change and persuasion.

As you have discovered in this chapter, researchers over the years have made, and will continue to make, strides in evaluating and understanding the many facets of attitudes and persuasion. We will continue to identify methods in which attitudes are measured and in doing so will be ever more capable of explaining how attitudes originate and can be altered. As social psychology research progresses, we will be able to further recognize and comprehend the complex interplay between our attitudes and the powerful force of persuasion that changes them.

Suggestions for Further Reading

Eagly, A. H., & Chaiken, S. (1993). *The psychology of attitudes*. Fort Worth, TX: Harcourt, Brace, Javanovich. doi:10.1207/s15327965pli0404_19

Maio, G., & Haddock, G. (2009). *The psychology of attitudes and attitude change*. London, England: Sage. doi:http://dx.doi.org/10.4135/9781446214299

Petty, R. E., & Cacioppo, J. T. (1996). *Attitudes and persuasion: Classic and contemporary approaches.* Boulder, CO: Westview Press.

Petty, R. E., Wheeler, S. C., & Tormala, Z. L. (2003). Persuasion and attitude change. In I. B. Weiner & M. J. Lerner (Eds.), *Comprehensive handbook of psychology* (2nd ed., Vol. 5). New York, NY: Wiley. doi:10.1002/0471264385.wei0515

References

Aguinis, H., Pierce, C. A., & Quigley, B. M. (1993). Conditions under which a bogus pipeline procedure enhances the validity of self-reported cigarette smoking: A meta-analytic review. *Journal of Applied Social Psychology, 23,* 352–373. doi:10.1111/j.1559-1816.1993.tb01092.x

Ajzen, I., & Fishbein, M. (1977). Attitude-behavior relations: A theoretical analysis and review of empirical research. *Psychological Bulletin, 84,* 888–918. doi:http://dx.doi.org.er.lib.k-state.edu/10.1037/0033-2909.84.5.888

Allport, G. (1954). The historical background of modern social psychology. In G. Lindzey (Ed.), *Handbook of social psychology* (Vol. 1). Cambridge, MA: Addison-Wesley.

Allport, G. W. (1935). Attitudes. In C. Murchinson (Ed.), *A handbook of social psychology* (pp. 798–844). Worcester, MA: Clark University Press.

Cacioppo, J. T., & Petty, R. E. (1979). Effects of message repetition and position on cognitive responses, recall, and persuasion. *Journal of Personality and Social Psychology, 37,* 97–109. doi:10.1037/0022-3514.37.1.97

Cacioppo, J. T., & Petty, R. E. (1980). Sex differences in influenceability: Toward specifying the underlying processes. *Personality and Social Psychology Bulletin, 6,* 651–656. doi:10.1177/014616728064016

Chaiken, S., & Eagly, A. H. (1976). Communication modality as a determinant of message persuasiveness and message comprehensibility. *Journal of Personality and Social Psychology, 34,* 605–614. doi:10.1037/0022-3514.34.4.605

Greenwald, A. G., McGhee, D. E., & Schwartz, J. L. K. (1998). Measuring individual differences in implicit cognition: The Implicit Association Test. *Journal of Personality and Social Psychology, 74*(6), 1464–1480. doi:http://dx.doi.org/10.1037/0022-3514.74.6.1464

Hass, R. G., & Grady, K. (1975). Temporal delay, type of forewarning and resistance to influence. *Journal of Experimental Social Psychology, 11,* 459–469. doi:10.1016/0022-1031(75)90048-7

Katz, E., & Lazarsfeld, P. F. (1955). *Personal influence.* Glencoe, IL: Free Press.

Kiesler, C. A., & Kiesler, S. B. (1964). Role of forewarning in persuasive communications. *Journal of Abnormal and Social Psychology, 68,* 547–549. doi:http://dx.doi.org/10.1037/h0042145

Kunst-Wilson, W. R., & Zajonc, R. B. (1980). Affective discrimination of stimuli that cannot be recognized. *Science, 207,* 557–558. doi:10.1126/science.207.4430.557

Likert, R. (1932). A technique for the measurement of attitudes. *Archives of Psychology, 140,* 1–55.

Petty, R. E., Cacioppo, J. T., & Goldman, R. (1981). Personal involvement as a determinant of argument-based persuasion. *Journal of Personality and Social Psychology, 41*(5), 847. doi:10.1037/0022-3514.41.5.847

Proshansky, J. (1943). A projective method for the study of attitudes. *Journal of Abnormal and Social Psychology, 38,* 393–395. doi:10.1037/h0056930

Skinner, B. F. (1953). *Science and human behavior.* Toronto, Canada: Macmillan.

Staats, A. W., & Staats, C. K. (1957). Meaning established by classical conditioning. *Journal of Experimental Psychology, 54,* 74–80. doi:http://dx.doi.org.er.lib.k-state.edu/10.1037/h0047716

Wise, R. (Producer & Director). (1965). *The sound of music* [Motion picture]. United States: 20th Century Fox.

Woodmansee, J. J. (1970). The pupil response as a measure of social attitudes. In G. F. Summers (Ed.), *Attitude measurement* (pp. 514–533). Chicago, IL: Rand McNally.

Zajonc, R. B. (1968). Attitudinal effects of mere exposure. *Journal of Personality and Social Psychology Monograph Supplement, 9,* 1–27. doi:http://dx.doi.org/10.1037/h0025848

Chapter Seven
Social Influence

Darin Challacombe

Fort Hays State University

Learning Objectives

- Describe the three types of social influence: conformity, compliance, and obedience
- Compare and contrast the two main types of conformity: normative and informational
- Describe compliance and ways to inducing compliance in other people
- Discuss the power of obedience to authority

Chapter Outline

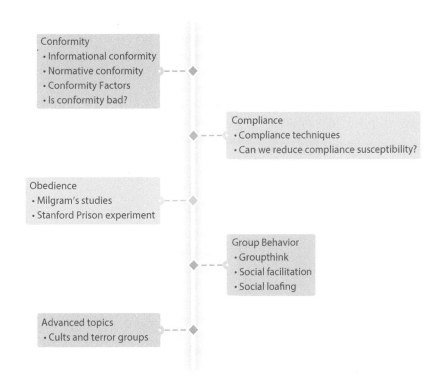

Conformity
- Informational conformity
- Normative conformity
- Conformity Factors
- Is conformity bad?

Compliance
- Compliance techniques
- Can we reduce compliance susceptibility?

Obedience
- Milgram's studies
- Stanford Prison experiment

Group Behavior
- Groupthink
- Social facilitation
- Social loafing

Advanced topics
- Cults and terror groups

Figure 7.1. The social influence spectrum.

Social Influence
Social influence is how your interactions with others can change behavior or attitudes.

Conformity
Conformity is when you are influenced by just the presence of other people.

Compliance
Compliance is when you are requested by others to do something you would not normally do.

Obedience
Obedience is when you are commanded to do something by others.

Social Influence

Why is it hard for you to say no to someone selling cookies door-to-door? Or, when you attempt to pass someone on the highway, why does the other car often increase their speed? Or, why are some people better sales people than others?

In this chapter, we focus on **social influence**, or how interactions with other people can change thoughts, behaviors, or actions. Social influence can be summarized by two words: behavior modification (Mehrabian, 1970). Behavior modification can be helpful (e.g., quit smoking, eat healthier) or harmful (e.g., underage drinking, participate in bullying). Generally, the social influence field is divided into three areas: conformity, compliance, and obedience.

You can think of social influence on a spectrum: on one end is a person, alone; and, on the other end is a completely subservient person. As you move from one end to the other, you encounter various levels of social influence. First, you have **conformity**: you change because of other people's mere or subtle presence. Then, you have **compliance**: you change because other people ask it. Finally, you have **obedience**: you change because someone tells you to change. This spectrum is visually depicted in Figure 7.1.

Conformity

Think of a time in which you were with a group of friends. One of your friends did something you disagreed with, then the next one did the same thing, and

so on. When it came to you, did you do what your other friends had done? This is called "peer pressure," which is descriptive of conformity.

There are two main types of conformity: informational and normative. Informational conformity is when we rely upon other people for an answer because we do not know the right answer (if there even is a right answer). Normative conformity is when we choose an answer based on others' answers in order to be more like them (and not stick out or be embarrassed).

Think back on the time in which you felt pressured to do something that your friends were doing. Maybe it was underage drinking or smoking. Most likely, you looked to your friends to determine what was the right thing to do in the situation. If all of your friends were drinking, then you probably also had a drink. This would be an example of normative conformity.

I like to travel. When I go to a new city, I normally will use a travel site to see which restaurants are rated best. There is not necessarily a right or wrong answer to which restaurant is the best, right? It all depends on the preference of the person. So, when I go to a site like this, I am using an aspect of informational conformity.

Informational Conformity

When I visit family or friends, I often go with them to attend a church service. When I was younger, I always would dress up for church, because that was the appropriate way to dress. Now, I see people in jeans and even shorts attending church. So, when I go to church with my family or friends, I look to them to tell me what I should wear. Should I put on a suit and tie, or should I just wear casual clothing?

When I follow my family or friends' suggestions on what to wear, I am succumbing to **informational conformity** because I am looking to someone else to help me understand an ambiguous situation. One of the first researchers of this effect was Mazuraf Sherif. In the 1950s, Sherif utilized the **autokinetic effect** to see if two people would make similar choices if asked to evaluate an ambiguous situation. Here is how the experiment worked:

Sherif conducted his experiment in a dark room with just a point of light so he could induce the autokinetic effect. He had participant pairs come into the room and then guess if the point of light moved and how far it moved during a certain period of time (e.g., five seconds). There was no right answer. This is because not only was the point of light not moving but each person's estimation of distance was different. Sherif, however, found the participant pairs would choose more similar answers as the experiment continued. To Sherif, this was fascinating. There was no right or wrong answer, yet the participants would progressively rely upon others for a right answer.

In order to evaluate left- vs. right-brain hemisphere activation, Challacombe, Turek, and Shrira (2005) replicated Sherif's (1935) study using 66 undergraduate students. Mirroring Sherif's setup, the researchers used a pinpoint of light in a completely dark room to generate the autokinetic effect. Challacombe and colleagues found the same rates of compliance Sherif found, along with an interesting twist. The researchers found those participants with greater right-brain activation complied more than those with greater left-brain activation. From these results, one could deduce that participants with more analytic minds (e.g., left-brain) were influenced less by the other participant than participants with more subjective minds (e.g., right-brain).

In review, informational conformity occurs in ambiguous events when we tend to look to others to know how to behave.

Normative Conformity

Similar to looking to others for how to behave in ambiguous situations, we often look to others to avoid not standing out. For example, if you have ever traveled on the highway in a big city during rush hour, you know that often drivers go faster than the posted speed limits. If I make a decision to go just the speed limit, I will stand out (and maybe put myself in a dangerous situation). So, I often try to match traffic in order to not stand out.

Around the same time as Sherif's experiments, psychologist Solomon Asch conducted his own set of experiments to explore conformity. Asch (1951/1955) used a visual perception test to determine the effects of peer pressure. Specifically, Asch had a participant go into a room with other individuals to take part in a line-matching exercise. Instead of the other individuals in the room being other participants, Asch had placed **confederates** in the room in order to control the experiment.

Informational Conformity
Informational conformity is when we look to others to determine how to act in an ambiguous situation.

Autokinetic Effect
The autokinetic effect is a phenomenon in which a point of light in dark space appears to move when you have no other point of reference (Sherif, 1965, 1967). This is often cited as the reason for people seeing unidentified flying objects (UFOs).

Confederates
Confederates are individuals used by the experimenter to act a certain way in order to induce a certain reaction from the participant.

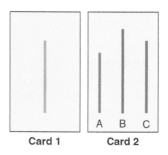

Figure 7.2. Stimuli from Asch's experiment on conformity.

·The participant and confederates were asked to compare a line with three other lines to determine which one was most accurate (see Figure 7.2). The first confederate would say that Card 1 line matched up to line A (clearly, incorrect). The second confederate would answer the same way, as would the third and fourth confederates. Asch was interested in how the true participants would reply when it was their turn. Nearly 40% of participants chose the same answer as the confederates; the incorrect answer! To Asch, this meant that the pressure to be like others in the group was very strong.

Asch (1955) conducted several variations on this experiment. For example, he would place the participant as the first person in a line of five. The participant would choose the correct answer, but the other four would choose the incorrect answer. Participants in this situation felt anxiety because they were clearly right but did not have the same answer as the others in the group. See the Thinking Critically Box below for more information on Ash's replications.

Conformity Factors

Researchers have identified several factors that can strengthen or reduce a person's susceptibility to conformity.

- **Group size**: Group size is an important factor for small to medium groups; however, this effect diminishes when the group gets larger (Stang, 1976). For instance, size factors more when your group is 10 people versus 100 people.
- **Self-esteem**: Researchers have found that an individual's self-esteem plays a role with conformity, and some individuals will conform in order to increase their self-esteem (Pool, Wood, & Leck, 1998). It takes someone with high self-esteem to not go along with the masses.

THINKING CRITICALLY

Many researchers have replicated Asch's (1955) experiments, often finding similar results to the original study. Several experiments have adjusted the experimental variables to see if the results are the same. For example, what do you think would happen if the person conducting the experiment were a male? Would the results be any different if this person was a female?

What about if all the confederates in the group were opposite gender of the participant? Would these factors have an effect on the outcome of the experiment?

Multiple studies have shown that men are slightly more influential than women on both genders, but have not shown significant gender effect differences in the ability to influence (Carli, 2001).

- **Unanimity**: The desire to conform to the group is greater when the group is unanimous (Asch, 1956). We will talk more about this when we discuss groupthink later in the chapter.
- **Culture**: Some have thought that culture plays a role in conformity's success; however, a Kuwait-based replication of the Asch experiment mirrored Asch's American culture findings (Amir, 1984). Bond and Smith (1996) conducted a meta-analysis of 133 studies and found **individualistic** cultures conformed less than **collectivistic** cultures.
- **Nature of task**: The nature of the task, such as its importance or difficulty, factors into conformity (Baron, Vandello, & Brunsman, 1996). Individuals completing an easy, important task would be less likely to conform than if they were completing a difficult, unimportant task.

Individualistic
Emphasis is on the individual and his/her contributions to society.

Collectivistic
Emphasis on the society as a whole as opposed to individual contributions.

Is Conformity Bad?

My mother would always say, "would you jump off a ledge if everyone else did?" when I would conform to negative or questionable group behavior. Although this is an extreme example, my mother did have a point: Conformity can be bad.

As pointed out above, we sometimes make decisions on whether to drink or smoke because of others. Conformity occurs in large settings, such as riots. Often, a small number of people start chaos, and others join to be part of the norm.

For me, conformity can have some positive effects. I try to surround myself with people who are healthy and make good life decisions. Therefore, when I am at a restaurant with some friends and everyone chooses something healthy to eat, I feel anxious if I choose something unhealthy. In the same fashion, I am often more inclined to workout or go for a run with my friends than I would be if I were friends with lazy or unhealthy people.

Compliance

Compliance occurs when you alter your behavior because someone requests this change. Even though most people think of compliance as having to do with large or important requests, all of us experience various levels of compliance every day.

It is hard to say no to people. Most online dating applications or sites have figured out a way to help people say no by allowing them to easily ignore someone. On one dating app, you see a photo of a potential date and you have the choice to either say "yes" or "no." This same potential date has the same choice on you. If you both say "yes," then you can start chatting; otherwise, game's over for this individual (at least in the app). Other times, you can simply ignore or block a person from chatting with you. This is much easier than saying "no" to a person.

In real-life situations, we often do not have the ability to ignore or block a person from talking to us. And, once the person has engaged us in conversation, then it is easier for them to get something from us than if they were to just ask for it outright. For example, you see an attractive individual at a bar, and you want his or her number. Will you get it if you just walk up to them and ask for it? Maybe. But, you would likely have a better chance if you start talking to them about something neutral, and then asked for their number. Although the individual may say no, it will be harder for him or her to say no since he or she have already tacitly said yes to talking to you.

Sometimes, saying "no" can be hard to do, especially when we have to say it to our friends.

Compliance Techniques

The easiest way of understanding compliance is to understand how it is operationalized. These techniques are ubiquitous; you use them without even knowing or considering what it is you are doing.

- **Foot-in-the-door**: The target is approached and a small request is made and accepted. Then, the requestor asks the target for something a bit larger. Since the target already agreed to the first item, the target is more likely going to agree to the second item (Freedman & Fraser, 1966). Sales people often use this when they first ask for a moment of your time, then see if you would be willing to spend five minutes talking to them.

- **Door-in-the-face**: The target is initially requested to comply with a very large request. Once the target refuses compliance, the requestor asks for a smaller request. Since the target refused the first request, it is difficult for the target to refuse the second request (Cialdini et al., 1975). Nonprofits often use this technique in pledge drives, suggesting monthly payments, then giving the option of one-time payments.

- **Low ball**: The target is presented with a price and agrees to the price. The requester then steps away for a few moments, returns, and then says that the price is now higher. Because the target already agreed to the lower price, the target is less likely to reject the higher price. Many sales companies use a version of the low ball technique on their advertisements (e.g., "you can get a trip to Hawaii for $250," but this price is only available for a limited number of customers).

- **But you are free**: This technique involves an initial request, followed by a statement like "but you are free to refuse or accept" (Carpenter, 2013). This technique showed promise in reducing any tension the target may have with helping the requestor. I often use this technique when I ask someone out for a date: "Would you like to grab coffee with me . . . you are free to say no. . ." This technique alleviates some of the pressure they would feel if I were to just ask them out for a drink.

- **Disrupt-then-reframe**: This is when the requestor presents the request in a novel fashion, followed by a pause, then restating the request followed by a positive statement (Davis & Knowles, 1999). For example: "Would you be willing to donate to XXX cause—we are only asking for 400 pennies per month. . .that's $4. It's a great deal!"

- **Ingratiation**: Restaurant servers' pay is usually partially dependent on their tips. In a field study, Seiter (2007) found servers who complimented their customers' food choices received significantly higher tips. The restaurant patrons responded positively to having their choices complimented.

- **That's not all**: The target is presented with an offer, then, after making the target wait a few seconds, presented with a second offer that either adds another product or lowers the price (Burger, 1986). Most infomercials use this technique.

Researchers continue to tweak these techniques in an attempt to increase understanding and effectiveness. For example, Hornik and Ellis (1988) found that nonevasive body contact during the request increased its effectiveness. In another study, Williams and Williams (1989) found slightly increased compliance when the requestor was viewed as high-strength, which they operationalized as wearing a suit versus wearing shorts.

Recently, researchers have turned to looking at social compliance online. Stefanone, Hurley, Egnoto, and Covert (2015) had participants pair up for online chat sessions. If participant A had more background information on participant B, then participant A had a greater chance to gain participant B's compliance. If both participants had the same amount of background information, then there was no significant compliance increase. This can happen in everyday situations. For example, suppose I match on Tender or another dating application with someone. If I am able to find out this person likes animals, I may invite them out on a first date to go to the local pet store or zoo. And, given what these researchers found, I have a better chance the potential date will agree to meet for this activity. It is very easy to search or Internet-stalk a potential date in order to find out about them before approaching them.

RomanSo/Shutterstock.com

Can We Reduce Compliance Susceptibility?

Compliance techniques are not fail-proof. Most techniques have only better-than-chance effectiveness rates. Numerous studies have shown greater effectiveness based on the requestor's attractiveness (Messner, Reinhold, & Sporer, 2008; Williams & Williams, 1989) or the target request amount (Burger, Reed, DeCesare, Rauner, & Rozolis, 1999), among other factors.

Recently, researchers have focused on looking at compliance rates when the target is fully aware the requestor is attempting to manipulate them. In one study (Messner et al., 2008), participants made a choice between a ball-point pen and a small amount of money. A requestor attempted to convince the target to choose the pen (e.g., the lesser of the two). These researchers found requestors who were more physically attractive were able to convince the target more than if the researcher was not attractive.

Other lines of research suggest that our susceptibility to compliance may be due in part to neurological processes (Falk et al., 2014). These researchers examined teenage male drivers' brain activity to determine the drivers' susceptibility to risk taking behavior. The teens first had their brain activity mapped while completing a social exclusion activity (e.g., the teen participants were socially excluded, or isolated, from their peers). Then, the researchers examined brain activity during driving simulations (e.g., alone vs. with a small-aged peer). The teenage males who had the most brain activity during the social exclusion exercise were more likely to have riskier driving behavior when with a peer versus when driving alone. This finding suggests that there may be neurological processes involved in the social influence.

Although there does not appear to be any empirically significant way to reduce our susceptibility to compliance techniques, you can focus on understanding and evaluating what is actually happening. For instance, when you are in a situation as a target of a technique, you can take a moment to classify the technique and then respond accordingly. It is still hard to say "no" to someone, but sometimes it is the best for you to do.

Obedience

If you recall history, most of the conformity experiments occurred around or just after World War II. At this time, the public was shocked to find out that normal German citizens were involved with killing thousands of Jews at Nazi concentration camps. How could this tragedy have happened?

Milgram's Studies

To answer these questions, psychologist Stanley Milgram (1963, 1965) conducted a series of experiments to determine the effects of **obedience**. These experiments, while controversial, significantly advanced our knowledge of obedience.

In his classic experiments, Milgram had participants administer increasingly powerful electric shocks to an individual every time the individual answered a question incorrectly. The individual, a confederate, actually did not receive any electric shocks; however, the confederate followed a script, crying out in relation to the strength of the shock.

Advertising his research project as a memory experiment, Milgram recruited his participants using fliers. He initially sought out nonstudent participants aged 20 to 50. Milgram paid participants $4 (or the equivalent of $30 today) for their time.

Milgram's experiments were structured very uniquely:

- Participants, after having the experiment explained to them, went into the room with the confederate and received a small test shock. This shock reinforced for the participant the shocking mechanism was real.
- The experimenter was the person in authority. Throughout the trials, the experimenter would tell any reluctant participant "you must continue" and other instructional statements.

Milgram found all of the participants administered shocks to the confederate up to the 300-volt level, with 26 of the original 40 participants administering fatal shocks (e.g., 450 volts). Milgram conducted several trials of this experiment with slightly different variables, but found similar results: Nearly 70% of participants would administer a fatal shock if instructed by an authority figure to do so.

Milgram's results helped explain some of the atrocities of the Nazis. These experiments also shaped how scientists conducted experiments with human participants, including a formalized process for reviewing experiments prior to their implementation, standardized informed consent and debriefing procedures, and stringent cost–benefit analysis on experiments with protected participants (e.g., children and the elderly).

Less than a decade ago, another researcher duplicated part of Milgram's study design in order to determine if Milgram's findings were still relevant today. Burger (2009) recruited participants in a similar fashion as Milgram and offered a $50 incentive for participation in two 45-minute sessions. In the initial session, participants completed several tests to measure anxiety, depression, and other factors, then interviewed by a licensed clinical psychologist. The psychologist made a determination on which individuals were psychologically prepared enough for this experiment.

Burger's (2009) experiment was structured nearly parallel to Milgram's (1963) studies; however, participants were only allowed to administer shocks up to 150-volts (only half as much as what Milgram's participants were allowed to administer). Interestingly, this researcher's results showed that obedience rates were only slightly lower than that in Milgram's study and found no remarkable difference on compliance based on gender.

Stanford Prison Experiment

As important as Milgram's experiments were to the understanding of obedience, Philip Zimbardo's 1971 Stanford Prison study helped researchers further understand obedience. In this case, Zimbardo's (2007) experiment provided insight into the expected cultural norms of a prison guard versus a prisoner.

In the Stanford study, the researchers selected 12 participants to be prison guards and 12 participants to be prisoners. Police arrested the prisoner participants and brought them to a basement converted into a makeshift prison. Once there, the guards treated the prisoners in as similar a fashion as prisoners are treated in real life (e.g., the guards stripped, searched, and deloused the prisoners). Following the initial intake, the guards told the prisoners that they must obey anything the guards told them to do.

This experiment ended on the sixth day (instead of the 14th, as originally planned). The experiment provided several interesting results:

- Both the guards and the prisoners, all regular college students, quickly assumed respective roles. The guards became demeaning of the prisoners; the prisoners began to reject the guards' authority, even revolting on the second day of the experiment.
- Several of the guards exhibited sadistic behavior. They punished the prisoners with exercise or manual labor.

Zimbardo's experiment further enhanced our understanding of obedience, and since this experiment, Zimbardo has dedicated a considerable focus of his research on this topic and its many variants. The Stanford Prison Experiment was documented in detail and can be found online at http://www.prisonexp.org/.

Group Behavior

In July 1999, a small town in New York State hosted the 30th anniversary of the Woodstock music festival (Vider, 2004). On the third and last day, the festival deescalated into a riot with several areas of the campground being set ablaze. Officials estimated out of the roughly 150,000 festival attendees present at that time, less than 300 youth participated in the riot with several thousand more watching the event unfold. How is it possible that an event steeped in a tradition of peace could end with a riot?

Even though we have focused on studying compliance's effect on an individual, social compliance can affects groups as well.

Groupthink is the phenomenon when highly cohesive groups in decision-making settings only accept congruent ideas and reject outside opinions (Janis, 1982). In groupthink settings, the group sees their viewpoint as the only correct one and assumes that all members of the group accept this viewpoint.

Groupthink can occur everywhere and can affect logical, analytical thinking. A group begins to only believe itself and rejects any other viewpoint. Recent examples of this include instances when fraternities will make poor, racially motivated decisions. Although not all the fraternity members likely agreed with the decision, all went along with it because of conformity.

During the 2002 Iraq conflict, a military detention center called Abu Ghraib was the site of systemic torture of Iraqi enemy combatants. The inmates were forced to remain naked for long periods of time and were subjected to other humiliation

Groupthink
Groupthink is when groups make decisions based solely on the views of a few group members instead of considering other, outside possibilities.

techniques. The United States' investigation into Abu Ghraib found groupthink as possible explanation for the soldiers' criminal actions (Post & Panis, 2011).

Social Facilitation

Social facilitation is when an individual does better on a task because there are others around.

Social facilitation is the tendency for people in groups to do better on tasks than if they were alone. Even individual sport athletes (e.g., distance running and wrestling) identified their teammates as a main source of their motivation to be better (Evans, Eys, & Wolf, 2013). For me, I like to go to a coffee shop or library when I write because I tend to stay more focused when I know other people are around and may be watching me. Although there are positive aspects of social facilitation, it can also have negative consequences. Beck, Ahmed, and Farkas (2011) found social facilitation as a prime factor in drinking behavior of young adults. People at a bar with friends may end up drinking more than if they were alone.

Social Loafing

Social loafing is the tendency for individual group members to participate in group tasks less actively than if they were alone.

Social loafing occurs when an individual in a group setting participates less on a task than if the individual was required to complete the task by him- or herself. One of the more famous experiments was when a researcher had people play tug-a-war and found the individuals themselves did not pull as hard when in a group as when they were by themselves (Ingham, Levinger, Graves, & Peckham, 1974).

Advanced Topics

Cults and Terror Groups

Almost 40 years ago, a religious leader named James Jones convinced over 1,000 people to leave their families, friends, and homes in the United States and move to a secluded jungle compound in the South American country of Guyana (Challacombe, 2005). Jones had progressively prepared his followers for this move. He preached about how he was a god, people were out to get him and his followers, and only through him would people be saved (Challacombe, 2005; Hochman, 1990). When Jones and his followers finally moved to Guyana, he had complete control over them.

The Guyana-based compound, nicknamed "Jonestown," was an agricultural community with the ability to self-sustain. Jones had all his followers engage

in ensuring Jonestown's success. In the evenings and at other, various times, Jones would conduct services, preaching the same rhetoric as when he was in California. Jones himself was very paranoid, and he appeared always fearful of unknown oppositional forces coming after him and his followers (Hochman, 1990).

Although only a handful, Jonestown defectors came back to the United States and raised concern about the living conditions in Guyana. About a year after Jones and his followers moved from California, United States Congressman Leo Ryan led a small group of people to visit Jonestown. When these visitors arrived, they were heartily greeted by Jones and his followers. The visitors initially found Jonestown as a healthy, positive community; however, the impression quickly changed as several Jonestown members secretly asked the visitors for help. When Congressman Ryan confronted Jones about this, Jones agreed to let any of his members leave with the visitors to return to the United States (Challacombe, 2005).

When Congressman Ryan, his original traveling party, and a few defectors tried to leave two days later, Jones ordered his men to intercept them at their plane and kill them. Meanwhile, back at Jonestown, Jones instructed his followers to consume a poison-induced liquid. On November 18, 1978, over 900 Jonestown residents died, including Jones himself (Challacombe, 2005).

As discussed above, researchers have identified groupthink as playing a significant role in this tragedy (Challacombe, 2005). Although this is an extreme example, how many companies, schools, or organizations have made unwise or unhealthy choices because of groupthink? How many times have you participated with your peer group in activities you did not agree with?

Social influence also plays a role in understanding terror or criminal groups. Individuals are often recruited one-on-one to participate in criminal activities, or entire groups are gradually led down paths in which the idea of committing criminal actions does not seem bad (Gill, 2012; Reedy, Gastil, & Gabbay, 2013).

References

Amir, T. (1984). The Asch conformity effect: A study in Kuwait. *Social Behavior and Personality, 12*(2), 187–190.

Asch, S. E. (1951). Effects of group pressure upon the modification and distortion of judgments. In H. Guetzkow (Ed.), *Groups, leadership and men: Research in human relations* (pp. 177–190). Oxford, England: Carnegie Press.

Asch, S. E. (1955). Opinions and social pressure. *Scientific American, 193*(5), 31–35.

Asch, S. E. (1956). Studies of independence and submission to group pressure: I. A minority of one against a unanimous majority. *Psychological Monographs, 70(9), 1–70.*

Baron, R. S., Vandello, J. A., & Brunsman, B. (1996). The forgotten variable in conformity research: Impact of task importance on social influence. *Journal of Personality and Social Psychology, 71*(5), 915–927.

Beck, K. H., Ahmed, A., & Farkas, Z. A. (2011). A descriptive analysis of the social context of drinking among first-time DUI offenders. *Traffic Injury Prevention, 12*(4), 306–311. doi:10.1080/15389588.2011.564693

Bond, R., & Smith, P. B. (1996). Culture and conformity: A meta-analysis of studies using Asch's (1952b, 1956) line judgment task. *Psychological Bulletin, 119*(1), 111–137.

Burger, J. M. (1986). Increasing compliance by improving the deal: The that's-not-all technique. *Journal of Personality and Social Psychology, 51*(2), 277–283.

Burger, J. M. (2009). Replicating Milgram: Would people still obey today? *American Psychologist, 64*(1), 1–11.

Burger, J. M., Reed, M., DeCesare, K., Rauner, S., & Rozolis, J. (1999). The effects of initial request size on compliance: More about the that's-not-all technique. *Basic and Applied Social Psychology, 21*(3), 243–249.

Carli, L. L. (2001). Gender and social influence. *Journal of Social Issues, 57*(4), 725–741. doi:10.1111/0022-4537.00238

Carpenter, C. J. (2013). A meta-analysis of the effectiveness of the "but you are free" compliance-gaining technique. *Communication Studies, 64*(1), 6–17. doi:10.1080/10510974.2012.727941

Challacombe, D. J. (2005). Exploring religious groups that end in tragedy by using principles of social influence to understand leader manipulation. *Journal of Psychological Inquiry, 9,* 19–33.

Challacombe, D. J., Turek, G. M., & Shrira, I. (2005). *Relative hemisphere activation as a moderator of information social influence in norm formation.* Poster presented at annual meeting of the Society for Personality and Social Psychology, New Orleans, LA.

Cialdini, R. B., Vincent, J. E., Lewis, S. K., Catalan, J., Wheeler, D., & Darby, B. (1975). Reciprocal concessions procedure for inducing compliance: The door-in-the-face technique. *Journal of Personality and Social Psychology, 31*(2), 206–215.

Davis, B. P., & Knowles, E. S. (1999). A disrupt-then-reframe technique of social influence. *Journal of Personality and Social Psychology, 76*(2), 192–199.

Evans, B., Eys, M., & Wolf, S. (2013). Exploring the nature of interpersonal influence in elite individual sports teams. *Journal of Applied Sports Psychology, 25*(4), 448–462. doi:10.1080/10413200.2012.752769

Falk, E. B., Cascio, C. N., O'Donnell, M. B., Carp, J., Tinney, F. J., Jr., . . . Simons-Morton, B. G. (2014). Neural responses to exclusion predict susceptibility to social influence. *Journal of Adolescent Health, 54*(5), S22–S31. doi:10.1016/j.jadohealth.2013.12.035

Freedman, J. L., & Fraser, S. C. (1966). Compliance without pressure: The foot-in-the-door technique. *Journal of Personality and Social Psychology, 4*(2), 195–202.

Gill, P. (2012). Terrorist violence and the contextual, facilitative and causal qualities of group-based behaviors. *Aggression and Violent Behavior, 17*(6), 565–574. doi:10.1016/j.avb.2012.08.002

Hochman, J. (1990). Miracle, mystery, and authority: The triangle of cult indoctrination. *Psychiatric Annals, 20*(4), 179–187.

Hornik, J., & Ellis, S. (1988). Strategies to secure compliance for a mall intercept interview. *Public Opinion Quarterly, 52*(4), 539–551.

Ingham, A. G., Levinger, G., Graves, J., & Peckham, V. (1974). The Ringelmann effect: Studies of group size and group performance. *Journal of Experimental Social Psychology, 10*(4), 371–384.

Janis, I. L. (1982). *Victims of groupthink* (2nd ed.). Boston, MA: Houghton Mifflin.

Mehrabian, A. (1970). *Tactics of social influence.* Englewood Cliffs, NJ: Prentice-Hall.

Messner, M., Reinhard, M. A., & Sporer, S. L. (2008). Compliance through direct persuasive appeals: The moderating role of communicator's attractiveness in interpersonal persuasion. *Social Influence, 3*(2), 67–83. doi:10.1080/15534510802045261

Milgram, S. (1963). Behavioral study of obedience and disobedience to authority. *Journal of Abnormal and Social Psychology, 67,* 371–378.

Milgram, S. (1965). Some conditions of obedience and disobedience to authority. *Human Relations, 18,* 67–76.

Mowen, J. C., & Cialdini, R. B. (1980). On implementing the door-in-the-face compliance technique in a business context. *Journal of Marketing Research, 17*(2), 253–258.

Pool, G. J., Wood, W., & Leck, K. (1998). The self-esteem motive in social influence: Agreement with valued majorities and disagreement with derogated minorities. *Journal of Personality and Social Psychology, 75*(4), 967–975.

Post, J. M., & Panis, L. K. (2011). Crimes of obedience: "Groupthink" at Abu Ghraib. *International Journal of Group Psychotherapy, 61*(1), 48–66.

Seiter, J. S. (2007). Ingratiation and gratitude: The effect of complimenting customers on tipping behavior in restaurants. *Journal of Applied Social Psychology, 37*(3), 478–485.

Sherif, M. (1935). A study of some social factors in perception. *Archives of Psychology, 27*(187), 23–46.

Sherif, M. (1956). *An outline of social psychology.* New York, NY: Harper & Brothers.

Sherif, M. (1967). *Social interaction: Process and products.* Chicago, IL: Aldine.

Stang, D. J. (1976). Group size effects on conformity. *Journal of Social Psychology, 98*(2), 175–183.

Stefanone, M. A., Hurley, C. M., Egnoto, M. J., & Covert, J. M. (2015). Information asymmetry and social exchange: Exploring compliance gaining online. *Information, Communication, & Society, 18*(4), 376–389.

Reedy, J., Gastil, J., & Gabbay, M. (2013). Terrorism and small groups: An analytical framework for group disruption. *Small Group Research, 44*(6), 599–626.

Vider, S. (2004). Rethinking crowd violence: Self-categorization theory and the Woodstock 1999 riot. *Journal for the Theory of Social Behavior, 34*(2), 141–166.

Williams, K. D., & Williams, K. B. (1989). Impact of source strength on two compliance techniques. *Basic and Applied Social Psychology, 10*(2), 149–159.

Zimbardo, P. G. (2007). *The Lucifer effect: Understanding how good people turn evil.* New York, NY: Random House.

Chapter Eight
Prosocial Behaviors

Dr. Fantasy T. Lozada
University of Michigan

Learning Objectives

- Understand the altruistic versus egoistic motives of prosocial behaviors
- Describe how emotion, morality, and personality impact willingness to help others
- Describe the bystander effect and the five steps that lead to helping behaviors in an emergency
- Understand how characteristics of the receiver/victim make them more or less likely to receive help
- Understand the impact that diverse samples can have on prosocial behavior research

Chapter Outline

Why do we help? Characteristics of the helper

When do we help? Situational Characteristics

Whom do we help? Victim/Receiver Characteristics

Diverse Samples in the Study of Prosocial Behavior

In today's electronic world, we have become avid consumers of constant news! Through our social network feeds, popular news network websites, and websites dedicated to bringing you fun, uplifting, or unusual viral stories, we are exposed to hundreds of stories a day about criminals and everyday heroes (human and four-legged a like). It is the latter, the heroes (the human ones), that the current chapter focuses on. For instance, the man who gave away his lunch to the hungry person on the street, the woman who donated life-saving bone marrow to a child she didn't know, and the little boy who donated half of the money he made from selling cocoa to a hospital all have something in common. They have engaged in **prosocial behaviors**. Prosocial behaviors are helpful acts or behaviors that benefit another individual. Prosocial behaviors may not directly benefit the helpful person and may at times even require a cost or sacrifice to that person. Many times when we hear stories of others' heroism and kind acts in their communities, we assume that we would be just as brave and helpful in that situation. However, 40 years of research on prosocial behavior has revealed that many of us are only helpful in certain situations, to people with certain characteristics, and when we feel a certain kind of way! Before you become disappointed in the disposition of the human race, you should recognize that there are many factors at play that either contribute to and/or inhibit our prosocial tendencies and understanding those factors may help us all become more altruistic on a daily basis. Whether it is stopping to help a neighbor carry a heavy load of groceries or giving to a disaster relief fund, we all have some inclination to be helpful at least some of the time.

Prosocial Behaviors
Helpful acts that benefit another individual.

Why Do We Help? Characteristics of the Helper

Altruistic
Motivated by selfless concern for others.

Think of a friend or family member that you consider particularly **altruistic**. How would you describe that person? One of my favorite descriptions of a selfless person is that "he/she will give you the shirt off his/her back!" This gives you the impression that someone is so helpful that they will take something of their very own, perhaps something that they need, just to help another person. Why would someone be *so* helpful? Why give when it means taking away something that you might need for yourself? Do people help out of the "goodness of their hearts" or do we only help others so that we can help ourselves? First, we discuss perspectives on whether or not any prosocial behavior is truly altruistic. Then, we turn to research that suggests why we might "give the shirts off our backs."

Altruistic or Egoistic Motivations

Egoistic
Motivated the concern for oneself or one's desires.

There are two sides to the debate on why we are motivated to help. The first side argues that humans have an inner desire to help others and that we are motivated to improve another's well-being (altruistic motivation). The other side argues that prosocial behaviors are motivated by selfish desires and are dictated by social expectations (**egoistic** motivation). For instance, Batson, Duncan, Ackerman, Buckley, and Birch (1981) define altruistic motivation in terms of being compelled to help another person because you identify with the victim and/or feel empathy for the victim's situation. He defined egoistic motivation in terms of feeling the obligation to do something for social pressure (so that you look good in front of others and receive potential rewards) or because you want to reduce the negative emotion that you feel from seeing the other person in need (which we will explore further below in the context of the costs and benefits to helping). Two researchers, Grace Lemmon and Sandy Wayne (2015), explored Batson's model within the workplace and examined organizational citizenship behaviors. Organizational citizenship behaviors are prosocial behaviors that go above and beyond job expectations and are not formally rewarded. The study examined 164 employees' feelings of obligation (egoistic motivation) and altruistic concern (altruistic motivation) toward both their supervisors and to the overall company. The employees' supervisors also participated in the study and reported on their employees' organizational citizenship behaviors toward the supervisor (e.g., assisting the supervisor with their workload without being asked) and organizational citizenship behaviors toward the organization (e.g., attends company functions that are not required but helps the company's image). Lemmon and Wayne found that when employees had greater altruistic concern for their company, they engaged in more organizational citizenship behaviors for the company. Feelings of obligation to the company did not relate to organizational citizenship behaviors for the company. However, for supervisors, when employees had more feelings of obligation toward the supervisor (and not altruistic concern toward the supervisor), they engaged in more organizational citizenship behaviors toward the supervisor. This is one of the few studies that examines prosocial behaviors in the workplace and it suggests that the motivation for our prosocial behaviors also depends on who will be the recipient of the prosocial behavior.

Kzenon/Shutterstock.com

To be motivated by altruism to do good things for your company means that you are willing to sacrifice or offer a helping hand just for the good of the company, without receiving anything in return. Do you think that people are motivated to help simply for the sake of being helpful to others? Think about the many ways that you are helpful to others from day-to-day. Why do you offer to help your roommate bring in her groceries? Why do you pick up the litter on the sidewalk on campus? Why do you stop to help someone who has dropped their books? Did you answer, "Because helping makes me feel good" or "I like to make others smile" or "Because I hope that someone would do the same for me"? Believe it or not, the only one of those reasons that would be considered altruistic is the motivation to make others smile. When you choose to help to make yourself feel better or because you feel bad for another person, theorists would argue that you are really responding to your own desires of wanting to feel positively. Below, we describe the way that your emotions may contribute to more egoistic motivations, whereas your moral code may contribute to more altruistic motivations. The research on prosocial behavior has not come to one solid conclusion about whether people help more from altruistic versus egoistic motivations. As you go through the rest of the chapter and learn about other studies and ways people have demonstrated prosocial behavior, see if you can determine whether the motivation is altruistic or egoistic.

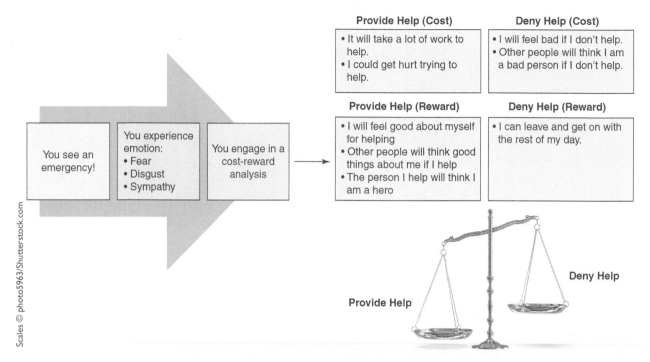

Scales © photos5963/Shutterstock.com

Figure 8.1. Arousal cost-reward model (Piliavin et al., 1969).

Emotion

Arousal Cost-Reward Model

A model that suggests that people respond to an emergency by engaging in a cost-reward analysis to reduce negative emotion.

On a daily basis, we listen to our emotional cues to guide us in our social interactions. With regard to our helping behaviors, our emotions can serve as a signal that moves us to help someone in need or as a reward we experience in response to helping someone. In the case of an emergency, the amount of negative emotion we feel motivates us to get involved. The **arousal cost-reward model** (Piliavin, Rodin, & Piliavin, 1969) suggests that when we see an emergency as a bystander, we feel emotions like fear, disgust, and/or sympathy (see Figure 8.1). In order to reduce this distress, the bystander engages in a cost-reward analysis to examine whether the potential rewards (to either the self or the victim) outweigh the potential costs (to either the self or the victim). Bystanders weigh the costs and rewards for both scenarios of choosing to help and choosing not to help. When costs for helping are perceived to outweigh the rewards for helping, the bystander is unlikely to help. However, when rewards of helping are perceived to outweigh the costs of helping, the bystander is likely to get involved and help in the situation.

Just as negative emotions may motivate us to get involved when someone needs help, positive emotions tend to surface after we have engaged in helpful behaviors. Simply put, when we help others, we feel good (Forest, Clark, Mills, & Isen, 1979). Helping other people can make us feel better when we are in a bad mood and can even improve our well-being (Aknin, Sandstrom, Dunn, & Norton, 2011). Feeling good for helping others may be a universal feature of being prosocial. Aknin, Broesch, Hamlin, and Van de Vondervoot(2015) found that even in the isolated village of Vanuata (an island in the South Pacific), with little to no influence of Western culture, people felt more positive emotion when they engaged in prosocial behaviors in comparison to when they did good things for themselves. For instance, village adults were given the opportunity to either buy candy for themselves or could buy candy for someone else. Those villagers who bought candy for someone else reported feeling happier than villagers who bought candy for themselves. Additionally, young children in the village (ages 2 to 5) were given the opportunity to engage in either costly giving (giving candy away from one's own supply of candy) or noncostly giving (giving candy away from the experimenter's supply of candy). These children also received candy themselves. Children expressed more happiness when they gave candy away in comparison to when they received candy and children expressed the most happiness when they engaged in costly giving in comparison to noncostly giving. Feeling good from helping others is obviously one of the great benefits to engaging in prosocial behaviors, but as we discussed earlier, if we always gain the benefit of feeling good after helping, are any of our prosocial behaviors truly altruistic?

Empathy
The emotional and cognitive experience of understanding another's perspective and feelings.

Another emotional component that has been suggested as a basic factor in prompting prosocial behavior is **empathy**. Empathy is the emotional and cognitive experience of understanding another person's perspective and feeling other-oriented emotions such as sympathy and compassion in response to another person's distress. Researchers suggest that when you take the perspective of another person, it creates *empathic concern* (the emotional component of empathy), which then prompts you to react in a way that reduces the other person's distress. However, when you witness someone in need and you do not or cannot take the perspective of the other person, you feel personal distress and react in a way that allows you to reduce your own stress (Batson, Early, & Salvarini, 1997). This is similar to what I described above in the arousal cost-reward model. Robert Cialdini and colleagues (1987) also highlighted the importance of empathic concern, stating in their **negative state relief model** that when a person feels bad he or she may be more likely to help someone in need to make him- or herself feel better. Specifically, when you see someone in need, this activates your empathic concern and increases your own feelings of sadness—which you then need to get rid of or relieve. The need to relieve this negative emotion motivates you to help the person in need.

Dragon Images/Shutterstock.com

Negative State Relief Model
A model that suggests that a person is more likely to help someone to make him- or herself feel better when he or she is in a negative mood.

Although many researchers have established that empathy contributes directly to prosocial behavior, new work has examined factors related to culture and gender that may also relate to the empathy–prosocial behavior connection. For instance, cultural artifacts such as music, books, and movies can cause emotional reactions, but did you know that certain types of music may be related to the likelihood that you will help other people? Australian researchers Clark and Giacomantonio (2013) examined the role of music preferences in fostering empathic concern and prosocial behavior among adolescents. The study examined adolescent music preferences for the genres of pop and dance music (genres that are typically considered to be upbeat, conventional, energetic, and rhythmic) and alternative, rap, and blues music (genres that are typically considered to be reflexive, complex, intense, and rebellious). Clark and Giacomantonio found that music preference was related to empathy and that specifically for adolescent boys, music preferences for alternative, rap, and blues music were related to more displays of cognitive and emotional components of empathy. This study is the first of its kind so there is still a lot for us to know about how music relates to

Moral Obligation

A sense of duty from one's beliefs of right and wrong.

Preconventional Morality

The early stage of moral development in which right and wrong is determined by punishments.

Conventional Morality

The middle stage of moral development in which right and wrong is determined by the majority's standards.

Moral Reasoning

The cognitive process of determining right from wrong.

Malchev/Shutterstock.com

Gregory James Van Raalte/Shutterstock.com

empathy and prosocial behaviors. For instance, do empathic, prosocial boys tend to choose to listen to rap and alternative music or do the lyrical content and complex rhythms of those genres help foster other-oriented thoughts and emotion?

Morality

Many people will tell you that they help others in need because they believe that it is the right thing to do. You may be familiar with the story of the fictional character Superman, who punishes villains by beating them up and stopping them from causing mayhem. But even when the villain is about to fall off the building to plunge to his death, Superman saves him to turn him into the proper authorities. Why does Superman help the villain when he is in danger? Some would say Superman follows a strict moral code, where you help others because they need help and you don't let anyone die if you can help it. (I should note that I and other comic book fans can debate whether Superman has truly ever followed this moral code, but in general Superman doesn't like to kill villains. See www.comicbookmovie.com to read more.)

When presented with the opportunity to help, it is often an opportunity to do what we think is right or what we think is our **moral obligation**. Moral obligation is a sense of duty arising from one's beliefs of right and wrong.

Kohlberg (1984) suggested that we develop our ideas of right and wrong through developmental stages during childhood and adolescence as shown in Table 8.1. We start at level 1 (before the age of 10), which is called **pre-conventional morality**, at which point we have not developed our own standards of what is moral (right or wrong), but instead believe that morality is dictated by what adults say and the consequences for breaking rules. During adolescence to early adulthood, we enter **conventional morality** in which we have internalized the moral code set in place by adults and the larger society. During this stage, we typically think that what is normal is right and that things that go against the majority are considered bad. Finally during adulthood (although many adults do not achieve this stage), we enter **postconventional morality** in which our moral standards are determined by personal principles and beliefs based on **moral reasoning** (the cognitive process by which you determine what is right or wrong) as opposed to predetermined societal standards. This postconventional morality allows us to think critically about laws or policies that might be good for some groups of people but are bad for others. Further, this type of morality helps us think about what is good for all people (human rights) and promotes justice and equality. As you might expect, the higher the level of someone's morality and moral reasoning, the more likely an individual is to help or to engage in prosocial behaviors across the lifespan (Erkut, Jaquette, & Staub, 1981; Schonert-Reichl, 1999).

Although by adulthood, we typically have a moral code, some researchers suggest that some of us like to appear moral to others without actually engaging in prosocial behaviors, known as moral hypocrisy. Moral hypocrisy can be in the form of someone saying that they care about a

Table 8.1: Kohlberg's Stages of Moral Development

Level	Stage	Description
Preconventional Morality (Infancy–age 9)	Obedience/Punishment	Right and wrong is determined by punishments. You do what is right so that you do not get punished.
	Self-Interest	Right and wrong is determined by self-interest and satisfaction. You do what is right because it benefits you.
Conventional Morality (Adolescence & Adulthood)	Conformity and Interpersonal Accord	Right and wrong is determined by the majority's standards. You do what is right to be liked by others.
	Authority and Social Order	Right and wrong is determined by your duty to society. You do what is right to show respect to authority and to the system.
Postconventional Morality (20+ Years; achieved by few adults)	Social Contract	Right and wrong is determined by personal belief and value systems. The society determines the laws, but if you don't agree with the law you choose to ignore them.
	Universal Principles	Right and wrong is determined by your own moral principles regardless of what society says is right.

certain issue or group in front of others, but engaging in the opposite behavior in private. For example, a friend who claims in front of others that she is a vegetarian because she is opposed to the treatment of animals, yet eats hamburgers when she thinks no one is looking engages in moral hypocrisy. The friend may perceive that others believe that becoming a vegetarian is the moral thing to do and wants to look moral in front of her friends, without giving up her favorite meal of hamburgers! The occurrence of moral hypocrisy suggests that having a moral code is not enough to make someone engage in prosocial behaviors. A particularly dangerous type of moral hypocrisy is when someone actually engages in an immoral act in private, like hurting someone or making them sick, and then engaging in helping behaviors to become the hero and save the day. This behavior mostly comes from the desire to look like a good person in front of others, even though the "helper" is actually the cause of harm. One notable case of this is a transit officer in New York City who planted a pipe bomb in a Times Square subway station. Shortly before the bomb exploded he warned everyone that he had discovered the bomb, evacuated the

Postconventional Morality

The last stage of moral development in which right and wrong is determined by one's own beliefs and standards.

Fotos593/Shutterstock.com

THINKING CRITICALLY

Morality and Helping Behaviors

Imagine this scenario: You are taking an exam in an empty room. Your professor told you that another student is also taking the same exam next door, and has left the two of you to complete the exam in separate rooms while she goes to another floor to handle other business. The exam is timed and you will only have a short amount of time to complete the exam before the professor comes back to collect it. If you don't complete the exam, you won't be able to make it up. While you are taking the exam, you hear loud groaning and moaning sounds coming from the room where the other student is completing the exam. What would you do? Would you leave your room to go check on the other student or leave the exam to go get help? Do you think that your response would be different if your professor had given you permission to go into the room of the other test-taker (perhaps to get an extra pen or pencil)? Or would you be worried that if you stopped the test to go see what's happening in the other room that you would get in trouble and/or not finish the test? Erkut and colleagues (1981) conducted a very similar study. Who do you think would be most likely to help the person next door: a person concerned with the timed test, a person who was given permission to go into the next room, or a person who wasn't told that the test was timed and was not told that they could go into the other room? How do you think your stage of moral reasoning would impact your willingness to help in this situation?

Applying Research: In Erkut and colleagues' study (1981), participants were invited to the lab and given a series of tests. They were then taken by a female experimenter to another room where she said she would measure the participants' reaction time. As the participant and experimenter were walking over, she mentioned that there was another participant in the room next door that she would also go and check on while he was working. The "other participant" in the room was a male confederate. After checking in on the "other participant," the experimenter gave the actual participant a timed test. Participants were given different instructions based on the condition that they had been unknowingly assigned. In the "permission condition," the experimenter told the participant that she had made some coffee in the other room (where the "other participant" was working) and that the participant could go get some in a moment. In the "prohibition condition," the experimenter told the participant that this was a timed task and that it must be worked on continuously and without breaks for it to be completed. In the "no information" condition, participants were not told about coffee *nor* were they told that the test was timed task. After the experimenter left and the task began, sounds of distress, moaning, and groaning began in the other room. The participants' behaviors were observed and recorded. Students who were in the conventional morality stage (the stages that are driven by compliance to the majority and authority figures) did not help in any of the conditions. However, participants in the postconventional morality stage (the stage driven by personal beliefs and principles) were likely to go and check on the confederate and to offer help by going to get someone. Postconventional stage participants were most likely to help when they had been given previous permission to enter the room. These results are presented in Figure 8.2.

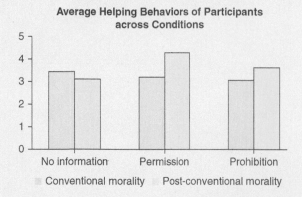

Figure 8.2. Average helping behaviors of participants across conditions in the Erkut and colleagues' (1981) morality and helping behaviors study.

area, and called for backup. When the bomb exploded, the man was the only one who was injured. Initially he was championed as a hero for identifying the bomb and evacuating the area, which was likely the reaction that the transit office wanted. However, further investigation revealed that the transit office was then one who planted and detonated the bomb (Brick, 2004). This example describes the desperate lengths some people will go to so that they *look* like they are helping and being moral! Have you heard of other cases of moral hypocrisy? See the Thinking Critically Box on page 124 for an example of how an individual's stage of moral development impacts helping behavior in a research setting.

Prosocial Personality

Would you describe yourself as a born-helper? Have you always liked to help others or can you point to one experience that prompted you to become more helpful? We might all agree that some people are nicer than others or at the very least that some people are willing to help more than others. In fact, research suggests that prosocial behaviors, empathic concern, perspective-taking, and sympathy are all aspects of being prosocial that appear to be stable over time. Children who tend to display a prosocial orientation grow up to be adults who display a prosocial orientation and adults who engage in frequent helping behaviors are the most likely to engage in helping behaviors in subsequent years (Eisenberg et al., 2002). However, there is no one factor that determines a person's tendency to be helpful. Some research suggests that there is a genetic component to prosocial behaviors and empathy (Knafo, Zahn-Waxler, Van Hulle, Robinson, & Rhee, 2008; Son & Wilson, 2010). Twin studies highlight that although prosocial tendencies can be attributed to genetics, there are a lot of environmental factors that relate to prosocial behaviors and empathy. For instance, childhood experiences like the way parents teach their children about helping, contribute to prosocial tendencies over time (Eisenberg, Hofer, Sulik, & Liew, 2014). There are other aspects such as characteristics of the situation, characteristics of the victim, and characteristics of the helper that dictate when, why, and who we help. I describe each of these types of characteristics below.

When Do We Help? Situational Characteristics

Imagine you are at home one night and you hear two people struggling and fighting in the street. When you look out your window to see what is happening, a man is attacking a woman with a knife. The woman calls out for help and you see lights turn on in almost all of the surrounding homes. It appears that everyone has heard the woman's cry for help! You think to yourself that surely, someone has called the police and help is on the way! What would you do in this situation? Would you go out and try to ward off the attacker? Would you yell out the window at the man to let him know that you see what he is doing? Would you call the police?

The scenario I described actually happened in the Queens borough of New York City in 1964. Catherine "Kitty" Genovese was walking home to her apartment after work at about 3:20 am. After parking her car, only 100 feet away from the entrance to her apartment building, she was suddenly attacked by a man wielding a knife. During the attack, Kitty screamed out for help—saying "He stabbed me! Please help me!" Lights came on in the apartments above where Kitty was being attacked. One neighbor called out of a window, "Let that girl alone!" Hearing this, the attacker shrugged and walked away. But after the lights went back out in the apartment building, the attacker came back for Kitty and stabbed her again. Kitty called out a second time, "I'm dying!" Although lights came on a second time in the apartments above, no one called out. The attacker left Kitty again and this time got in a car and drove away. Kitty tried to get into the safety of an apartment building, but never made it inside. The attacker came back once more and finally killed her. No one called the police until 30 minutes into the attack, when Kitty had already been murdered. Police arrived in 2 minutes to the scene of the crime and discovered Kitty's body. Had the police been called earlier, Kitty might have survived the attack. When the neighbors in the apartment building were asked why they didn't call the police even though they heard the attack many said, "I didn't want to get involved" or many wives said, "I didn't want my husband to get involved." One woman said she believed that it was a "lover's quarrel" while another man said that he was tired and went back to bed (Gansberg, 1964).

The response of Kitty's neighbors baffled people across the United States and many people blamed a decline in morals to the lack of help offered during such an obvious emergency situation. It was noted that 38 people witnessed Kitty's attack. Could it really be that out of 38 people, only one person realized that calling the police was the right thing to do? Kitty's case caught the attention of two social psychologists, John Darley and Bibb Latané who began a series of social experiments to understand when people are most likely to help. Below we review their work and other studies that may help us understand in what type of situations we are most likely to be helpful.

The Bystander Effect

The surprising aspect of the Kitty Genovese case was the number of witnesses that did not offer help. Latané and Darley wondered if the number of witnesses to an emergency had an impact on whether or not someone would help. The researchers set up an experiment in which participants were told to communicate about their experiences as a college student over an intercom to other participants. Some students were told that they were only speaking with one other person on the intercom. Other students were assigned to talk in groups of three or six. In truth, participants were only hearing the recordings of people speaking to make them think that they were in a group with others. During the "conversation," one of the group members, who had mentioned earlier that he suffered from occasional seizures, began to stutter, asked for help because he was beginning to seize, made choking noises, and then suddenly went silent. Over 80 percent of the participants who believed that they were the only other person in their group immediately responded by leaving the room to go get help. However, in scenarios where the participants believed that they were in the three-person or six-person group, participants responded more slowly, if at all. In fact, in the six-person group 38 percent of the participants never left the room (Darley & Latané, 1968).

Bystander Effect
The effect in which an increased number of witnesses decreases the likelihood that someone will help another.

Diffusion of Responsibility
The belief that other bystanders will/should take responsibility for helping others in need.

Darley and Latané's study suggested that the more witnesses or bystanders in an emergency situation, the less likely an individual will get involved to help, even if you can't see the other witnesses. This phenomenon is known as the **bystander effect**. The bystander effect occurs because of **diffusion of responsibility**. This means that a person feels less responsible to help as the bystander group becomes larger. Diffusion of responsibility occurs because the presence of other people decreases feelings of personal responsibility, lessens the feeling of guilt for not acting, and provides the opportunity to look to others for guidance in what to do in response to the emergency. However, when there is only one witness to an emergency, there is no one else to share responsibility or blame with and no one to suggest what should be done to help, making a person feel fully responsible for saving the victim and increasing the likelihood that they will help. Similarly, if in an emergency the person who needs help asks one person directly to get involved, that one person is more likely to feel fully responsible for helping and will, in most cases, help.

A more recent study by Tobias Greitemeyer and Dirk Oliver Mügge (2015) found that the bystander effect could be reversed as the number of help-givers needed in the situation increased. Specifically, participants were asked if they would help a fellow student who needed more participants for an unrelated study. Participants were told that either the student needed only one person to help or four people to help and were additionally told that either they were the only person asked or that they were one of a group of people that was asked. The study found that in conditions when only one helper was needed, the bystander effect still remained and participants assumed that someone else would help unless they were specifically told that they were the only one asked to help. However, in conditions where four people were needed to help, helping intentions increased if more individuals were asked to help. Greitemeyer and Mügge concluded that when helping requires teamwork or interdependence, a "safety in numbers" mentality emerges, encouraging people to work with other bystanders to help.

Helping in an Emergency

Latané and Darley (1968) also outlined other aspects of both the situation and an individual's cognitive process in an emergency situation that helps determine when a person will help in an emergency, as depicted in Figure 8.3. The first step toward helping in an emergency is noticing that someone is in danger or in need of help. However, distraction and self-concern can often get in the way of noticing that there is an emergency. For example, if you are late for a very important meeting and you walk by a man who is slumped over and groaning, you might be too distracted by the fact that you are running late and too worried about getting reprimanded if you are delayed any further, that you may not even notice the man who appears to need medical attention. Even if you do notice that something is wrong with the man, the fact that you are busy and believe that someone else will be available to help soon could make you less likely to stop to help. The second step toward helping is interpreting that someone is currently experiencing an emergency. Three aspects of the situation that may get in the way of recognizing an event as a situation are the ambiguity (vagueness) of the situation (has the man been injured or is he drunk), **pluralistic ignorance** (no one else who

Pluralistic Ignorance
The state in which people in a group believe that their individual thoughts and feelings are different from those of others; no one reacts to an emergency because they think that others know it is not an emergency.

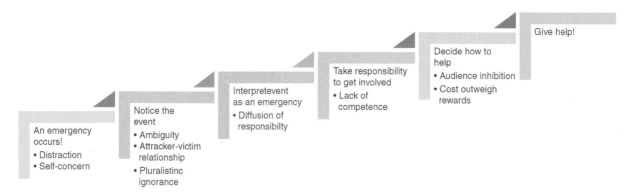

Figure 8.3.   Latané and Darley's (1968) Five steps to helping in an emergency.

sees the event is worried), and the relationship between the attacker and the victim (is this a quarreling husband and wife or a strange man attacking a woman). Once you determine that there is an emergency to respond to, you must then take responsibility for helping, which can be hindered by diffusion of responsibility as described earlier. If you do feel that it is your responsibility to respond, you must decide how you will help the victim. However, you still might not act if you lack the "know-how" or the confidence to help. Finally, if you decide that you know how to help, you still may not provide help if you fear that the costs to helping outweigh the benefits, as described earlier in the chapter.

Latané and Darley's (1968) Five Steps to Helping in an Emergency
These five steps represent the cognitive processes related to recognizing and responding to an emergency. Below each step are the possible barriers that could prevent making it to the next step and would stop the process of responding to an emergency situation.

Geographic Location

Do you think that someone is more likely to receive help if he or she lives in an urban area versus a rural or suburban area? The Kitty Genovese case described above did not surprise some people because they expected that you are less likely to receive help in an urban city than in a rural city. Nancy Steblay (1987) did a review of 65 studies that examined helping behaviors in rural versus urban settings and found that the geographic differences in helping were not because individuals in urban cities were less helpful people than people in rural areas. Instead, she found that the situational characteristics of the urban city made it less likely that one would help a stranger. One possible explanation of this rural–urban difference is that urban cities have more stressful environmental stimulation than rural cities, which contributes to higher distraction and more attention to one's own personal concerns as an adaptive response to the sensory overload that can occur in urban cities (Milgram, 1970). For instance, if you were walking in a city where there are typically many people on the sidewalks quickly moving past you and speaking loudly with others and the constant noise of city traffic and construction, do you think you would be able to pick out a plea for help or notice if someone had passed out near an alley? Milgram suggested that a way to handle the vast amount of sight and sound, one has to tune out much of the environmental stimuli of the city to be able to effectively and efficiently attend to one's own needs and tasks. Similarly, **deindividuation theory** (Zimbardo,

Deindividuation Theory
Theory that suggests that overwhelming social stimulation leads to a loss of thinking of people as individuals.

1969) suggests that overwhelming stimulation in urban cities contributes to a loss of thinking of people as individuals leading to a decrease in empathic concern and a decrease in prosocial behaviors. Another explanation is that there is more diversity of behaviors and people in urban cities compared to rural cities. The diversity of behavior may make it more likely that you interpret a possible emergency as vague or ambiguous and less likely that you interpret a situation as an emergency. The diversity of individuals makes it more likely that you will find yourself among people who are unfamiliar and dissimilar to you, leading you to feel less secure and less likely to help if you see an emergency. Consider your own personal experience with urban cities versus rural cities. Did you notice differences in the way that people interacted with strangers or helped one another? Did you grow up in an urban or rural area? Do you believe that the explanations of helping behavior in urban areas are valid?

Thomas La Mela/Shutterstock.com

Social Norms

Another characteristic of the situation that impacts helping behaviors are the **social norms** established by a culture or society. Social norms are the general rules for behavior that reflect acceptable ways of interacting with others. Some norms reflect fair treatment of others. For instance, the **norm of reciprocity** is that we should treat other people the way that those people have treated us. With regard to helping, we tend to help those who have helped us in the past (Gross & Latané, 1974) and those who we see have been helpful to others in the past (Nowak & Sigmund, 2005). The **norm of equity** suggests that in order to maintain equitable balance, we should give away extra benefits that we receive to those who received few benefits. However, some studies have shown that people typically choose to maintain advantage (having more benefits or resources than the other person), than to give away resources to establish balance or equity (Fiske, 2011). Those who follow social norms of fairness tend to help based on whether or not the person in need *deserves* their help. However, other social norms reflect a sense of morality or what is considered right. For instance, the **norm of social responsibility** is the standard that you should help someone in need simply because he or she is in need and it is the right thing to do. Those who follow this norm feel a sense of obligation when they encounter someone in need and give more help to those who display a greater amount of need.

Social norms can vary across cultures. Miller, Bersoff, and Harwood (1990) found that participants in India adhered to standards of the norm of social responsibility, regardless of who was in need of help and no matter the conditions under which help was requested. However, American participants believed that moral social norms only applied in life-threatening situations and in some situations in which parents responded to the needs of their children. Additionally, Soosai-Nathan, Negri, and Fave (2013) conducted interviews with participants in India and Italy to examine beliefs and norms about prosocial behaviors across the two cultures. Although both cultures described prosocial behaviors as valuable for social interactions and relationships, there were differences in how people in

Norm of Reciprocity
A norm of fairness that says we should treat other people the way that they have treated us.

Norm of Equity
A norm of fairness that suggests that we should give away extra resources to those with fewer resources to maintain equitable balance.

Norm of Social Responsibility
A moral norm that emphasizes helping others just because they are in need.

Collectivism
A cultural orientation that emphasizes group identity and needs over individual identity and needs.

Individualism
A cultural orientation that emphasizes individual identity and needs over group identity and needs.

both cultures described the nature of prosocial behaviors. Indian participants described engaging in prosocial behavior as a value to and a virtue of an individual, whereas Italian participants described engaging in prosocial behavior as coming from an individual's feeling of care and concern for others. Indian culture reflects stronger beliefs in the importance of interdependence and group harmony (**collectivism**), which is consistent with beliefs that helping is a moral behavior and that people should help because it is the right thing to do. On the other hand, Italian and American cultures reflect more of an **individualist** orientation, which is consistent with beliefs that helping behaviors are dependent on the norm of reciprocity and/or an individual's feelings. Such differences and norms across cultures also lead to differences in the rates of helping across cultures. For instance, in a study that examined willingness to spontaneously help a stranger across 23 countries, Levine and colleagues (2001) found that helping behaviors were highest among countries that emphasize the social well-being of others (e.g., Brazil, Costa Rica, and Spain) and lowest among countries that had higher economic well-being (e.g., Netherlands and the United States).

Whom Do We Help? Victim/Receiver Characteristics

Imagine that you won a cash prize while participating in a research study. There are two others who are participating in the study at the same time, but who did not win a cash prize. The researcher allows you to decide which other participant will also get a cash prize—but it can only be given to one of the other participants, not both. How do you decide who gets the cash prize? Would you make your decision based on outward characteristics such as gender, race, or attractiveness? Would you choose the cash prize recipient by the way he or she interacted with you or the researcher earlier? Perhaps you would choose someone who reminded you of yourself in some way. This next section explores three of the factors that impact whom we help: attributions of responsibility, attractiveness, and similarity of the victim/receiver in relation to the helper.

Attributions of Responsibility

Helping behaviors can be influenced by our own perceptions of how responsible the person in need is for his or her own situation. For example, studies show that homeless individuals are often thought to be responsible for their lack of resources (Kluegel & Smith, 1986; Pellegrini, Quierolo, Monarrez, & Valenzuela, 1997) and that these attitudes toward the homeless have an impact on whether individuals helped or interacted with the homeless (Hocking & Lawrence, 2000). On the other hand, when an impoverished group is believed to be less responsible for their current situation, people tend to be more sympathetic and express greater intention to offer help to this group. For example, Michael Halloran and Glynn Chambers (2011) examined the attitudes and helping intentions toward homeless and indigenous Australians among Australian college students. The study revealed that after highlighting the social identity of being an Australian, students expressed a greater intention to help indigenous Australians but did not express a greater intention to help homeless Australians. Halloran and Chambers suggested that helping intentions did not increase for the homeless because of the general belief that the homeless were responsible for their current conditions.

Another example of the impact of attribution of responsibility is found in a recent study that examined participants' willingness to donate money to a nonprofit organization. At the beginning of the study, participants were given two envelopes, one marked "compensation" and the other marked "donation." After reading the description of the nonprofit organization, participants indicated how much money they wanted to donate to the organization by putting it in the "donation" envelope. The description of the nonprofit organization said, "This nonprofit organization supports the largest network of community health centers in Pennsylvania. Community health centers provide medical treatment for patients who are unable to afford the necessary medical treatment for serious illnesses and diseases." The last sentence of the description differed by two conditions. In the "low-responsibility" condition, the last sentence of the description said, "The majority of the patients community health centers serve are individuals who have been working hard at multiple low-wage jobs but are unable to obtain medical insurance due to poor benefits and economic conditions." The "high-responsibility" description said, "The majority of the patients community health centers serve are individuals who do not have medical insurance because they do not hold a steady job due to their drug and alcohol abuse or gambling addiction" (Lee, Winterich, & Ross, 2014). Participants also completed a moral identity questionnaire that measured the degree to which moral traits (e.g., caring, compassionate, and kind) were part of their identity. Participants who said that moral traits were an important part of their identity (high moral identity) and who were a part of the low-responsibility condition gave more money to the organization than participants who said that moral traits were not an important part of their identity (low moral identity). However, in the high-responsibility condition, participants with high moral identity were less likely to donate than participants with lower moral identity. Participants with high moral identity felt empathy for the organization when they believed that the people in need were not responsible for not having medical insurance, but felt that it was not fair for them to donate to people who did not have health insurance because their addictions hindered them from keeping a steady job.

Rawpixel/Shutterstock.com

Attractiveness

The Internet and other media sources are filled with articles, blogs, and social media posts that indicate that life is better or easier for beautiful or attractive people for a whole host of reasons (e.g., perceptions of health, intelligence, and trustworthiness and persuasive ability). The advantages of being attractive may be up for debate but studies indicate that there is a beauty bias with regard to helping behaviors. W. Andrew Harrell (1978) examined male participants' willingness to stop and help a female who needed directions to the health services building on a college campus. Males were asked for directions either by an attractive female (the female confederate was dressed in a neat pants suit, neatly combed hair, and makeup) or by an unattractive female (the female confederate wore wrinkled clothing with a food stain, had uncombed hair, and wore no makeup). The female confederate also varied in whether or not she disclosed her name while asking for directions. Males spent more time giving directions (and even offering to walk the female confederate to the health services building) when in the attractive condition, particularly when the attractive confederate disclosed her name. Males spent the least amount of time giving directions to the female confederate if the unattractive confederate disclosed her name. Harrell suggested that males spent more time helping the attractive confederate when she gave her name because the disclosure was viewed as valuable given the attractive nature of the participant. However, when the unattractive confederate disclosed her name, the male participants may have seen the name disclosure as an attempt to foster a personal relationship, which was seen as undesirable given the unattractive nature of the confederate.

Maksim Denisenko/Shutterstock.com

Help is offered more readily not only to the physically attractive but also to those who appear to be friendlier or to engage in behavior that reflect social connection. For instance, college students were more likely to help a confederate in a study who dropped a stack of folders if the confederate had previously spoken with the participant using a warm tone of voice, made eye contact while speaking, or touched the participant while speaking (Goldman & Fordyce, 1983). However, the study noted that helping behaviors toward the confederate were low if the confederate engaged in all three of these "connecting behaviors" (the eye contact, touching, and using the warm tone of voice). It may be that too many behaviors that are meant to signal connection may be perceived as inappropriate when coming from a stranger! Another study in Amsterdam showed that when researchers approached passers-by with a request to participate in a study, smiling researchers elicited more help to participate in the study than un-smiling researchers. Male researchers in particular were more likely to gain participants when smiling (Vrugt & Vet, 2009).

Similarity

Are we more likely to help when we see someone in need with whom we can identify with? A large body of work supports that we tend to help others who are more similar to us across several group identities such as gender (Emswiller, Deaux, & Willits, 1971), race (West, Whitney, & Schnedler, 1975), religious affiliation (Yinon & Sharon, 1985), personal attitudes (Suedfeld, Bochner, & Wnek, 1972), and similar styles of dress (Hensley, 1981). Guéguen, Pichot, and Le Dreff (2005) in France found that we are even more likely to help others when we perceive similarity by our last names only. College students received an e-mail asking if they would help a fellow university student by filling out a 40-item survey for a class project. Half of the students received the e-mailed request from a student who had the same last name as themselves while the other half of the students received the e-mailed request from a student who had a different last name. Results from the study showed that both the agreement to complete the survey was higher and the response time to the request was shorter in the same last name condition than in the different last name condition. Our willingness to help individuals that are similar to ourselves may come from an over-identification with the person in need, which fosters more empathic concern for the other because we can imagine "being in their shoes." Although this **intergroup bias** in helping is beneficial for those that share our similarities (and who are considered in-group members), one can see how this can be problematic in diverse settings where you must work with and cooperate with people from various backgrounds. However, research suggests that these biases can be reduced if you can get members of different groups to see themselves as part of one larger, common group. For instance, in the Australian study described earlier in the section discussing attributions of responsibility, Australian college students increased helping intentions toward indigenous Australians when their common Australian group identity was activated and they were able to see themselves as more similar than dissimilar to indigenous Australians (Halloran & Chambers, 2011).

Closeness

If you were asked if you would rather help a friend or family member over a stranger, most of us would obviously choose to help the person that we are close to rather than someone else. For our **communal relationships** (i.e., relationships with family, friends, and romantic partners), we feel a sense of mutual responsibility for attending to one another's needs. Additionally, we tend to have more empathic concern for those whom we are in communal relationships with in comparison to strangers (Maner & Gailliot, 2007). For our **exchange relationships**, such as relationships with work and school acquaintances, we tend to give help based off of ideas of **direct reciprocity**. Direct reciprocity is the expectation that you will receive something in return for giving to or helping another. Those who are in communal relationships tend to help

Monkey Business Images/Shutterstock.com

their relationship partner more and are less likely to attend to the costs and benefits of helping the other (Williamson, Clark, Pegalis, & Behan, 1996).

Although helping those we care about most often makes us feel good and aids in relationship maintenance, there are times when relationship closeness can hinder the help we offer to our loved ones. Specifically, when our relationship partner does well at something, the **self-evaluation maintenance model** (Tesser & Smith, 1980) says that we will either respond with happiness or with resentment. We experience happiness when our loved one has done well in an area or domain that we don't care about, but we experience resentment when the great performance has occurred in a domain that is important to us. To test this model, Abraham Tesser and Jonathan Smith had 52 friendship pairs participate in a word identification task with strangers. Friendship pairs were assigned to either a low-relevance condition (participants were told the word identification task was a game and that performance on the task didn't indicate anything about a person's skill level) or a high-relevance condition (participants were told the word identification task mapped onto skills typically measured by standardized aptitude tests and indicated how well one will do in school). Each member of the friendship pair was given the opportunity to give clues to their friend during the task. The clues that each member could choose to offer their friend would either make the task easier or more difficult. Results from the study supported

Intergroup Bias
Showing favoritism to members of your own group over members of another group.

Communal Relationships
Relationships in which partners exchange benefits out of concern for each other's well-being.

Exchange Relationships
Relationships in which partners exchange benefits with the expectation that a similar benefit will be given in the future.

Direct Reciprocity
The expectation that you will receive something in return for giving to or helping another.

Self-Evaluation Model Maintenance Model
A model that says when a relationship partner experiences success, you will be happy for the partner if it is in a domain you do not care about or resentful of them if it is in a domain you care about.

the self-evaluation maintenance model in that friends gave their partners harder clues in the high-relevance condition than in the low-relevance condition. The authors believed that participants felt that their ego would be threatened in the high-relevance condition, such that their performance on the word identification task would be compared with the performance of their friend and thus they gave harder clues in an attempt to sabotage their friend's performance.

Diverse Samples in the Study of Prosocial Behaviors

Forty years of research on prosocial and helping behaviors has highlighted the many factors related to the helper, the victim/receiver, and the situation that prompt us to act when someone is in need. However, most of the research described above has been conducted among predominately European American, college-age samples. For the most part, the only diversity we find in these samples is with regard to gender. When research samples have included both males and females, studies have noted gender differences in prosocial behavior, with women typically engaging in more prosocial behaviors than men (Espinosa & Kovářík, 2015). Although this pattern of findings seems consistent with our beliefs about male and female behavior (we typically think of women as more responsive, empathic, and helpful than men), these differences are not found in every study on prosocial behaviors. It is important that researchers make efforts to understand the gender differences in helping behaviors, particularly if we want better representation of both genders in participating in charitable and volunteerism acts.

It is also important to understand age-related differences in helping behaviors, particularly so we can understand how prosocial behaviors develop and how they can be maintained into old age. Recent work has examined the occurrence of prosocial behaviors throughout the entire lifespan. Although it may be clear to you what prosocial and helping behaviors are in adulthood, what does help look like in infancy? Can you think of a time when you have seen a little brother or sister try to help around the house? In infancy, helping behaviors can be picking up something that someone has dropped, handing someone an object that is out of their reach, sharing an object with another person, or engaging in acts of comfort (e.g., patting someone's arm or leg). A review by Alia Martin and Kristina Olson (2015) highlights that helper, receiver, and situational factors dictate helping and

Pavel L Photo and Video/Shutterstock.com

sharing behaviors among children as young as 18 months old. For instance, reciprocity seems to be a factor that dictates helping among children at 21 months. Infants were more likely to give a toy to an adult who had previously tried to give the child a toy truck (although the adult did not successfully give the child the toy) than to an adult who refused to help the child (by withholding the toy from the child), or did not respond to the child (by not interacting with toy or the child; Dunfield & Kuhlmeier, 2010). Infants also display selective helping with regard to close relationships (Young, Fox, & Zahn-Waxler, 1999) and similarity (Kinzler, Dupoux, & Spelke, 2012).

Research examining prosocial behaviors among older adult samples find that both empathic concern and prosocial behaviors increases into old age (Sze, Gyurak, Goodkind, & Levenson, 2012). Older adults also engage in more other-focused cognitions such as problem solving in relationship maintenance, taking others' needs into account, and perspective taking than younger adults (Hoppmann, Coats, & Blanchard-Fields, 2008), which are cognitions that contribute to engagement in prosocial and helping behaviors. Although helping behaviors may not look different for older adults as it does for younger adults, the amount of certain types

of helping behaviors may increase over time just as others may decrease. For instance, it is unlikely that older adults are able to engage in more active forms of helping, like offering to carry someone's heavy groceries, into their later years. However, they may increase the amount that they give in monetary donations or in volunteering a service, such as cooking for a neighbor. What type of prosocial behaviors have you seen older adults engage in?

Research examining prosocial behaviors within ethnic/racial groups in the United States has broadened conceptions of the helper and situation factors that contribute to helping behaviors. For instance, work on altruism in predominately African American communities highlights that the combination of multiple identities (*intersectionality*) across race, gender, class, age, and urbanicity relate to the type of helping behaviors community members engage in on behalf of their neighbors (Mattis et al., 2008). Additionally, experiences related to racial discrimination, racial ideology, and civic education also contribute to prosocial behaviors in African American adults and adolescents (Hope & Jagers, 2014; White-Johnson, 2012). Specifically, African Americans who experienced more racial discrimination tended to engage in more helping behaviors that benefited members of the African American community (White-Johnson, 2012). Additional work with Latino American, Asian American, and American Indian youth has highlighted that cultural experiences and connectedness foster prosocial behaviors among these groups (Rivas-Drake et al., 2014). Racial/ethnic experiences and belief systems often teach ethnic minority youth about the value of interconnectedness in their communities and so it is not surprising that these experiences have an impact on the way that they help and interact with others. For instance, Latin American culture promotes beliefs in *familismo* and *simpatía* (Díaz-Loving & Draguns, 1999; Marín & Marín, 1991). Familismo is the concept of prioritizing the needs of family members above your own needs. Simpatía is the concept of promoting positive interactions and respect within relationships. These concepts can be thought of as social norms among the Latino community and thus, they encourage prosocial behaviors among both family and other community members. As described earlier, Levine, Norenzayan, and Philbrick's (2001) study examining the rate of helping behaviors across countries found the rate of helping a stranger to be highest among Latin American countries that promote these norms.

By examining prosocial behavior in diverse groups of people, we can begin to get a better understanding of the variety and process of prosocial behaviors. Would the five stages of helping in an emergency be the same for young children

in comparison to adults? How would the process of helping look different for children who choose to intervene to stop the bullying of a classmate? Do the same biases in helping behaviors still apply in old age or do older people help less discriminately? How does knowing about your cultural heritage foster empathic concern and helping behaviors? Do our ideas about being a male or female impact the way we think we should help others? These are questions about prosocial behavior that have yet to be explored, but the answers have important implications to fully understanding the how, when, why, and who of helping.

Conclusion

In summary, the concepts and theories reviewed in this chapter make one thing clear: prosocial behaviors are derived out of our sense of wanting to relate to others. Regardless of the motive, when you engage in acts of helping and kindness, you are making an impact on another person and contributing to the well-being of your community at large. As you consider the news coverage on your social media feeds about the everyday heroes that find big and small ways to get involved, think of the costs that this hero had to overcome to help another. Consider each of the five steps and the barriers that the hero had to go through just to make a difference in another person's life. And the next time that you find yourself faced with the opportunity to help someone, either in an emergency or some everyday task, consider how helping this one person may inspire others to do their part too.

References

Aknin, L. B., Broesch, T., Hamlin, J. K., & Van de Vondervoot, J. W. (2015). Prosocial behavior leads to happiness in a small-scale rural society. *Journal of Experimental Psychology: General, 144,* 788–795. doi:http://dx.doi.org/10.1037/xge0000082

Aknin, L. B., Sandstrom, G. M., Dunn, E. W., & Norton, M. I. (2011). It's the recipient that counts: Spending money on strong social ties leads to greater happiness than spending on weak social ties. *PLos ONE, 6,* e17018. doi:10.1371/journal.pone.0017018

Batson, C. D., Early, S., & Salvarani, G. (1997). Perspective taking: Imagining how another feels versus imagining how you would feel. *Personality and Social Psychology Bulletin, 23,* 751–758. doi:10.1177/0146167297237008

Batson, C. D., Duncan, B. C., Ackerman, P., Buckley, T., & Birch, K. (1981). Is empathic emotion a source of altruistic motivation? *Journal of Personality and Social Psychology, 40,* 290–302. http://doi.org/10.1037/0022-3514.40.2.290

Brick, M. (2004). Officer charged in bomb blast at subway. Retrieved from http://www.nytimes.com/2004/08/01/nyregion/officerchargedinbombblastatsubway.html

Cialdini, R. B., Schaller, M., Houliham, D., Arps, K., Fultz, J., & Beaman, A. L. (1987). Empathy-based helping: Is it selflessly or selfishly motivated. *Journal of Personality and Social Psychology, 52,* 749–758. doi:10.1037/0022-3514.52.4.749

Clark, S. S., & Giacomantonio, S. (2013). Music references and empathy: Toward predicting prosocial behavior. *Psychomusicology: Music, Mind, and Brain, 23,* 177–186. doi:http://doi.org/10.1037/a0034882

Darley, J. M., & Latané, B. (1968). Bystander intervention in emergencies: Diffusion of responsibility. *Journal of Personality and Social Psychology, 8,* 377–383. doi:10.1037/h0025589

Darley, J. M., & Latané, B. (1970). Norms and normative behavior: Field studies of social interdependence. In J. McCauley & L. Berkowitz (Eds.), *Altruism and helping behavior* (pp. 83–101). New York, NY: Academic Press.

Díaz-Loving, R., & Draguns, J. G. (1999). Culture, meaning, and personality in Mexico and in the United States. In Y.-T. Lee, C. R. McCauley, & J. G. Draguns (Eds.), *Personality and person perception across cultures* (pp. 103–126). Mahwah, NJ: Lawrence Erlbaum.

Dunfield, K. A., & Kuhlmeier, V. A. (2010). Intention-mediated selective helping in infancy. *Psychological Science : A Journal of the American Psychological Society / APS, 21,* 523–527. doi:http://doi.org/10.1177/0956797610364119

Eisenberg, N., Guthrie, I. K., Cumberland, A., Murphy, B. C., Shepard, S. A., Zhou, Q., & Carlo, G. (2002). Prosocial development in early adulthood: A longitudinal study. *Journal of Personality and Social Psychology, 82,* 993–1006. doi:10.1037//0022-3514.82.6.993

Eisenberg, N., Hofer, C., Sulik, M. J., & Liew, J. (2014). The development of prosocial moral reasoning and a prosocial orientation in young adulthood: Concurrent and longitudinal correlates. *Developmental Psychology, 50,* 58–70. doi:http://doi.org/10.1037/a0032990

Emswiller, T., Deaux, K., & Willits, J. E. (1971). Similarity, sex, and requests for small favors. *Journal of Applied Social Psychology, 1,* 284–291. doi:10.1111/j.1559-1816.1971.tb00367.x

Erkut, S., Jaquette, D. S., & Staub, E. (1981). Moral judgment-situation interaction as a basis for predicting prosocial behavior. *Journal of Personality, 49,* 1–14. doi:10.1111/j.1467-6494.1981.tb00842.x

Espinosa, M. P., & Kovářík, J. (2015). Prosocial behavior and gender. *Frontiers in Behavioral Neuroscience, 9,* 1–9. doi:http://doi.org/10.3389/fnbeh.2015.00088

Fiske, S. T. (2011). *Envy up, scorn down: How status divides us.* New York, NY: Russel Sage Foundation.

Forest, D., Clark, M. S., Mills, J., & Isen, A. M. (1979). Helping as a function of feeling state and nature of the helping behavior. *Motivation and Emotion.* doi:http://doi.org/10.1007/BF01650601

Gansberg, M. (1964). Thirty-eight who saw murder didn't call the police. *New York Times.* New York, NY.

Goldman, M., & Fordyce, J. (1983). Prosocial behavior as affected by eye contact, touch, and voice expression. *The Journal of Social Psychology, 121,* 125–129. doi:10.1080/00224545.1983.9924474

Greitemeyer, T., & Mügge, D. O. (2015). When bystanders increase rather than decrease intentions to help. *Social Psychology, 46,* 116–119. doi:http://doi.org/10.1027/1864-9335/a000215

Gross, A. E., & Latané, J. G. (1974). Receiving help, reciprocation, and interpersonal attraction. *Journal of Applied Social Psychology, 4,* 210–223. doi:http://doi.org/10.1111/j.1559-1816.1974.tb02641.x

Guéguen, N., Pichot, N., & Le Dreff, G. (2005). Similarity and helping behavior on the Web: The impact of the convergence of surnames between a solicitor and a subject in a request made by E-mail. *Journal of Applied Social Psychology, 35,* 423–429. doi:http://doi.org/10.1111/j.1559-1816.2005.tb02128.x

Halloran, M., & Chambers, G. (2011). The effects of a common in-group prime on intentions to help indigenous and homeless Australians. *Australian Psychologist, 46,* 163–170. doi:http://doi.org/10.1111/j.1742-9544.2010.00004.x

Harrell, W. A. (1978). Physical attractiveness, self-disclosure, and helping behavior. *The Journal of Social Psychology, 104,* 15–17. doi:10.1080/00224545.1978.9924033

Hensley, W. E. (1981). The effects of attire, location, and sex on aiding behavior: A similarity explanation. *Journal of Nonverbal Behavior, 6,* 3–10. doi:http://doi.org/10.1007/BF00987932

Hocking, J. E., & Lawrence, S. G. (2000). Changing attitudes toward the homeless: The effects of prosocial communication with the homeless. *Journal of Social Distress and the Homeless, 9,* 91–110. doi:http://doi.org/10.1023/A:1009466217604

Hope, E. C., & Jagers, R. J. (2014). The role of sociopolitical attitudes and civic education in the civic engagement of Black youth. *Journal of Research on Adolescence, 24,* 460–470. doi:http://doi.org/10.1111/jora.12117

Hoppmann, C. A., Coats, A. H., & Blanchard-Fields, F. (2008). Goals and everyday problem solving: Examining the link between age-related goals and problem-solving strategy use. *Neuropsychology, Development, and Cognition. Section B, Aging, Neuropsychology and Cognition, 15,* 401–423. doi:http://doi.org/10.1080/13825580701533777

Kinzler, K. D., Dupoux, E., & Spelke, E. S. (2012). "Native" objects and collaborators: Infants' object choices and acts of giving reflect favor for native over foreign speakers. *Journal of Cognition and Development, 13,* 67–81. doi:http://doi.org/http://dx.doi.org/10.1080/15248372.2011.567200

Kluegel, J. R., & Smith, E. R. (1986). *Beliefs about inequality: Americans' views of what is and what ought to be.* Hawthorne, NY: Aldine de Gruyter.

Knafo, A., Zahn-Waxler, C., Van Hulle, C., Robinson, J. L., & Rhee, S. H. (2008). The developmental origins of a disposition toward empathy: Genetic and environmental contributions. *Emotion, 8,* 732–752. doi:http://doi.org/10.1037/a0014179

Kohlberg, L. (1984). *The psychology of moral development: The nature and validity of moral stages (Essays on moral development, Volume 2).* Harper & Row.

Latané, B., & Darley, J. M. (1968). Bystander intervention in emergencies: Diffusion of responsibility. *Journal of Personality and Social Psychology, 8,* 377–383. doi:http://doi.org/10.1037/h0026570

Lee, S., Winterich, K. P., & Ross, W. T. (2014). I'm Moral, but I won't help you: The distinct roles of empathy and justice in donations. *Journal of Consumer Research Inc., 41,* 678–696. doi:http://doi.org/10.1086/677226

Lemmon, G., & Wayne, S. J. (2015). Underlying motives of organizational citizenship behavior: Comparing egoistic and altruistic motivations. *Journal of Leadership and Organizational Studies, 22,* 129–148. doi:http://doi.org/10.1177/1548051814535638

Levine, R. V, Norenzayan, A., & Philbrick, K. (2001). Cross-cultural differences in helping strangers. *Journal of Cross-Cultural Psychology, 32,* 543–560. doi:http://doi.org/10.1177/0022022101032005002

Maner, J. K., & Gailliot, M. T. (2007). Altruism and egoism: Prosocial motivations for helping depend on relationship context. *European Journal of Social Psychology, 37,* 347–358. doi:http://doi.org/10.1002/ejsp.364

Marín, G., & Marín, B. V. (1991). *Research with Hispanic populations.* Newbury Park, CA: Sage.

Martin, A., & Olson, K. R. (2015). Beyond good and evil: What motivations underlie children's prosocial behavior. *Perspectives on Psychological Science, 10,* 159–175. doi:http://doi.org/10.1177/1745691615568998

Mattis, J. S., Grayman, N. A., Cowie, S. A., Winston, C., Watson, C., & Jackson, D. (2008). Intersectional identities and the politics of altruistic care in a low-income, urban community. *Sex Roles, 59,* 418–428. doi:http://doi.org/10.1007/s11199-008-9426-2

Milgram, S. (1970). The experience of living in cities. *Science, 167,* 1461–1468. doi:http://doi.org/10.1126/science.167.3924.1461

Miller, J. G., Bersoff, D. M., & Harwood, R. L. (1990). Perceptions of social responsibilities in India and in the United States: moral imperatives or personal decisions? *Journal of Personality and Social Psychology, 58,* 33–47. doi:http://doi.org/10.1037/0022-3514.58.1.33

Nowak, M. A., & Sigmund, K. (2005). Evolution of indirect reciprocity. *Nature, 437,* 1291–1298. doi:10.1038/nature04131

Pellegrini, R. J., Quierolo, S. S., Monarrez, V. E., & Valenzuela, D. M. (1997). Political identification and perceptions of homelessness: Attributed causality and attitudes on public policy. *Psychological Reports, 80,* 1139–1148. doi:10.2466/pr0.1997.80.3c.1139

Piliavin, I. M., Rodin, J., & Piliavin, J. A. (1969). Good Samaritanism: An underground phenomenon? *Journal of Personality and Social Psychology, 13*(4), 289–299. doi:10.1037/h0028433

Rivas-Drake, D., Seaton, E. K., Markstrom, C., Quintana, S., Syed, M., Lee, R. M., . . . Sellers, R. M. (2014). Ethnic and racial identity in adolescence: Implications for psychosocial, academic, and health outcomes. *Child Development, 85,* 40–57. doi:http://doi.org/10.1111/cdev.12200

Schonert-Reichl, K. A. (1999). Relations of peer acceptance, friendship adjustment, and social behavior to moral reasoning during early adolescence. *The Journal of Early Adolescence, 19,* 249–279. doi:http://doi.org/10.1177/0272431699019002006

Son, J., & Wilson, J. (2010). Genetic variation in volunteerism. *The Sociological Quarterly, 51,* 46–64. doi:10.1111/j.1533-8525.2009.01167.x

Soosai-Nathan, L., Negri, L., & Fave, A. D. (2013). Beyond pro-social behaviour: An exploration of altruism in two cultures. *Psychological Studies, 58,* 103–114. doi:http://doi.org/10.1007/s12646-013-0184-z

Steblay, N. M. (1987). Helping behavior in rural and urban environments: A meta-analysis. *Psychological Bulletin, 102,* 346–356. doi:http://doi.org/10.1037/0033-2909.102.3.346

Suedfeld, P., Bochner, S., & Wnek, D. (1972). Helper-sufferer similarity and a specific request for help: Bystander intervention during a peace demonstration. *Journal of Applied Social Psychology, 2,* 17–23. doi:10.1111/j.1559-1816.1972.tb01260.x

Sze, J. A., Gyurak, A., Goodkind, M. S., & Levenson, R. W. (2012). Greater emotional empathy and prosocial behavior in late life. *Emotion, 12,* 1129–1140. doi:http://doi.org/10.1037/a0025011

Tesser, A., & Smith, J. (1980). Some effects of task relevance and friendship on helping: You don't always help the one you like. *Journal of Experimental Social Psychology, 16,* 582–590. doi:http://doi.org/10.1016/0022-1031(80)90060-8

Vrugt, A., & Vet, C. (2009). Effects of a smile on mood and helping behavior. *Social Behavior and Personality: An International Journal, 37,* 1251–1258. doi:http://doi.org/10.2224/sbp.2009.37.9.1251

West, S. G., Whitney, G., & Schnedler, R. (1975). Helping a motorist in distress: The effects of sex, race, and neighborhood. *Journal of Personality and Social Psychology, 31,* 691–698. doi:http://doi.org/10.1037/0022-3514.31.4.691

White-Johnson, R. L. (2012). Prosocial involvement among African American young adults: Considering racial discrimination and racial identity. *Journal of Black Psychology, 38,* 313–341. doi:http://doi.org/10.1177/0095798411420429

Williamson, G. M., Clark, M. S., Pegalis, L. J., & Behan, A. (1996). Affective consequences of refusing to help in communal and exchange relationships. *Personality and Social Psychology Bulletin, 22,* 34–47. doi:http://doi.org/10.1177/0146167296221004

Yinon, Y., & Sharon, I. (1985). Similarity in religiousness of the solicitor, the potential helper, and the recipient as determinants of donating behavior. *Journal of Applied Social Psychology, 15,* 726–734. doi:10.1111/j.1559-1816.1985.tb02270.x

Young, S. K., Fox, N. A., & Zahn-Waxler, C. (1999). The relations between temperament and empathy in 2-year-olds. *Developmental Psychology, 35,* 1189–1197. doi:http://doi.org/10.1037/0012-1649.35.5.1189

Zimbardo, P. (1969). The human choice: Individuation, reason, and order vs. deindividuation, impulse and chaos. In W. J. Arnold & D. Levine (Eds.), *Nebraska symposium on motivation* (pp. 237–307). Lincoln: University of Nebraska Press.

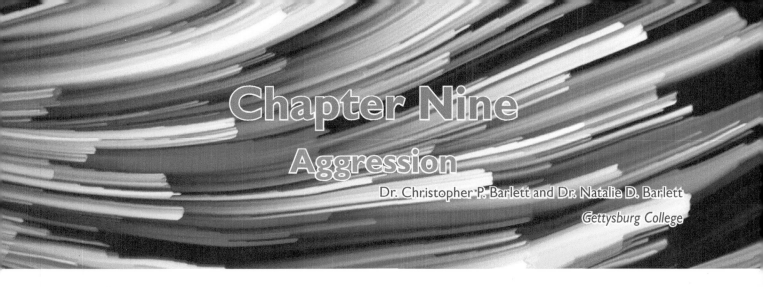

Chapter Nine
Aggression

Dr. Christopher P. Barlett and Dr. Natalie D. Barlett

Gettysburg College

Learning Objectives

- Develop fluency in aggression research terminology
- Demonstrate proficiency in aggression theory
- Understand personal and situational factors that increase one's likelihood of aggressing
- Recognize ways to decrease one's likelihood of aggressing
- Appreciate the complexity of aggressive behavior

Chapter Outline

Defining Aggression

General Aggression Model

Sex Differences in Aggression

Narcissism and Aggression

Alcohol Consumption and Aggression

The Weapons Effect

Heat and Aggression

Media Violence and Aggression

Risk and Resiliency Approach

Violence Escalation Model

Re-Appraisal Reducing Aggression

Agreeableness Reducing Aggression

Reducing Hostile Attributions

Aggression

On November 11, 2014, off-duty Deputy Constable Kenneth Caplan was driving when a woman allegedly changed lanes cutting him off. Mr. Caplan pulled out his firearm and fired at the woman, grazing the left side of her head. Mr. Caplan was charged with aggravated assault with a deadly weapon (McCormack, 2014). At her home in Alaska, Jessica Beagley was angered by her 7-year-old son's behavior and punished him by placing him in a cold shower and having him consume hot sauce. The authorities got involved when a video surfaced of the punishment. Beagley was charged with child abuse and sentenced to prison (Hopper, 2011). Finally, on October 12, 2013, Scott Jones, an openly gay comedian, was out celebrating his friend's art studio opening when Shane Matheson stabbed him twice in the back, severing his spinal cord leaving Jones paralyzed from the waist down. Matheson was arrested and sentenced to 10 years in prison for attempted murder, aggravated assault, and possession of a dangerous weapon (CBC, 2014).

These examples differ in several ways; however, they share at least one common denominator: they exemplify aggressive behavior. Unfortunately, examples like these are commonplace all over the world. Some get extensive news coverage, such as the September 11, 2001, terrorist attacks on the United States or the genocide reported in Syria. The hundreds of thousands of murders, assaults, incidents of abuse, attempted murders, bullying, gang violence, and other behaviors often receive little to no news coverage. Indeed, the examples at the beginning of this chapter are rather extreme forms of aggression that are typically overrepresented in the news but get dwarfed by the number of less severe aggressive acts that happen daily. The FBI uniform crime statistics report includes the numbers of violent crimes that are committed and reported in the United States annually and found that, in 2013, a violent crime (i.e., murder, rape, robbery, or aggravated assault) occurred every 27.1 seconds; a total of 1,163,146 violent crimes occurred nationwide (FBI, 2013). Although the numbers we reported are specific to the United States in 2013, aggressive behaviors are commonplace all over the world and over the course of human history. Given the prevalence and wide array of behaviors that could be classified as aggressive, the current chapter will describe (a) how aggression is conceptualized, (b) aggression theory, (c) causes of aggressive behavior, and (d) methods to reduce aggression.

Defining Aggression

Aggression

Behavior intended to harm another who is motivated to avoid that harm.

Contemporary social psychologists define **aggression** as behavior intended to harm another who is motivated to avoid that harm (Anderson & Bushman, 2002). There are several aspects of this definition that are crucial to understanding aggression. First, aggression must be a behavior—not a feeling or thought. Second, there must be intent to harm another person. Thus, if someone tries to punch you but misses, that would still be considered aggressive behavior because the intent to harm was there. If someone accidentally bumps into you in the hallway causing pain, that may not be aggression because it was an accident. Finally, there must be motivation to avoid that harm. Most humans are motivated to avoid harm and will evade a punch or duck if they hear a gunshot, but sometimes people will seek out painful behaviors and are not motivated to avoid it. For instance, individuals who enjoy S&M sexual behaviors are not being aggressive or aggressed against because they are not motivated to avoid that harm.

Using the Anderson and Bushman (2002) definition, one can see that myriad different behaviors could be categorized as aggressive. Indeed, researchers have categorized aggression into various forms. **Physical aggression** includes physically touching an individual with their body or object with the intent to harm, whereas **verbal aggression** is yelling, teasing, or threatening another with the intent to harm (Buss & Perry, 1992). **Relational aggression** is hurting someone by damaging his or her social relationships, such as social exclusion and rumor spreading (Crick & Grotpeter, 1995). Although all forms of aggression are important to study, physical aggression has received the most research attention, and as you will see, is the focus of the majority of research discussed in this chapter.

Using the various forms of aggression, researchers have conceptualized aggression on a continuum ranging from low physical harm to the victim to extreme physical harm to the victim. This is termed the aggression continuum (Anderson & Huesmann, 2003). On the low end are verbal and relational aggressive acts and on the high end are instances of assault, murder, and genocide. Thus, the higher any one aggressive act lies on the continuum is representative of how much physical harm the victim is experiencing. If you turn the continuum on its side and add a frequency dimension, then you get the aggression pyramid. This pyramid details the relative frequency of the types of aggressive actions as they relate to the continuum, and you can clearly see that those behaviors that are low on the continuum are more frequent than those high on the continuum. See Figure 9.1.

Physical Aggression
Physically touching an individual with his or her body or object with the intent to harm.

Verbal Aggression
Yelling, teasing, or threatening another with the intent to harm.

Relational Aggression
Hurting someone through damage to their social relationships.

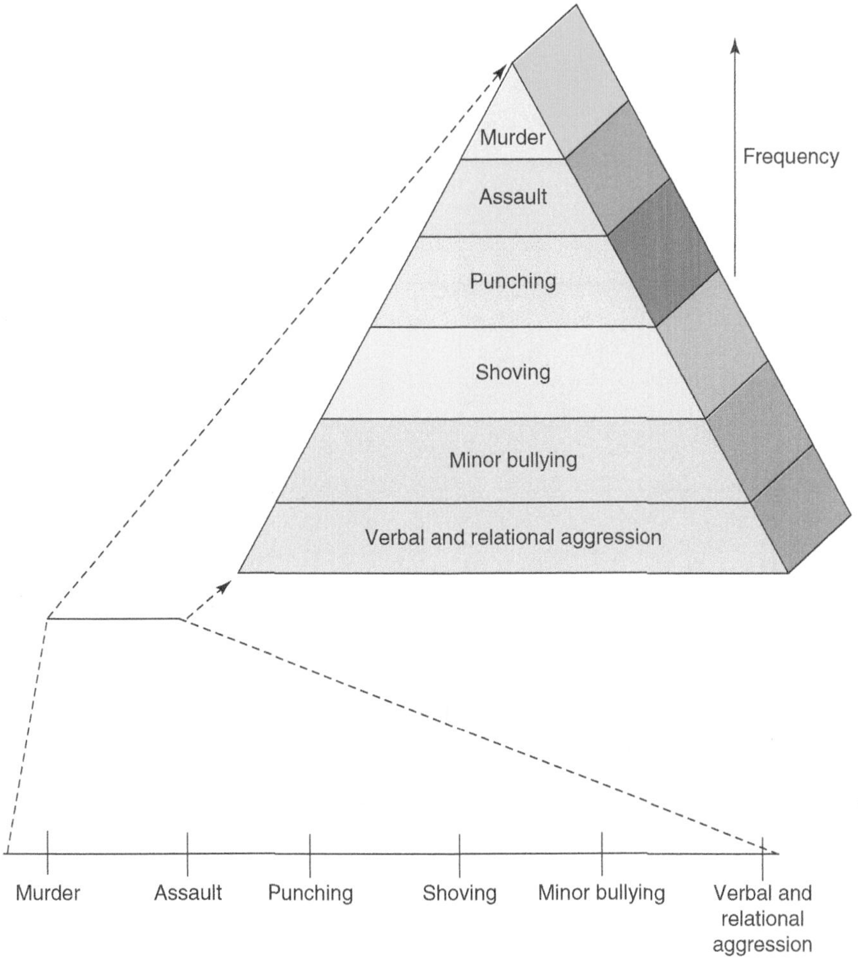

Figure 9.1. Representation of Aggression Continuum and Frequency Pyramid

Gentile and Sesma (2003) extracted data from the US Secret Service regarding aggression in schools and, consistent with the frequency pyramid, found that bullying was more prevalent than physical fights, which was more prevalent than serious injuries and death. Applying the Gentile and Sesma data to our conceptualization of the frequency pyramid, we will see that verbal and relational aggression should be more frequent than physical aggression, which should be more frequent than violence. One possible reason why the pyramid works is because there are more serious consequences to the aggressor the higher up the pyramid the behavior. For example, a college student will likely not get in trouble with authorities for spreading a rumor about a peer (lowest on the continuum and most frequent on the pyramid) but will likely go to prison for murdering a peer (highest on the continuum and less frequent on the pyramid).

Of course, the frequency pyramid and aggression continuum are not perfect. As we noted, both organize aggressive behaviors by the physical harm they cause the victim. At one level, this makes sense since such organization allows for violence to be at the end of the continuum (and therefore the top of the pyramid); however, we believe that the continuum and pyramid would likely categorize behaviors differently if emotional harm was used as the organizational criteria. For instance, relational aggression would likely be placed higher on the continuum if emotional harm was the criterion. Additional problems using such categorization would be apparent too, such as not having the aggression continuum align with the frequency pyramid if emotional harm was the criterion. Despite these issues, the representation of the frequency pyramid depicted in Figure 9.1 is a good starting point for our understanding of aggressive behavior.

General Aggression Model

Several domain-specific and more general theories have been posited to describe aggressive behavior. For the purposes of this chapter, we will focus on the General Aggression Model (Anderson & Bushman, 2002) because we believe it is the most complete model to describe the complex interplay between various aggression-related factors.

General aggression model (GAM) is a dynamic social-learning model of aggressive behavior (Anderson & Bushman, 2002). The short-term portion of GAM (termed the proximate model) starts with two inputs: person and situation factors. **Person factors** are variables that are correlated with aggressive behavior that are related to one's personality, such as narcissism (Baumeister, Bushman, & Campbell, 2000) and sex (Archer, 2004). These factors will be discussed in more depth later. **Situational factors** are variables that are currently in the situation that should be related to aggressive behavior, such as alcohol (Ito, Miller, & Pollock, 1996), video game violence exposure (Anderson et al., 2010), and heat (Anderson, 2001). These factors will also be discussed in more detail later. Person and situational factors likely interact to influence one's present internal state, which consists of correlated aggressive affect (e.g., anger), aggressive cognitions (e.g., thinking about harming an individual), and physiological arousal (e.g., heart rate increases). Any one or combination of these internal state variables will lead to a decision and appraisal process that predicts behavior. Figure 9.2 shows this model.

The appraisal and decision-making processes in GAM are the immediate precursors to behavior and are depicted in Figure 9.3. After one's internal state is heightened by personality and/or situational factors, one will likely make an initial appraisal (or attribution) about another's behavior. If one does not have

General Aggression Model (GAM)

A dynamic social-learning model of aggressive behavior.

Person Factors

Variables that are related to one's personality and are correlated with aggressive behavior.

Situational Factors

Variables that are currently in the situation that should be related to aggressive behavior.

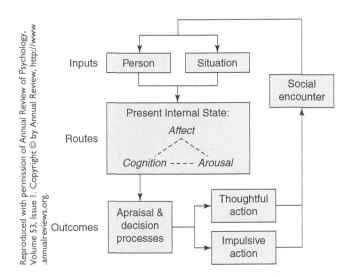

Figure 9.2. Proximate GAM from Anderson and Bushman (2002).

the time, motivation, or cognitive ability to further process this appraisal, then an impulsive action is likely. If that immediate appraisal is hostile and these resources are not sufficient, then aggressive behavior is likely. Indeed, research has shown that when provoked participants must make quick decisions, they aggress (Finkel, DeWall, Slotter, Oaten, & Foshee, 2009), and when participants have consumed alcohol (presumably reducing cognitive ability) aggression is likely (Giancola, Josephs, DeWall, & Gunn, 2009). If one does have these resources sufficient and they view the outcome of the immediate appraisal as important but unsatisfying, then re-appraisal processes are engaged. **Re-appraisal** is defined as actively seeking additional information to clarify the situation or one's own psychological state (Barlett & Anderson, 2011). Any number of re-appraisals may be processed and, if successful, will change the immediate attribution to something more benign and aggression will be reduced. If unsuccessful, rumination processes are likely to increase aggressive behavior (Bushman, 2002).

Barlett and Anderson (2011) tested re-appraisal processes in regard to how aggressive behavior is reduced. Participants entered the lab and were told they would be working with a partner on decision-making games. The participant had to first write an essay on abortion for their partner to grade. There really was no partner and the essay was used to set up the provocation. Once the essay was

Re-Appraisal
Actively seeking additional information to clarify the situation or one's own psychological state.

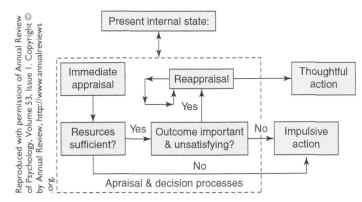

Figure 9.3. Appraisal processes in GAM (Anderson & Bushman, 2002).

written, participants were randomly assigned to get harsh feedback on their essay, praise on their essay, or no feedback. However, after the participants got their grades, the participants were then randomly assigned to get an excuse (e.g., the reason I graded your essay that way was because I broke up with my boy-/girl-friend last night and I am still angry) from their partner delivered online. Barlett and Anderson (2011) posited that the excuse would prompt re-appraisal processes. Findings showed that those who were provoked and got the excuse had significantly lower aggression compared to provoked participants who did not get the excuse.

Understanding how GAM works is not an easy task and hopefully the following real-life example will demonstrate how one situational and personality variable can interact to predict aggressive behavior. On November 19, 2004, two NBA basketball teams were playing each other—the Detroit Pistons and the Indiana Pacers. With less than a minute left in the game, a scuffle broke out between Ben Wallace (Piston player) and Ron Artest (Pacer player). The fight was broken up and Ron Artest laid down on the scorer's table. Before we go any further, it is important to note that Ron Artest has a history of physical fights during basketball games and would be considered an aggressive person by some. While lying on the table, a cup full of liquid is thrown and hits Artest who flies into the crowd and starts physically attacking a spectator. If we analyze this from GAM, we know that Ron Artest is an aggressive person (a personality factor) and had just been in a physical altercation with Ben Wallace (a situational factor). According to GAM, Artest is likely feeling angry, aroused, and thinking hostile thoughts, which makes him attribute hostility toward Wallace. However, he must have the cognitive resources available to not continue fighting Wallace or any other Piston player. Thus, he is able to re-appraise his hostile attribution of Wallace and not fight. When the spectator throws the liquid at Artest, a new short-term GAM cycle begins. Artest perceives this as a provocation (a situational factor), is likely now feeling angry, aroused, and thinking hostile thoughts, and then attributes hostile intent on the fan. Artest had his resources depleted from not engaging Wallace earlier and behaves impulsively attacking the fan. This was called the Malice in the Palace and some credit it with the worst day in NBA history.

The previous paragraphs describe a single episodic cycle of the proximate GAM. After a behavior is enacted (whether aggressive, nonaggressive, impulsive, or thoughtful), a social encounter occurs that feeds back into the input factors of GAM. Recall that GAM is a learning model. Each single cycle within GAM is a learning trial with that stimulus. It is predicted that continual positively reinforced learning with these aggression stimuli in the input will lead to the development and automatization of learned aggressive knowledge structures. Anderson and Bushman (2002) posit that such learning is related to the formation of aggressive attitudes and the creation and availability of aggressive expectations and beliefs. These, and other, knowledge structures help create one's aggressive personality, which feeds back into the personality input factor in the proximate GAM.

Factors That Influence Aggression

As mentioned above, several person and situational variables have been shown to increase aggression. Here we discuss several that have received much research support while acknowledging that there are many other factors that space does not allow us to delve into. We will begin with the personal variables of sex and narcissism and then continue with some situational variables: alcohol consumption, exposure to weapons, heat, and violent media exposure.

Sex Differences

The common perception by laypeople and social scientists alike is that males are more aggressive than females. Although this assumption is mostly correct, researchers have begun to unravel when this is the case and why. Archer (2004) conducted a meta-analysis testing whether sex differences in aggression are specific to the forms of aggressive behavior—physical, verbal, and relational. Results showed that males were more aggressive than females for physical and verbal aggression independent of how aggression was measured across the studies. However, Archer found mixed results for relational aggression such that females were more relationally aggressive than males when assessed by teacher and peer reports, but no difference was observed when self-reports were used. Overall, findings showed that males are more physically aggressive than females, a finding observed in other meta-analytic reviews (e.g., Bettencourt & Miller, 1996).

Understanding why males tend to be more physically aggressive than females is highly debated. One hypothesis, rooted in evolution, is that males have more testosterone than females that surges when confronted with a perceived provocation (Archer, 2006). Testosterone has been positively correlated with aggression (see Archer, 1994). A second hypothesis is a social role interpretation, which argues that males and females have socially governed and learned rules and expectations about appropriate behaviors. In this vein, males are taught that it is socially acceptable to be physically aggressive when appropriate relative to females (Eagly & Wood, 1991). Indeed, Eagly and Steffen (1986) found that males were more physically aggressive than females. But, the same meta-analysis also found that females perceived that their aggressive behavior would harm the target more and would make them feel more guilty and anxious than males.

Narcissism

Researchers have defined **narcissism** as a personality trait characterized by a grandiose pattern of unstable high self-esteem and self-focused belief about oneself (Morf & Rhodewalt, 2001). Twenge, Konrath, Foster, Campbell, and Bushman (2008) conducted a meta-analysis of college student's narcissism levels (assessed using a valid self-report; the Narcissistic Personality Inventory) across time, and found that the average narcissism scores have increased approximately 30% from the 1980s to mid-2000s. The important aspect of linking narcissism with aggression is the *unstable* high self-esteem narcissists have. Indeed, Bushman and colleagues (2009) found that self-esteem was not correlated with aggression. This suggests that having high self-esteem is not a predictor of aggression; however, it is the instability of the high self-esteem that likely manifests into aggressive behavior after a provocation.

When the self-esteem of a narcissist is challenged or attacked, termed **ego threat**, that is when the highly unstable self-esteem often results in aggression. Bushman and Baumeister (1998; Study 1) randomly assigned participants to be provoked or not from a partner (really there was no partner, but the participants did not know that) before engaging in an aggressive behavioral task. To provoke the participants, Bushman and Baumeister had participants write an essay about abortion, and those who were provoked were given negative feedback from their presumable partner. Because abortion is a highly debated topic and whether one is pro-choice or pro-life is a reflection of one's moral values, this constituted an ego threat. Results showed that aggression was highest for provoked participants who were high on narcissism. In a follow-up study, Bushman and Baumeister

Narcissism
A personality trait characterized by a grandiose pattern of unstable high self-esteem and self-focused belief about oneself.

Ego Threat
A provocation targeting some aspect of the self that one finds important.

(Study 2) had a similar procedure except some participants were told that they would be engaging in the aggression task with the person who graded their essay or with a new partner. Results showed a similar pattern as Study 1 when the aggression was aimed at the provocateur but not the new partner. In other words, narcissists tend to aggress after an ego threat to the original person they perceived as wronging them but not to others in general.

Alcohol Consumption

According to the US Department of Justice (DOJ, 1998) in 1996, 36% of convicted offenders had been drinking alcohol when they committed their offence, and alcohol was likely involved in 21% of aggravated assault incidents. Given such staggering numbers, aggression scholars have been interested in testing whether a link between alcohol consumption and aggression exists and, if so, why. To answer the first question, much research has shown a link between alcohol consumption and aggression (e.g., Giancola et al., 2009). Ito and colleagues (1996) found that the relationship between alcohol consumption and aggression was positive and significant, but was especially strong for men (compared to women). This result was also found by DeWall, Bushman, Giancola, and Webster (2010) who hypothesized that on average males, compared to females, are heavier, which plays a role in the amount of alcohol consumed to be intoxicated.

Attention-Allocation Model

After consuming alcohol one's attention gets narrowed to focus on salient factors while downplaying peripheral information.

After researchers found the link between alcohol consumption and aggression, subsequent research examined why the effect occurs. Giancola and Corman (2007) tested and found evidence for an **attention-allocation model**. This model states that consuming alcohol narrows one's attention to the social environment, allowing one to focus on the most salient factors of the environment while ignoring information in the periphery. For instance, if Person A has been drinking at a bar and Person B bumps into them, the attention allocation model would be supported if Person A only notices that Person B bumped into them without regarding how crowded the bar is, likely leading to a physical altercation. However, if Person A is not drinking, then they are more apt to notice how crowded the bar is and be able to reduce the likelihood of aggression. Such theorizing fits within the GAM framework. Impulsive aggression will be likely when a person is drinking (a situational factor) and perceives a provocation (another situational factor) because they lack the cognitive ability to re-appraise the situation. In other words, drinking impairs cognitive functioning that narrows attention given to outside inhibitory cues and focuses the attention on the perceived provocation (see also Giancola et al., 2009).

Exposure to Weapons

In their seminal work, Berkowtiz and LePage (1967) had 100 college-aged male participants interact with a confederate to write down how a car salesman and publicity agent would succeed at their jobs. Both the participant and confederate were separated into different rooms to evaluate the essays using electric shocks. Participants randomly assigned to the provocation condition received seven shocks and participants who were not provoked got one shock. Participants were then informed that it was their turn to evaluate the confederate's essay and provide shocks in return. Thus far, this study is a basic provocation study; however, Berkowitz and LePage randomly assigned the participants to see a revolver, a badminton racquet, or no object on their desk. Results showed that provoked participants were more aggressive when a revolver was on the desk compared to the badminton or no object conditions. This effect has been named the **weapons effect**. Within the framework of GAM, the presence of a weapon is a situational cue that could influence the internal state. Anderson, Benjamin, and Bartholow (1998) posited that priming of aggressive cognitions was the prime mediator in this relation. Anderson et al. had participants either view words (Study 1) or pictures (Study 2) of firearms or nonaggressive objects (e.g., plants) and then had them complete an aggressive thought task. Results showed that participants who viewed the weapon stimuli had higher aggressive thought accessibility than those who viewed the nonaggressive stimuli. In other words, weapons prime aggressive thoughts. Geen (1990) and Collins and Loftus (1975) offer theoretical insight into how this works. These researchers argue that humans have many nodes in our long-term memory that represent our world. If you close your eyes and think of a duck, your node would then be activated along with other duck-related nodes, such as feathers, bread, water, and Donald Duck. If I showed you a picture of a gun, your node of a gun would be activated and it would prime other related nodes, such as shoot, death, and blood. These nodes get connected to form a network through a process called **spreading activation**. If the gun network gets big enough, then it primes an aggressive script centered on aggression. This explains why having the gun present caused participants in the Berkowtiz and LePage (1967) study to aggress.

GAM also suggests that the situational input (gun presence) along with personality variables enhances the aggression effect. In an interesting study, Bartholow, Anderson, Carnagey, and Benjamin (2005) had hunters and non-hunters view pictures of hunting or assault rifles before engaging in aggressive thought and aggressive behavior tasks. Results showed that aggressive thoughts and behaviors were low for hunters who viewed the hunting guns but were high when hunters viewed the assault rifles. Bartholow and colleagues reasoned that the networks primed when viewing hunting rifles were different than when viewing assault rifles for hunters. For hunters, hunting is associated with family, gun safety, and happy moments, whereas assault rifles still cued violence and death.

Heat

Reifman, Larrick, and Fein (1991) conducted a field study looking at whether heat was related to aggression within the context of a baseball game. They conceptualized aggression as when a pitcher intentionally threw a baseball at a batter. They collected data from 826 games during the 1986–1988 baseball seasons and assessed whether the batter was hit by a baseball and the temperature. In addition, they controlled for other variables that could offer alternative hypotheses, such as number of wild pitches, number of walks, number of errors, attendance, and number of homeruns. Results showed that temperature positively predicted number of players hit by a pitch even while controlling for these other extraneous factors. Further, looking at more sociological-level data, Anderson, Bushman, and Groom (1997) analyzed crime data and temperature data from various cities across the United States. Results showed that as the temperature rose, more assaults were committed, and this effect remained when only looking into the summer months. The Thinking Critically Box on page 150 provides another example of the impact of heat; this time its effect on thoughts and feelings.

Weapons Effect
The presence of a weapon (e.g., gun) in one's environment can increase one's likelihood of behaving aggressively.

Spreading Activation
Process of forming a cognitive network by connecting nodes from long-term memory.

THINKING CRITICALLY

This clearly establishes heat as a risk factor for aggression. Think about times when you are really hot and cannot escape the heat, do you feel more angry, irritable, and aggressive? In accordance with GAM, heat is a situational variable that should predict changes in the internal state, but which one(s)? We already showed how gun exposure works primarily though the cognition route, but heat does not.

Anderson, Deuser, and DeNeve (1995) had participants complete validated measures of aggressive thoughts and aggressive feelings while working in a room that was either comfortable (72–78 degrees F), warm (79–86 degrees F), or hot (87–94 degrees F). Can you guys interpret how aggressive thoughts and feelings varied based on the temperature in the room?

Results showed that hot temperatures increased aggressive affect. Thus, according to these findings coupled with GAM's theoretical power, heat causes increases in aggressive affect to influence the likelihood of aggressive behavior.

Media Violence Exposure

Literature from countless longitudinal, correlational, experimental, and meta-analytic findings clearly shows that media violence exposure is related to aggression. The GAM processes are fairly clear and straightforward. Primary research has shown that playing a violent (versus nonviolent) video game is related to aggressive thoughts (Bushman & Anderson, 2002), aggressive feelings (Anderson & Carnagey, 2009), physiological arousal (Arriaga, Esteves, Carneiro, & Monteiro, 2006), and aggressive behavior (Anderson & Dill, 2000). In other words, media violence exposure has the ability to influence all three internal state variables and aggressive behavior.

These aforementioned effects highlight the short-term, or proximate, GAM processes; however, extensive research has been conducted on the long-term, or distal, processes that determine how media violence exposure influences aggression over time. It is important to note the key theoretical difference in proximate versus distal GAM processes. If you watch a violent TV program right now, that is a situational variable in the proximate GAM; however, if I ask you how many hours during the week you watch violent TV programs, we are getting at more distal learning processes. Using correlational and longitudinal research designs that have asked participants how often they have played violent video games and assessed aggressive personality and aggression knowledge structures has shown that violent video game exposure predicts aggressive behavior (Anderson et al., 2008).

Overall, Figure 9.4 shows the results of the Anderson et al. (2010) meta-analysis that separated the effect sizes relating violent video game exposure to aggressive behavior into the type of research design each study employed, and results show that across all types of experimental designs, violent video game exposure is related to aggressive behavior.

As multiple factors related to aggression have been discussed, it is necessary to point out that often research is conducted on one factor at a time to understand the specific influence that the factor has on aggression. In the real world, we realize that multiple factors will be at play at any given time. As such, aggression is often a multifaceted social behavior. No one single aggression-related factor is likely to elicit an aggressive response in isolation. For example, are you likely to aggress against a peer if you catch him or her making fun of you? For a few, that

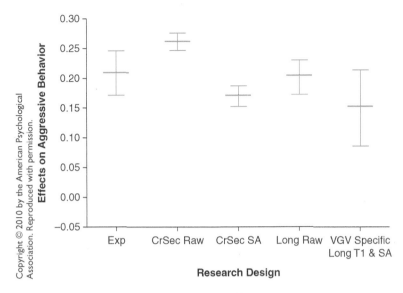

Figure 9.4. Violent video game effects on aggressive behavior (Anderson et al., 2010).

Effects of playing violent video games on aggressive behavior. Averages and 95% confidence intervals by research design. Exp = experimental studies (same in best raw and best partials data); CrSec = cross-sectional studies; Raw = data from best raw samples; SA = sex adjusted (data from best partials samples); Long = longitudinal studies; VGV Specific = studies that used the more specific type of video game violence exposure measure; T1 & SA = Time 1 and sex adjusted.

is sufficient to warrant an aggressive response, but for most it is not. However, what if you hear a peer making fun of you and you are tired? And hungry? And just got a bad grade on a test? And saw that your best friend was laughing at you? In theory, the more situational variables added to this seemingly benign example should increase the likelihood of an aggressive retaliation. This is termed the **risk and resiliency approach** (Gentile & Bushman, 2012).

Risk and Resiliency Approach

The medical field uses the risk and resiliency approach when discussing complex diseases that have multiple causes. For instance, the risk of a heart attack increases when certain risk factors are present, such as lack of exercise, poor diet, and family history of heart disease. Aggressive behavior operates in a similar fashion. One's risk of behaving aggressively will increase with the presence of variables that predict aggressive behavior. As per the example above, if the person is being provoked, tired, hungry, has general negative affect, and feels betrayed by a friend, the likelihood of aggression goes up compared to when any one or several of these factors are missing. In a longitudinal study, Gentile and Bushman (2012) showed that the likelihood of being in a physical fight at Wave 2 was 82% when four risk factors were present (e.g., high media violence exposure, being male, history of fighting, and high hostile attribution bias) at Wave 1, and if one risk factor is removed (e.g., media violence exposure) but all other risk factors are present, that percentage will drop (50% likelihood; see Figure 9.5).

Risk and Resiliency Approach
The combination of various risk and protective factors for aggression that determine the probability of future aggressive action.

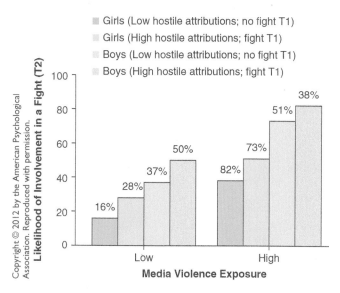

Figure 9.5.   Risk and resiliency findings from Gentile and Bushman (2012).

Overall, there are multiple factors that increase aggressive behavior. Indeed, the Surgeon General (2001) reported that substance use, low IQ, low SES (poverty), antisocial parents, history of violence, hyperactivity, risk taking, and others are risk factors for aggression. The key advantage to the risk approach to studying aggression is the ability to theoretically connect multiple risk factors together to predict aggressive behavior.

Violence Escalation Model

Let's connect the pieces of what we know about aggression thus far. There are hundreds of individual risk factors of aggression. We named only a few; however, each of these is likely not sufficient to cause an aggressive response in isolation. As previously stated, aggression scholars contend that when more risk factors are present, aggressive behavior will be likely (Gentile & Bushman, 2012). This leads to the next question: how can one risk factor start the path to aggressive responding? Anderson, Buckley, and Carnagey (2008) answered this with their study of the **violence escalation model** (VEM).

Violence Escalation Model (VEM)

An approach that explains why seemingly benign or minor aggressive acts often lead to more aggressive and violent actions.

The VEM is shown in Figure 9.6 and assumes that there are two units (people, groups, etc.) interacting with one another. Let's say Person A makes a negative joke about Person B who now feels provoked. Person B then publicly chastises Person A and feels justified in doing so. Person A is now mad and feels provoked, so Person A yells at Person B. Person B feels more provoked and pushes Person A, who punches Person B. At a theoretical level, the VEM would say that the aggression elicited by both parties escalated up the aggression continuum, starting with a joke and ending in a physical fight. The primary method by which VEM works is the perceived provocation each person felt. In their study, Anderson et al. (2008) had participants engage in the Competitive Reaction Time (CRT) task. This is a validated task used to measure aggression and has participants respond to a tone on the computer as quickly as possible. The winner gets to deliver a white noise blast at any intensity to the loser of each trial. There are 25 trials. Higher scores indicate that more painful/higher intensity noise blasts were given. Anderson and colleagues found that Person A's aggressive personality predicted

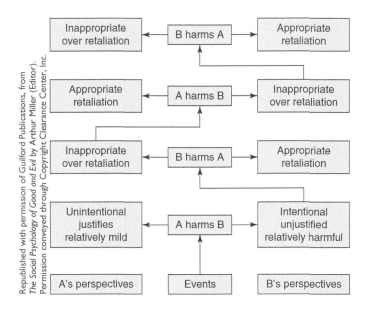

Figure 9.6. Violence escalation cycle from Anderson and Carnagey (2004).

how intense the early noise blasts were to Person B, which significantly predicted how intense the later noise blasts Person B delivered to Person A. In other words, if Person A was aggressive and gave high-intense noise blasts, Person B often retaliated in a more intense fashion. Revisiting the earlier example, the violence escalation model would predict that a joke leads to yelling that leads to pushing and shoving that leads to hitting that leads to violence. In other words, each aggressive act escalates up the aggression continuum until intervention efforts are applied (e.g., people stopping the fight) or someone gets seriously injured.

Reducing Aggression

Akin to how risk factors for aggression increase the likelihood to aggress, researchers have also looked at the protective factors for aggression; those variables that decrease the likelihood of aggressive behavior. Understanding the psychological processes that govern how protective factors work is paramount for delving into aggression reduction techniques.

Re-Appraisal

We have already discussed one aggression-reduction technique, re-appraisal. Recall, that re-appraisal is defined as actively seeking additional information to change an initially hostile appraisal of someone to other benign causes. For example, if someone bumps into you in the hallway, your first inclination may be to think that person did it on purpose and he or she is a jerk. However, according to GAM, if you have the time, cognitive resources, and motivation to continue to rethink this attribution of jerkiness, then you may look around and notice that the hallway was particularly crowded and it was probably an accident. The shift from attributing you getting bumped into from the person (he is a jerk) to the crowded hallway (it was an accident) reduces the likelihood of an aggressive response and does not start the upward violence cycle. It is in these re-appraisal processes that **mitigating information** (e.g., excuses, justifications, and apologies) has their affect. Barlett (2013) conducted a meta-analysis regarding such relations and

Mitigating Information
Excuses, justifications, or apologies that cue re-appraisal processes.

found that mitigating information is negatively correlated with aggression after a provocation; however, this effect differed by excuse strength and provocation severity. Barlett found that if the provocation was severe, mitigating information did not reduce aggression. If someone punches you in the face and says "sorry," that is probably not going to make you re-appraise! Also, if the quality of the excuse was lacking, aggressive behavior did not decrease. These findings suggest that the mitigating information must fit the provocation in order for re-appraisal processes to work.

The work by Barlett and Anderson (2011) treats mitigating information delivered after a provocation in the moment as a cue to engage in state re-appraisal processes. Additionally, re-appraisal is a stable personality variable. High re-appraisers are individuals who have the ability to change a negative situation into a positive one. Mauss, Cook, Cheng, and Gross (2007) attached participants to a physiological arousal monitor before counting numbers backward over an intercom. In addition to assessing various arousal outcomes, Mauss et al. used this as a way to provoke participants. Participants were provoked by having the researcher (in a rude voice) tell the participants that they were moving too much and eventually stopped the study. Results showed that high re-appraisers were less angry at the experimenter than low re-appraisers, suggesting that individuals high on this individual difference variable have the cognitive ability to change their emotional status to be less angry.

Overall, re-appraisal is a sufficient personality trait and process that can reduce aggressive behaviors. Barlett and Anderson (2011) devised a short-term intervention aimed at reducing aggression-related variables using re-appraisal tactics. For eight weeks, the researcher would teach re-appraisal definitions, tactics, and present data demonstrating how re-appraisal reduces all negative emotions to participants in the intervention group. Trait levels of re-appraisal and vengeance were administered at baseline and at the end of the study for intervention and control (those who did not receive any training) participants. Results showed that the re-appraisal training worked only for those low on re-appraisal at baseline, and increases in trait re-appraisal as a function of the intervention were related to decreases in trait vengeance.

Agreeableness

Agreeableness
One of the Big Five personality traits that is characterized by being trustworthy, good-natured, and cooperative.

Situational Modifier
A variable that disrupts aggressive learning.

Agreeableness is one of the Big Five personality traits that is characterized by being trustworthy, good-natured, and cooperative (John & Srivastava, 1999). In a correlational study, Barlett and Anderson (2012) found that agreeableness was negatively related to physical aggression through the reduction of aggressive emotions and attitudes. All these variables were assessed at the trait level. Using distal GAM, this suggests that highly agreeable individuals have the ability to reduce their aggressive attitudes and beliefs. Therefore, Anderson and Bushman (2002) would term agreeableness as a **situational modifier**; a variable that disrupts the aggression-related learning postulates of the distal GAM. In other words, those who are highly agreeable will likely find it difficult to pair positive reinforcement with aggressive-related stimuli, which disrupts the learning and automatization of learned aggressive knowledge structures.

Experimental evidence also alludes to the ability for agreeable people to not be aggressive in the current situation. Meier, Robinson, and Wilkowski (2006) found that highly agreeable people who were given an aggression prime were less aggressive than low agreeable people given the same prime. A follow-up study confirmed that highly agreeable people have the ability to cognitively shift the meaning of aggressive words to prosocial words. In other words, highly agreeable people are not easily primed with aggressive thoughts relative to individuals low on agreeableness. Meier, Wilkowski, and Robinson (2008) randomly assigned participants to receive training to learn to pair aggressive primes with prosocial targets (experimental group) or receive training related to activating helpful thoughts absent of social meaning (control group). Aggressive behavior was significantly lower for those in the experimental versus control group.

Reducing Hostile Attributions

The discussion on re-appraisal and agreeableness gives strong theoretical and practical reasons to investigate the personality and situational variables needed to be trained to help reduce aggression. However, the intervention of Barlett and Anderson (2011) and Meier et al. (2008) teach people a new skill. Research has also found that removing an aggression-related process is also beneficial at reducing aggression. One method is to reduce **hostile attributions**. Recall that GAM posits that the first step in the appraisal and decision-making process, the process that is the precursor to aggressive behavior, begins with an initially hostile interpretation of another's behavior, which is governed by the input factors and internal state. Thus, according to GAM, if one has the ability to change their attribution or not even make an initially hostile attribution in the onset, aggression should be reduced. Hudley and Graham (1993; Hudley, Graham, & Taylor, 2007) devised a curriculum aimed at training such attributional skills. In their intense intervention, children are taught how to detect intentions of others accurately, how to attribute ambiguous information to an accident rather than hostile intent, and understanding what social behaviors are appropriate. Results from their work clearly show the success of this program at reducing aggressive attributions and subsequent aggressive behavior (Hudley & Graham, 1993).

Hostile Attributions
Inferring hostile intent from the actions of another.

Conclusion

Aggression is a complex social behavior: there are several different forms, positive predictors, and negative correlates. Understanding the psychological processes that outline why one individual aggresses is important to predict future aggressive behaviors. This is why theory, such as the General Aggression Model, is so important to understand. The GAM offers a theoretical rationale for why, how, and for whom various personality (sex, narcissism) and situational (heat, media violence, weapon exposure) variables predict aggression. Understanding such processes is paramount for developing interventions aimed at training people to be less aggressive. Whether it's through agreeableness, re-appraisal, attributional changes, or other techniques, reducing aggressive behavior is an important step at making the world a less violent place.

Additional Readings

Card, N. A., Stucky, B. D., Sawalani, G. M., & Little, T. D. (2008). Direct and indirect aggression during childhood and adolescence: A meta-analytic review of gender differences, intercorrelations, and relations to maladjustment. *Child Development, 79*(5), 1185–1229. doi: 2121/10.1111/j.1467-8624.2008.01184.x

Crick, N. R., & Dodge, K. A. (1994). A review and reformulation of social information processing mechanisms in children's social adjustment. *Psychological Bulletin, 115*(1), 74–101. doi: 2121/10.1037/0033-2909.115.1.74

Gentile, D. A. (Ed.). (2003). *Media violence and children: A complete guide for parents and professionals.* Westport, CT: Praeger.

Huesmann, L. R., Eron, L. D., Lefkowitz, M. M., & Walder, L. O. (1984). Stability of aggression over time and generations. *Developmental Psychology, 20*(6), 1120–1134. doi: 2121/10.1037/0012-1649.20.6.1120

Shaver, P. R., & Mikulincer, M. (Eds.). (2011). *Human aggression and violence: Causes, manifestations, and consequences.* Washington, DC: American Psychological Association.

References

Anderson, C. A. (2001). Heat and violence. *Current Directions in Psychological Science, 10,* 33–38.

Anderson, C. A., & Bushman, B. J. (2002). Human aggression. *Annual Review of Psychology, 53,* 27–51.

Anderson, C. A., & Carnagey, N. L. (2009). Causal effects of violent sports video games on aggression: Is it competitiveness or violent content? *Journal of Experimental Social Psychology, 45,* 731–739.

Anderson, C. A., & Dill, K. E. (2000). Video games and aggressive thoughts, feelings, and behavior in the laboratory and in life. *Journal of Personality and Social Psychology, 78,* 772–790.

Anderson, C. A., & Huesmann, L. R. (2003). Human aggression: A social-cognitive view (pp. 296–323). In M.A. Hogg & J. Cooper (Eds.), *The sage handbook of social psychology.* London, England: Sage.

Anderson, C. A., Benjamin, A. J., & Bartholow, B. D. (1998). Does the gun pull the trigger? Automatic priming effects of weapon pictures and weapon names. *Psychological Science, 9,* 308–314.

Anderson, C. A., Buckley, K. E., & Carnagey, N. L. (2008). Creating your own hostile environment: A laboratory examination of trait aggression and the violence escalation cycle. *Personality and Social Psychology Bulletin, 34,* 462–473.

Anderson, C. A., Bushman, B. J., & Groom, R. W. (1997). Hot years and series and deadly assault: Empirical tests of the heat hypothesis. *Journal of Personality and Social Psychology, 73,* 1213–1223.

Anderson, C. A., Deuser, W. E., & DeNeve, K. M. (1995). Hot temperatures, hostile affect, hostile cognition, and arousal: Tests of the General Model of Affective Aggression. *Personality and Social Psychology Bulletin, 21,* 434–448.

Anderson, C. A., Sakamoto, A., Gentile, D. A., Ihori, N., Shibuya, A., Yukawa, S., . . . Kobayashi, K. (2008). Longitudinal effects of violent video games on aggression in Japan and the United States. *Pediatrics, 122,* 1067–1072.

Anderson, C. A., Shibuya, A., Ihori, N., Swing, E. L., Bushman, B. J., Sakamoto, A., ... & Saleem, M. (2010). Violent video game effects on aggression, empathy, and prosocial behavior in Eastern and Western countries: A meta-analytic review. *Psychological Bulletin, 136,* 151–173.

Archer, J. (1994). Testosterone and aggression. *Journal of Offender Rehabilitation, 21,* 3–25.

Archer, J. (2004). Sex differences in aggression in real-world settings: A meta-analytic review. *Review of General Psychology, 8,* 291–322.

Archer, J. (2006). Testosterone and human aggression: An evaluation of the challenge hypothesis. *Neuroscience and Biobehavioral Reviews, 30,* 319–345.

Arriaga, P., Esteves, F., Carneiro, P., & Monteiro, M. B. (2006). Violent computer games and their effects on state hostility and physiological arousal. *Aggressive Behavior, 32,* 146–158.

Barlett, C. P. (2013). Excuses, excuses: A meta-analytic review of how mitigating information can change aggression and an exploration of moderating variables. *Aggressive Behavior, 39,* 472–481.

Barlett, C. P., & Anderson, C. A. (2011). Re-appraising the situation and its impact on aggressive behavior. *Personality and Social Psychology Bulletin, 37,* 1564–1573.

Barlett, C. P., & Anderson, C. A. (2012). Direct and indirect relations between the Big 5 personality traits and aggressive and violent behavior. *Personality and Individual Differences, 52,* 870–875.

Bartholow, B. D., Anderson, C. A., Carnagey, N. L., & Benjamin, A. J. (2005). Interactive effects of life experience and situational cues on aggression: The weapons priming effect in hunters and nonhunters. *Journal of Experimental Social Psychology, 41,* 48–60.

Baumeister, R. F., Bushman, B. J., & Campbell, W. K. (2000). Self-esteem, narcissism, and aggression: Does violence result from low self-esteem or from threatened egotism? *Current Directions in Psychological Science, 9,* 26–29.

Berkowitz, L., & LePage, A. (1967). Weapons as aggression-eliciting stimuli. *Journal of Personality and Social Psychology, 7*, 202–207.

Bettencourt, B. A., & Miller, N. (1996). Gender differences in aggression as a function of provocation: A meta-analysis. *Psychological Bulletin, 119*, 422–447.

Bushman, B. J. (2002). Does venting anger feed or extinguish the flame? Catharsis, rumination, distraction, anger, and aggressive responding. *Personality and Psychological Bulletin, 28*, 724–731.

Bushman, B. J., & Anderson, C. A. (2002). Violent video games and hostile expectations: A test of the General Aggression Model. *Personality and Social Psychology Bulletin, 28*, 1679–1686.

Bushman, B. J., & Baumeister, R. F. (1998). Threatened egotism, narcissism, self-esteem, and direct and displaced aggression: Does self-love or self-hate lead to violence? *Journal of Personality and Social Psychology, 75*, 219–229.

Bushman, B. J., Baumeister, R. F., Thomaes, S., Ryu, E., Begeer, S., & West, S. G. (2009). Looking again, and harder, for a link between low self-esteem and aggression. *Journal of Personality, 77*, 427–446.

Buss, A. H., & Perry, M. (1992). The Aggression Questionnaire. *Journal of Personality and Social Psychology, 63*, 452–459.

CBC. (2014). Scott Jones says he forgives his attacker, Shane Edward Matheson. Retrieved from http://www.cbc.ca/news/canada/nova-scotia/scott-jones-says-he-forgives-his-attacker-shane-edward-matheson-1.2673052

Collins, A. M., & Loftus, E. F. (1975). A spreading activation theory of semantic processing. *Psychological Review, 31*, 272–292.

Crick, N. R., & Grotpeter, J. K. (1995). Relational aggression, gender, and social-psychological adjustment. *Child Development, 66*, 710–722.

Department of Justice. (1998). Alcohol and crime. Retrieved from http://www.bjs.gov/content/pub/pdf/ac.pdf

DeWall, C. N., Bushman, B. J., Giancola, P. R., & Webster, G. D. (2010). The big, the bad, and the boozed-up: Weight moderates the effect of alcohol and aggression. *Journal of Experimental Social Psychology, 46*, 619–623.

Eagly, A. H., & Steffen, V. J. (1986). Gender and aggressive behavior: A meta-analytic review of the social psychological literature. *Psychological Bulletin, 100*, 309–330.

Eagly, A. H., & Wood, W. (1991). Explaining sex differences in social behavior: A meta-analytic perspective. *Personality and Social Psychology Bulletin, 17*, 306–315.

FBI. (2013). Crime in the United States: 2013. Retrieved from https://www.fbi.gov/about-us/cjis/ucr/crime-in-the-u.s/2013/crime-in-the-u.s.-2013/offenses-known-to-law-enforcement/browse-by/national-data

Finkel, E. J., DeWall, C. N., Slotter, E. B., Oaten, M., & Foshee, V. A. (2009). Self-regulatory failure and intimate partner violence perpetration. *Journal of Personality and Social Psychology, 97*, 483–499.

Geen, R. G. (1990). *Human aggression.* Pacific Grove, CA: Brooks/Cole.

Gentile, D. A., & Bushman, B. J. (2012). Reassessing media violence effects using a risk and resilience approach to understanding aggression. *Psychology of Popular Media Culture, 1*, 138–151.

Giancola, P. R., & Corman, M. D. (2007). Alcohol and aggression: A test of the Attention-Allocation Model. *Psychological Science, 18*, 649–655.

Giancola, P. R., Josephs, R. A., DeWall, C. N., & Gunn, R. L. (2009). Applying the Attention-Allocation Model to the explanation of alcohol-related aggression: Implications for prevention. *Substance Use and Misuse, 44*, 1263–1279.

Giancola, P. R., Levinson, C. A., Corman, M. D., Godlaski, A. J., Morris, D. H., Phillips, J. P., & Holt, J. C. D. (2009). Men and women, alcohol and aggression. *Experimental and Clinical Psychopharmacology, 17*, 154–164.

Hopper, J. (2011). Alaska's hot sauce mom found guilty of child abuse. Good Morning America (8/23/2011). Retrieved from http://abcnews.go.com/US/hot-sauce-mom-jessica-beagley-found-guilty-child/story?id=14366615

Hudley, C., & Graham, S. (1993). An attributional intervention to reduce peer-directed aggression among African-American boys. *Child Development, 64*, 124–138.

Hudley, C., Graham, S., & Taylor, A. (2007). Reducing aggressive behavior and increasing motivation in school: The evolution of an intervention to strengthen school adjustment. *Educational Psychologist, 42*, 251–260.

Ito, T. A., Miller, N., & Pollock, V. E. (1996). Alcohol and aggression: A meta-analysis on the moderating effects of inhibitory cues, triggered events, and self-focused attention. *Psychological Bulletin, 120,* 60–82.

John, O. P., & Srivastava, S. (1999). The Big-Five trait taxonomy: History, measurement, and theoretical perspectives. In L. Pervin & O. P. John (Eds.), *Handbook of personality: Theory and research* (pp. 102–138). New York, NY: Guilford Press.

Mauss, I. B., Cook, C. L., Cheng, J. Y., & Gross, J. J. (2007). Individual differences in cognitive reappraisal: Experiential and physiological responses to an anger provocation. *International Journal of Psychophysiology, 66,* 116–124.

McCormack, S. (2014). Off-duty cop allegedly shoots woman in head during road range incident. Huffington Post (11/29/2014). Retrieved from http://www.huffingtonpost.com/2014/11/29/cop-shoots-woman-in-head-road-rage_n_6237910.html

Meier, B. P., Robinson, M. D., & Wilkowski, B. M. (2006). Turning the other cheek: Agreeableness and the regulation of aggression-related primes. *Psychological Science, 17,* 136–142.

Meier, B. P., Wilkowski, B. M., & Robinson, M. D. (2008). Bringing out the agreeableness in everyone: Using a cognitive self-regulation model to reduce aggression. *Journal of Experimental Social Psychology, 44,* 1383–1387.

Morf, C. C., & Rhodewalt, F. (2001). Unraveling the paradoxes of narcissism: A dynamic self-regulatory processing model. *Psychological Inquiry, 12,* 177–196.

Reifman, A. S., Larrick, R. P., & Fein, S. (1991). Temper and temperature on the diamond: The heat-aggression relationship in Major League Baseball. *Personality and Social Psychology Bulletin, 17,* 580–585.

Surgeon General. (2001). Youth violence: A report of the Surgeon General. Retrieved from http://www.ncbi.nlm.nih.gov/books/NBK44293/

Twenge, J. M., Konrath, S., Foster, J. D., Campbell, W. K., & Bushman, B. J. (2008). Egos inflating over time: A cross-temporal meta-analysis of the Narcissistic Personality Inventory. *Journal of Personality, 76,* 875–901.

Chapter Ten
Prejudice

Dr. Holly Krech Thomas and Prof. Andrea Ring

Bethany College

Learning Objectives

- Define prejudice, stereotype, discrimination, and implicit prejudice
- Explain how prejudice is a natural byproduct of the way our brain categorizes information
- Understand how evolutionary processes can lead to prejudice, and analyze how these processes play out in current events
- Explore various ways categorization of people influences our perceptions and judgments
- Understand stereotype threat and how it influences people's performance
- Describe effective ways to reduce prejudice

Chapter Outline

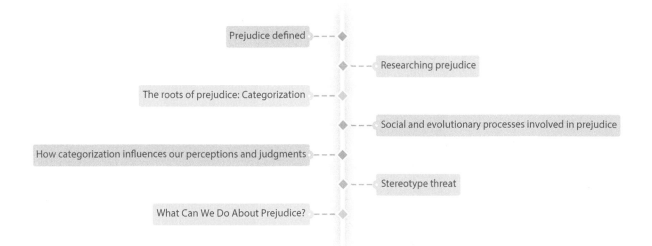

Prejudice defined

Researching prejudice

The roots of prejudice: Categorization

Social and evolutionary processes involved in prejudice

How categorization influences our perceptions and judgments

Stereotype threat

What Can We Do About Prejudice?

Prejudice is a learned trait. You're not born prejudiced; you're taught it.

~ Charles R. Swindoll

…The less secure a man is, the more likely he is to have extreme prejudice.

~ Clint Eastwood

If people are informed they will do the right thing. It's when they are not informed that they become hostages to prejudice.

~ Charlayne Hunter-Gault

(Quotes retrieved from www.brainyquote.com)

Consider the quotes above. If nothing else, they certainly speak to the fact that prejudice is something that concerns our society, from religious leaders like Charles Swindoll, to movie stars like Clint Eastwood, to those in the civil rights movement, like Charlayne Hunter-Gault. But these quotes also demonstrate the many misconceptions there are about prejudice. The claims they make are all, to a great extent, false. Prejudice has been a major focus of research in psychology for over 50 years. Prompted by the atrocities of World War II and inspired by Gordon Allport's (1954) seminal work, *The Nature of Prejudice*, generations of researchers have dug into the topic of prejudice.

Initially, researchers sought to determine how personality types, particularly the authoritarian personality, were associated with prejudice (Dovidio, Hewstone, Glick, & Esses, 2010; Fiske, 1998). The assumption was that certain people were prone to prejudice; the actions of the Nazis in Germany made this assumption a reasonable place to start. However, by the 1970s, the focus of discrimination research shifted to more subtle forms of racism, as well as how cognitive and social processes lead to prejudice. More recently, research has expanded to include the ways that emotions, neural processes, social systems, and other aspects of our mental and social life influence people's prejudices.

PathDoc/Shutterstock.com

With such a rich history of research, this chapter will highlight some of the key theories and findings about prejudice, but by no means can it give an exhaustive overview of the topic. We encourage you to check out the additional resources listed at the end of the chapter, if you would like to explore this topic in more depth or breadth. By the end of this chapter, you will be able to explain what is misguided or just plain wrong with the way the quotes above characterize prejudice. You will also, we hope, come to appreciate the wisdom in Herbert Spencer's (1851, p. 176) observation, "We all decry prejudice, yet are all prejudiced." We cannot point fingers at others without realizing, as the adage goes, that three fingers are pointing right back at us.

Prejudice
A negative attitude toward a group of people which involves cognitive, emotional, and behavioral components.

Prejudice Defined

Before we explore the topic of prejudice, pause for a moment to consider how you would define these terms: prejudice, stereotype, and discrimination. You might jot down your definitions now, so you can compare them to how researchers have defined the terms. A common way to explain **prejudice** is that it is a negative attitude toward a group of people which involves cognitive, emotional, and behavioral components (Aronson, 2012; Dovidio et al., 2010). The cognitive component of prejudice involves a set of beliefs about a person or group of people, generalizations that are based on incomplete or inaccurate information. The emotional component is often expressed as dislike of a group or feeling hostility toward it. The behavioral component is a predisposition to act in negative ways toward a group.

Given this approach, prejudice is something of an umbrella term, and the concepts of stereotypes and discrimination basically represent different aspects of prejudice (see Figure 10.1). **Stereotypes** are the generalizations that people make about others: the cognitive component of prejudice. Stereotypes can be about people's characteristics, motives, or behavior. For example, a stereotype that Asians do well in math is about that group's behavior, but a stereotype that men are insensitive is more about their personal characteristics. **Discrimination** is the behavioral component of prejudice, the biased treatment of a group. In contrast with how the media in our society seem to fanatically report and denounce instances of discrimination, researchers tend to focus on stereotypes and attitudes when investigating the topic of prejudice (Fiske, 1998).

Although prejudice usually involves negative attitudes, as the definition above indicates, some prejudices lead to positive stereotypes, such as the belief that Asians do well in math. Research has focused on negative attitudes and negative stereotypes because they are by far the most common forms of prejudice. But it is important to note that sometimes we have ill-informed positive attitudes about others, too, and they can also be considered prejudice.

An alternative way to understand prejudice, stereotypes, and discrimination is to treat all three terms as separate phenomena (Fiske, 1998, p. 357). From this perspective, stereotypes and discrimination are not simply aspects of prejudice. Rather, all three are facets of a person's attitude toward others in groups that seem different from his or her own group (see Figure 10.1). Stereotypes are the most cognitive facet, prejudice is the most emotional, and discrimination is the most behavioral. Regardless of which approach to the terms researchers adopt, prejudice, stereotypes, and discrimination are clearly related to each other. For the purposes of this chapter, stereotypes and discrimination are treated as components of prejudice, but this approach does not really affect the interpretation of the vast amount research that has been done on these topics.

Stereotypes
Generalizations people make about others based on incorrect or incomplete information.

Discrimination
Acting in negative ways toward a group of people.

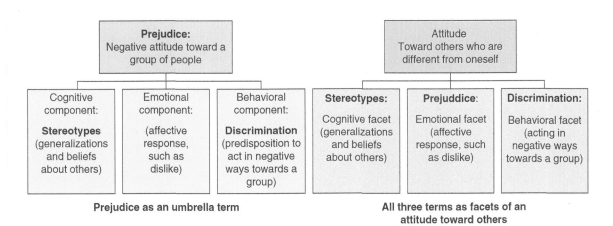

Figure 10.1. Two ways of defining prejudice, stereotypes, and discrimination.

Researching Prejudice

Demand Characteristics

The experimenter's expectations about participants' performance in an experiment influence their actual performance; participants may or may not be aware that they are inferring these expectations.

Researching prejudice can be tricky. It can be difficult to get accurate measures of people's true attitudes for a number of reasons. First, people may be unwilling to admit socially unacceptable attitudes. If you ask them point blank a question like, "How comfortable do you feel around Hispanic people?" they may indicate that they feel more comfortable than they actually do because admitting their true discomfort is frowned on in our society. The more sensitive a topic, the less truthful responses to explicit questions tend to be (Greenwald, Poehlman, Uhlmann, & Banaji, 2009). Second, people may try to impress a researcher or give the "right" answer, something known as **demand characteristics**. In a study about world religions, participants might assume that the researcher would approve of responses that are positive toward all religions.

Implicit Prejudice

A negative attitude toward a group of people that someone holds with little or no conscious awareness.

Third, people may be unaware of their prejudice. This sort of prejudice is called **implicit prejudice**, the negative attitudes toward a group of people that someone holds with little or no conscious awareness. You might know someone who is generally acknowledged to be sexist, yet he does not think of himself that way. If he were asked about his attitude toward women, he might respond in ways that appeared respectful and sincere, and he might believe that he really is respectful.

Ways to Obtain More Accurate Responses

One way that researchers can address the problems inherent with **self-report methods** for measuring prejudice is to phrase questions in terms of behaviors rather than attitudes (Greenwald et al., 2009). Instead of asking, "How comfortable do you feel around Hispanic people?" a questionnaire might ask, "How likely would you be to choose someone who is Hispanic for a roommate?" Another method for addressing the issue of inaccurate responses is to capitalize on the relationship between the behavioral and cognitive/emotional components of prejudice

(see Figure 10.1). Behaviors are typically easy to measure, which makes them a useful tool. Some research looks at correlations between behaviors and self-reported attitudes (e.g., Greenwald, McGhee, & Schwartz, 1998), and other research infers cognitive or emotional processes from behaviors (e.g., Dovidio & Gaertner, 2000). In both cases, behaviors provide a less biased reflection of people's actual prejudices than their self-reported attitudes might give.

A nonscientific demonstration of how behaviors can reveal implicit prejudice comes from the ABC news show *What Would You Do?* In 2010, the show staged an attempted bike theft in a city park (Pyle, 2010). The would-be thief sawed away on a chain that locked the bicycle to a pole, and the cameras caught the reactions of passersby. Although the bystanders insisted when interviewed that they would have responded the same way regardless of the race of the thief, there were clear differences in responses to a thief who was a young Black male, a young White male, and a young White female. You can probably guess which thief had more people stop, angrily demand to know what was going on, and threaten to call 911. The young Black male. What you might not guess is how many people, males in particular, stopped to help the young lady thief. That's right, they actually helped her steal the bicycle. Clearly, actions speak louder than words when it comes to implicit prejudice.

The Implicit Association Test: Praise and Criticism

The Implicit Association Test (IAT, see Chapter 6 for an introduction to what it is and how it works) has given researchers yet another way to ferret out people's true attitudes. Many researchers have used various versions of the IAT since it was first introduced in 1998 in an article by Anthony Greenwald and his colleagues. Research using the IAT has measured people's implicit prejudices about race, gender, political preferences, drug and alcohol use, and many other topics. Based on a **meta-analysis** of well over a hundred studies using the IAT, Greenwald et al. (2009) conclude that a decade of research using the IAT has demonstrated that the IAT effectively predicts people's behaviors and attitudes, and is a better measure than self-reports for sensitive topics such as race. What this conclusion means is that if your score on a race IAT indicates strong negative associations with Blacks, you probably have some hidden biases against Blacks. Furthermore, those biases might express themselves as discrimination or prejudice under the right conditions.

Although there are many fans of the IAT, it is not without its critics. Blanton and Mitchell (2011), for instance, reanalyzed data from two prior studies that used the IAT. They found that what the original articles touted as significant results supporting the IAT's ability to predict prejudice were actually **nonsignificant results**, which showed no relationship between implicit attitudes and discriminatory behaviors. Based on these results, Blanton and Mitchell caution that the IAT does not necessarily predict latent racism. In other words, strong associations on an IAT do not predict overt prejudice or discrimination, contrary to what Greenwald et al. (2009) claim.

One of the main benefits of the IAT is that, unlike self-report measure, the IAT cannot be faked. You can pretend to like Hispanics when you answer explicit questions on a survey, but you cannot pretend to have an implicit association between "Hispanic" and "good." Or so researchers thought. A study by Fiedler and Bluemke (2005) calls this assumption into question. Fiedler and Bluemke show in a series of experiments that participants actually can fake implicit associations, and they can do it in a way that even expert IAT testers cannot detect the cheating. Other research (Cvencek, Greenwald, Brown, Gray, & Snowden, 2010) argues that authentically faking IAT results is not possible, and test takers who try to fake their results can be reliably detected.

Obviously, the IAT is not a silver bullet, solving all the problems of establishing truthful, accurate information about people's prejudices. The IAT has provided many insights into the issues around prejudice, but we still need to know more about the test as a measurement tool (e.g., what it really tests and what it predicts) before we can be sure that an IAT score gives us a clear window into someone's hidden prejudices. If you want to learn more about the IAT test or try it yourself, read the Thinking Critically Box on the top of page 164.

Self-Report Methods
Data collection that involves the participant answering questions about his or her thoughts and behaviors.

Meta-Analysis
A study that statistically analyzes the results of many similar experiments in order to identify patterns, disagreements, or other insights.

Nonsignificant Results
Results that do not reach statistical significance; any trend or pattern that appears in the data is likely due to chance, not to actual relationships or true differences.

THINKING CRITICALLY (A)

Try out the IAT for yourself by going to https://implicit.harvard.edu/implicit/takeatest.html.

There are many different versions of the IAT, but we suggest you begin by taking the Race IAT. Take the test at least twice.

A. The first time you take the test, simply follow the instructions. When you finish and receive your results, either jot them down or save them somewhere.

B. The second time you take the test, try to fake your results, as the participants in Fiedler and Bluemke (2005). So if you scored a "strong" association the first time you took the test, can you reverse that or change it to "slight?" Or if you scored a "slight" association the first time, can you make it "strong?"

Questions:

1. Reflect on your score—do you agree with it?
2. Reflect on how easy or difficult it was to fake the test.
3. How does your experience with the IAT inform your understanding of the test as a measure of implicit prejudice? How does it inform your perspective on the criticisms of the IAT, particularly criticisms that participants may be able to fake the test?

See the end of the chapter for ideas and hints.

The Roots of Prejudice: Categorization

herjua/Shutterstock.com

Humans think in categories. From our earliest interactions with the world, we are busy categorizing. Babies who are only days old recognize and prefer their mother's voice, smell, and face. They have already formed a mental category for "Mama." Granted, early categories tend to be broad and often flawed. When my (Holly's) son was a year old, he would be in his stroller as we walked down the streets ofi New York City, where we lived at the time, and he would point to all the dogs he saw, delightedly calling out, "Moo! Moo!" Having only seen cows in picture books, the dogs on the street apparently looked like cows to him, and were lumped into that category.

Categories are essential for our daily functioning in the world. In a sense, they provide shortcuts, or **heuristics**, that allow us to interact competently with our environment and each

Heuristics
Methods that help you solve problems or make judgments faster than if you went through all the steps that would otherwise be involved; rules of thumb.

other. As Gordon Allport wrote in *The Nature of Prejudice* (1954, p. 20), "The human mind must think with the aid of categories .... Once formed, categories are the basis for normal prejudgment. We cannot possibly avoid this process. Orderly living depends upon it." To put Allport's (1954) comment in perspective, imagine what would happen if you did not have a category for "doors," for instance. Every time you came to a new flat wall-like object with hinges, you would have to examine it to figure out its purpose and how to manipulate it. By identifying an object as a door, you instantly have a wealth of information about its structure, function, and some likely ways to successfully get past it. We cannot avoid categorizing our world, nor would we want to. "Orderly living depends on it."

However, our natural propensity to categorize information has serious implications for our social interactions. Children are not the only ones with flawed categories. Adults may not mistake dogs for cows, but we do have biases in how we group things and people, and these biases can lead to skewed perspectives that we are often unaware of. As Allport (1954) recognized, the development of prejudices is at least partly due to the normal cognitive process of categorization. Social, economic, historical, and personality factors play a role in the development prejudice, but at its root, prejudice is arguably about categorization.

Prejudice is a great time saver. You can form opinions without having to get the facts.

E. B. White

Retrieved from www.brainyquote.com

Social Categories
Categories, usually of people, based on social information.

Babies' Social Categories

Some fascinating research by Karen Wynn, Paul Bloom, and their colleagues has revealed that as early as three months of age, babies are forming **social categories** (e.g., Bloom, 2013). These categories may be based on trivial similarities between the babies and others, such as food preferences, or they may be based on judgments of moral character. Babies like others who are like themselves, and they dislike others who are unkind.

Trivial Similarities In one study, 11-month-old babies got to choose a snack: Cheerios or graham crackers (Mahajan & Wynn, 2012). Then they watched two puppets choose snacks. One puppet chose the same snack as the baby, making happy, "Yum!" responses and chewing noises, after rejecting the other snack with a disgusted, "Yuck!" The other puppet had the opposite response, choosing the snack that was different from the baby's selection, and exclaiming "Yum!" and "Yuck!" appropriately. After the snacks were removed, the babies could choose a puppet to play with. The babies overwhelmingly chose the puppet that had selected the same snack they had chosen (see Figure 10.2).

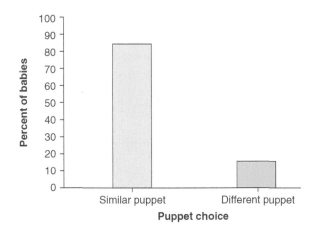

Figure 10.2. Percentage of 11-month-olds who chose puppets with food preferences that were similar to or different from their own (graph created from results in Mahajan & Wynn, 2012).

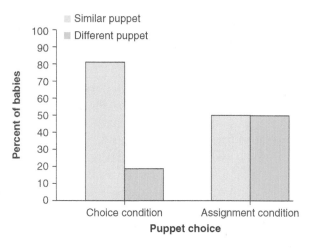

Figure 10.3. Percentage of 11-month-olds who chose puppets with mittens that were similar to or different from their own, depending on whether they had a choice of mitten color or were assigned mittens (graph created from results in Mahajan & Wynn, 2012).

Another experiment in Mahajan and Wynn's (2012) study involved 11-month-olds either choosing a yellow or orange pair of mittens, or being given one of the pairs of mittens. The babies got to wear their chosen or assigned mittens. For those babies who chose their mittens, they watched two puppets select yellow or orange mittens; as in the snack experiment, the puppets expressed a positive attitude toward the mittens they chose and a negative one toward the mittens they rejected. For the babies who were assigned mittens, they watched two puppets also be given mittens.

Finally, the babies selected which puppet they wanted to play with. The babies who chose their mittens responded like those in the snack experiment, consistently selecting the puppet that had selected the same color mittens (see Figure 10.3). Those babies who had been given mittens, however, randomly chose one of the puppets. They did not appear to be influenced by the color of mittens the puppet was wearing.

As Mahajan and Wynn (2012) point out, these experiments suggest a couple of things. First, babies prefer those who are similar to themselves, just as adults do. Second, babies' preferences may be based on trivial similarities in choices, such as food or clothing, but they are not influenced by arbitrary similarities. When babies and puppets were given mittens, having no say in the matter, babies apparently did not assume the puppet with the same color mittens was like themselves, and so were not drawn to play with that puppet any more than the other puppet. Adults, in contrast, do appear to be influenced by even arbitrary or random similarities (see also Aronson, 2012).

Moral Judgments Perhaps it is too strong a statement to claim that babies make moral judgments, categorizing others' behavior as good or bad, but that is exactly what Paul Bloom (2013) suggests. He bases his assertion on numerous studies with preverbal infants. In one such study with 3-month-olds (Hamlin, Wynn, & Bloom, 2010), infants appear to be attracted to prosocial individuals who are kind to others, and they avoid antisocial individuals who are unkind. Because 3-month-olds lack the motor control needed to reach for a toy they prefer, the experiments in Hamlin et al. (2010) measure their eye gaze instead. The eye gaze technique takes advantage of the fact that infants look longer at things they like or are interested in; longer looking times are essentially equivalent to reaching for a toy.

The infants first watched a scene in which a wooden block tried to "climb" a hill; another block came along and either helped or hindered the climber. For infants in the social condition, the climber had googly eyes, making it look like a character; for infants in the inanimate control condition, the climber was a plain block with no eyes. For all infants, the helper and hinderer blocks had googly eyes. After the scene was over, infants were shown the helper and hinderer blocks, and the amount of time they spent looking at each was measured.

Results showed that infants preferred the helper blocks and avoided the hinderer blocks, but only in the social condition. In other words, when the infants perceived that the helper blocks were kindly assisting another block to the top of the hill, they looked longer at the helper. But when it appeared that the helper block was merely pushing an inanimate object up a hill, the helper was not preferred over the hinderer.

A follow-up experiment with a neutral block, in addition to the helper and hinderer blocks, showed that infants avoided looking at the hinderer, but treated the helper and neutral blocks similarly. This strong rejection of the hinderer may indicate that infants key in on negative social information, much as older children and adults do. People in general appear to be more sensitive to negative information about others, noticing angry faces more than neutral or happy ones, for example (Hamlin et al., 2010).

Arunas Gabalis/Shutterstock.com

Cognitive Origins of Prejudice

Clearly, the 3-month-olds are categorizing characters based on the characters' actions, much as the 11-month-olds categorized based on food and color preferences. Other research with older babies (e.g., Hamlin, Wynn, Bloom, & Mahajan, 2011) clarifies that babies not only dislike those who are unkind to others, but they like those who are unkind to bad guys. So babies appear to think that bad guys deserve to be punished. That seems reasonable, but Wynn and Bloom (as interviewed by Stahl, 2012) also note a darker side to babies' preferences. Babies treat those who are unlike themselves (for example, choosing Cheerios instead of graham crackers) similar to the way they treat bad guys: They prefer those who harm individuals who are unlike themselves. In other words, babies seem to think that those who are different from themselves deserve punishment merely because they are different.

Potapenko Ivan/Shutterstock.com

Here is where we see most clearly the roots of prejudice in the innate human drive to categorize. If babies not only dislike those who are unlike themselves, but think they should be harmed, we can see that there is an innate cognitive tendency toward prejudice that is evident before any social, historical, or even personality factors could be prompting this behavior.

Social and Evolutionary Processes Involved in Prejudice

In-Groups and Out-Groups

Since the beginning, humans have lived and survived in communities. As a result, we tend to categorize ourselves and others into in-groups and out-groups.

sezer66/Shutterstock.com

In-groups are those similar to us, those with whom we identify. **Out-groups** are others we do not identify with, whom we see as different. The babies in Wynn and Bloom's research (Bloom, 2013) essentially were classifying puppets and blocks into in-groups and out-groups: The objects that were like themselves were in the babies' in-group but objects that were different were in the babies' out-group. With adults, in-group and out-group categorizations can fall along the lines of race, gender, class, age, or sexuality. But adult categorizations can also be based on something as simple as arbitrary group labels in a class activity, with students in Group A seeing those in Group B as an out-group, at least for the duration of the activity (Tajfel, Billig, Bundy, & Flament, 1971).

In-Groups

Individuals similar to us, those with whom we identify; people in our group.

Out-Groups

Individuals outside our group; those with whom we do not identify and whom we see as different.

Us Versus Them

Henri Tajfel is given credit for the popularity of the terms in-group and out-group in a study he and his colleagues did on social categorization (Tajfel et al., 1971). A group of adolescent male students participated in the experiment. These males all attended the same school and identified as an in-group (schoolmates) prior to the experiment.

First, the students completed a simple estimation task (Tajfel et al., 1971). Next, the experimenters divided the students into two groups, "overestimators" and "underestimators," with no feedback about how accurate either group was. The experimenters then asked each student to allocate rewards to others in the experiment based on their scores on the estimation task. The booklet the students used to record their allocation suggestions identified individuals as either in their group or in the other group (overestimators versus underestimators). The rewards were for individuals only, meaning that giving more allocations to their own group members did not affect their own reward amount.

The results showed that students tended to favor their in-group and allocated more rewards to them regardless of the actual scores on the estimation task (Tajfel et al., 1971). In other words, after just a short period of time being in the estimation groups, students tended to show an in-group mentality and discrimination towards the out-group. These results suggest that identifying with an in-group is a very natural behavior. Furthermore, this natural tendency to identify with in-groups can create an "us versus them" mentality, which we also saw in the studies on babies' categorization (Mahajan & Wynn, 2012).

A Connection Between Evolutionary Theory and Prejudice

This "us versus them" mentality can be understood as an integral part of our survival instinct. In 1859 Charles Darwin first published *The Origin of Species*, in which he introduced his theories on natural selection and survival of the fittest (Darwin, 1896). In simplistic terms, Darwin believed that the goal of humanity is to survive and reproduce so our genetic make-up can continue on after we die. You could argue that the innate desire to categorize and label in-group/us and out-groups/them is for the purpose of survival of our species. Those like us, those with whom we share similar genes, our in-group.

A recent study looked at the connection between evolutionary theory and prejudice. Krupp and Taylor (2015) were interested not just in in-group favoritism and out-group discrimination but also to what extent those behaviors may occur based on how similar we are to the in-group and the level of diversity in the in-group. They worked with a simple **inclusive fitness model** to demonstrate the role that genetic similarity of group members plays in how altruistic or spiteful members are to non-members. According to their model, if we share more genes with a group and the group has less diversity, our identity becomes stronger and our prejudice can become worse. This model can explain the behavior of a variety of species, including ground squirrels and the weaver ant, as well as humans.

Rena Schild/Shutterstock.com

You could apply Krupp and Taylor's (2015) model to the protests in Ferguson, Missouri, over the Michael Brown shooting. A brief background, according to a *New York Times* article ("Tracking the Events," 2014): On August 9, 2014, Michael Brown, an 18-year-old Black man, was shot and killed by Darren Wilson, a Caucasian police office. Brown was unarmed and there was disagreement as to whether Wilson acted in self-defense or if he used excessive force. Eye witness testimonies were conflicting. Some reported that Brown had his hands up in a surrendering manner, others reported that Brown was approaching Wilson in a "threatening manner" (p. 5). Race quickly became an issue. Protests began the next day. Most protests were peaceful, but others became violent. On August 18, the National Guard was brought in to help. On November 24, a Grand Jury made the announcement that no charges would be brought against Wilson.

A separate *New York Times* article (Smith, 2014, p. 1) explains, "Ferguson's demographics have shifted rapidly: in 1990, it was 74 percent White and 25 percent Black; in 2000, 52 percent black and 45 percent white; by 2010, 67 percent black and 29 percent white." The article also suggests that the police force is predominantly White. According to Krupp and Taylor's (2015) model, these demographics would create a hot bed for prejudice. The Ferguson in-group is rather homogenous (being predominately Black), suggesting their discrimination toward the out-group (White police force) would be greater. The characteristics of the in-group and out-group may help us understand why the reaction to the Michael Brown shooting was so extreme. By no means does this excuse any violence or illegal behavior, but it helps us understand that these are not bad people, but individuals engaging in behaviors they may feel are necessary for their survival and the survival of their in-group.

Terror Management Theory

Another theory that addresses reasons for violence toward out-groups is **Terror Management Theory**, which posits that fear leads to prejudice and violence. The basis for Terror Management Theory comes from Ernest Becker (1971), a cultural anthropologist. He believed that people are unable to accept the idea that we are all going to die someday. He felt that humans are able to avoid the

Inclusive Fitness Model
A model for social behaviors that promote evolutionary success; importantly, evolutionary success is predicted not just by an individual's offspring but also by its relatives or others that may share its genes (such as siblings and cousins).

Terror Management Theory
The theory that believes in order for humans to manage anxiety about their own mortality they create culture and worldviews and cling to these beliefs when their survival is threatened.

Derogation

The belief that we should dismiss others' worldviews that are different than ours.

Assimilation

The belief that if an individual's worldview is different than ours, we must help him or her change his or her worldview to ours.

Accommodation

When an individual only accepts appealing aspects of the out-groups worldview and only if it benefits them.

Annihilation

The belief that one's worldview will and should prevail.

anxiety of facing their own death by creating "culture," which in turn helps create a worldview that gives us purpose and meaning and decreases our anxiety about our own mortality. This worldview and culture also creates an in-group. Individuals from other cultures then become out-groups and can become a threat to the meaning and purpose of the in-group.

Jeff Greenberg and his colleagues took Becker's ideas and created Terror Management Theory in the 1980s. Initially the theory was met with "stunned silence, shock and dismay" (Greenberg & Arndt, 2012, p. 399). The basic claim of Terror Management Theory is:

> . . . *that to manage the potential for terror engendered by the awareness of mortality, humans sustain faith in worldviews which provide a sense that they are significant beings in an enduring, meaningful world rather than mere material animals fated only to obliteration upon death... [and] reminders of mortality instigate worldview bolstering and self-esteem striving. . . . (Greenberg & Arndt, 2012, p. 398).*

In simpler terms, the theory says that as humans when we feel threatened we are more likely to hold to our beliefs, culture, and worldview to make us feel better. And in doing so, we are also more likely to discriminate against those who have different beliefs, cultures, and worldviews. In even simpler terms, we want to feel good and do not get along with people different from us.

Everett Historical/Shutterstock.com

Four Types of Discrimination, According to Terror Management Theory Greenberg and Arndt (2012) believe that discrimination can play out in four different behaviors (see Figure 10.4). **Derogation** is the belief that we should dismiss others' beliefs that are different than ours. If their worldview is different, they must be "ignorant or evil" (p. 403). An example is when someone criticizes another person for having a different religious belief than his or her own. **Assimilation** is the belief that if an individual's worldview is different than ours, we must help him or her "see the light." They must adopt our worldview and join our in-group. Greenberg and Arndt use the example of missionaries traveling to other countries to share the "correct" religion and worldview. **Accommodation** is when individuals only accept appealing aspects of the out-group's worldview and only if it benefits themselves. An example given by Greenberg and Arndt is when a business may dislike rap music but use the popular genre of music in a marketing ad because it helps sell a product. **Annihilation** is the belief that our worldview will and should prevail, and all others will be obliterated. An example would be Hitler and Nazi Germany: Hitler felt the Jews had the wrong worldview, and he chose to eliminate them so his worldview could prevail.

Greenberg and Arndt (2012) imply that these behaviors are the core to all human behavior. This does not present humans in the best light, so one can see why the initial reaction to the theory

Ken Tannenbaum/Shutterstock.com

Behavior	Definition
Derogation	Dismissing others' beliefs
Assimilation	Helping others "see the light"
Accommodation	Accepting only beneficial aspects of a different worldview
Annihilation	Believing other worldviews will be wiped out

Figure 10.4. A summary of the four ways discrimination plays out, according to Terror Management Theory.

was not favorable. Despite the initial lack of enthusiasm for these ideas, there have now been over 400 empirical studies across the world published on Terror Management Theory.

Terror Management Theory Applied to Current Events Terror Management Theory saw a revival in popularity after the 9/11 terrorist attacks. Obviously, this was a time when Americans felt their survival was threatened and the fear of death became a prominent thought. As Terror Management Theory would predict, Americans faced this renewed awareness of their mortality by doing things to bolster their worldview and their self-esteem. Some ways we saw these predictions play out in our country:

1. The day after the attacks, Wal-Mart sold over 88,000 flags. The year before on the same day, September 12, 2000, it sold only 6,000 in comparison (Mullen, 2015).
2. *God Bless America* by Lee Greenwood, originally released in 1983 and not a big hit, received massive airplay after 9/11 and was even covered by powerhouse popstar Beyoncé (Weiser, 2015).
3. Churches and synagogues saw a 25% increase in attendance (Zelizer, 2002).
4. Hate crimes against Muslims (the out-group Americans blamed for the attack) increased exponentially (Khan & Ecklund, 2012). According to FBI records, in the year before the attacks, there were 28 hate incidents reported. The year after the attacks 481 incidents were reported (Schevitz, 2002).

Americans clung to their patriotism, identity as American citizens, and belief in their faith. However, once the threat was less salient, flag sales and church attendance returned to normal.

A more recent example of how Terror Management Theory has played out in the United States is the legalization of gay marriage. Back in 1996 President Bill Clinton signed the Defense of Marriage Act (DOMA). This stated that, for the purposes of the federal government, the legal definition of marriage was between a man and a woman. This legislation was initiated to protect the sanctity of marriage. Many believed marriage was between a man and a woman. This was their worldview. Since then the LGBT population and its supporters have been trying to get the act repealed.

On June 26, 2015, the Supreme Court ruled that the Constitution of the United States guarantees the right to same-sex marriage nationwide (Liptak, 2015). Some people saw this ruling as a "threat," prompting many examples

of what would be, according to Terror Management Theory, out-group discrimination and "worldview bolstering" on both sides. That day I (Andrea) opened Facebook to see some of my "friends" had changed their Facebook profile pic to the representative Gay Pride Rainbow; showing their worldview supported the landmark decision. Other "friends" posted scripture and threatened to move out of the country, showing their worldview did not support the decision. Some posts got ugly! Names were called and virtual punches were thrown as both sides engaged in derogation, each group thinking its worldview was right and the other was "ignorant or evil." Neither side seemed willing to listen to or try to understand the other's beliefs, as would be predicted by Terror Management Theory for people who felt their in-group identity was being threatened.

Politicians have put forward various arguments on both sides of the same-sex marriage issue. Many of these arguments, like the fiery Facebook responses to the Supreme Court's decision, can also be viewed through the lens of Terror Management Theory. Here are a few examples:

Example 1—David Blankenhorn, who describes himself as a liberal Democrat, argues against same-sex marriage in his book, *The Future of Marriage*. Blankenhorn explains (as cited by Steinfels, 2007, para. 12):

> *The real conflict is between one good and another: the equal dignity of all persons and the worth of homosexual love, versus the flourishing of children. On each side, the threat to something important is real. It wastes everyone's time to pretend that this question is an easy one, and that only bad people can fail to see the right answer.*

Blankenhorn identifies the debate about same-sex marriage as a threat to something of value for both sides. From a Terror Management Theory perspective, our values and worldview give our lives meaning, so fighting to maintain our worldview feels vital to our survival and worth. Feeling threatened never justifies demeaning or disrespecting another group, but perhaps it helps us understand why some individuals are so passionate about the topic of same-sex marriage.

Example 2—In Claire Snyder's book *Gay Marriage and Democracy: Equality for All*, she frames the issue in terms of gay citizens' rights to be treated equally before the law (Snyder, 2006, p. 11):

> *The political theory of liberal democracy outlined in this book both requires the legalization of same-sex marriage (legal equality) and protects the right of consenting adults to engage sexually with other consenting adults without state interference (right to privacy, individual autonomy). In fact, reinforcing the principles of liberal democracy should actually help secure not only legal equality but also the right of individuals to self-determination in personal matters….*

In other words, Snyder argues that a democracy protects people's rights to hold their own worldview and to pursue their own significance as human beings. These rights are threatened or denied, Snyder claims, by laws that prohibit same-sex marriage. Terror Management Theory predicts that protecting one's worldview and self-esteem become increasingly important as they are increasingly threatened, so again, it comes as no surprise that people are passionate about this topic. See the Thinking Critically Box on page 173 for another example of Terror Management Theory in current events.

THINKING CRITICALLY (B)

According to an article in *The Atlantic*, Freddie Gray, a 25-year-old Black man, was arrested on April 12 (Graham, 2015). During the transition to the police station there was a question of whether excessive force was used by the arresting officers. By the time Gray arrived at the station he was "unable to breathe or talk" (Graham, 2015, para. 1). Gray later died on April 19 from his injuries. Six officers were placed on suspension following the incident. Three of the officers involved were Caucasian. Like the Michael Brown case, this prompted questions of race and police's use of force as well as protests in the streets of Baltimore.

In a PBS Blog (Shalby & Barajas, 2015, para. 4), Reverend Delman Coates was quoted as saying the following about Freddie Gray's death and the protests that followed:

> *In the absence of jobs, decent education, healthcare and opportunity, people are going to respond in these ways. If you leave a hot stove on the oven too long, the top is going to blow off.*

How might Terror Management Theory and the concept of in-groups versus out-groups apply to this quote?

1. Who is the in-group?
2. Who is the out-group?
3. According to Terror Management Theory when there is a salient threat to our survival, in-group bolstering and out-group discrimination gets worse. What does the quote suggest about the "threat" to the Black population of Baltimore?

See the end of the chapter for sample answers.

How Categorization Influences Our Perceptions and Judgments

Having established some of the cognitive, social, and evolutionary sources of prejudice, this section moves on to explore how our bent to categorize influences our perceptions and judgments. One of the consequences of grouping people into categories is that we tend to make generalizations about out-groups in a way we do not about our in-group. We know our in-group pretty well. We recognize differences between its members. But because we are not as familiar with out-groups, we tend to see members of out-groups as very similar to one another, a phenomenon known as **out-group homogeneity bias** (Linville, Fischer, & Salovey, 1989).

Out-Group Homogeneity Bias
The tendency to see members of out-groups as very similar to one another.

Physical Perceptions of Out-Groups

I (Holly) experienced out-group homogeneity bias first-hand when I was in China teaching English for a year. The first few weeks of class, I looked out on the sea of Asian faces in my classroom and despaired of ever being able to tell my students apart. They all looked alike to me. I memorized where they sat, what they wore, and how they did their hair as I attempted to distinguish between them. By the end of the year, of course, I had gotten to know the students, and I was rather taken aback when my sister, who came to visit me, remarked that the students all looked alike. They looked nothing alike to me by that time.

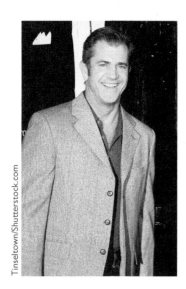

An amusing counterpart to my initial bias about Chinese faces was the Chinese bias toward Americans. My American colleagues who were male would laugh about how Chinese people would tell them they looked just like Mel Gibson. Men who were half Mel Gibson's age, had blond hair, or were short and stocky … all looked like Mel Gibson to the Chinese people they ran into on the street.

Perceiving out-group members as looking alike, as I did with my Chinese students, has also been attested in research. In one early study (Taylor, Fiske, Etcoff, & Ruderman, 1978), for instance, participants were part of a discussion that included in-group and out-group members. After the discussion, participants were asked to recall who said what. They generally remembered their in-group members' comments better, and, importantly, they had trouble remembering which out-group member said what. They could recall that *someone* in the out-group said the comment, but not exactly who it was. It was as though the out-group members all blended together. Obviously, this perception of out-group members as looking alike can have important consequences for eye-witness accounts or even identifying a suspect from a line-up.

Inferences About Out-Groups

Patricia Linville and her colleagues (1989) report several experiments demonstrating how inferences can be made on the basis of out-group homogeneity bias. In the experiments, participants rated their in-group and an out-group on personal characteristics, such as friendliness. They had to indicate what percentage of people were, for example, very friendly, somewhat friendly, and somewhat unfriendly, making sure that the percentages totaled 100. In one experiment comparing college students and senior citizens, results showed strong out-group homogeneity bias, with both groups assuming that members of the other age group had similar personality traits, but members of their own group were quite diverse. However, another experiment comparing males and females did not show this same effect.

The authors suggest that the experiment comparing males and females demonstrates how the more familiar someone is with members of an out-group, the less likely the person is to assume that the out-group members share similar characteristics (Linville et al., 1989). In contrast, the experiment comparing college students and senior citizens indicates that less familiarity leads to stronger assumptions of homogeneity within the out-group.

Ultimate Attribution Error

In addition to assuming out-group members share similar personal characteristics, out-group homogeneity bias has another effect. People tend to assume that negative behavior of an out-group member reflects the behavior typical of all members. For instance, if you see a football player at your college litter, you might think to yourself, "Ugh. How typical of football players. They litter and don't clean up after themselves." However, if you are on the softball team and you see one of your teammates litter, you might be more inclined to either dismiss the littering as "something only Kris would do," or to give your teammate the benefit of the doubt: "I bet she didn't even realize that candy wrapper dropped." You may recall learning about the **ultimate attribution error** (Pettigrew, 1979) in Chapter 3. When applied to prejudice attributions, the ultimate attribution error is the tendency to give in-group, but not out-group, members the benefit of the doubt when they do something negative.

As Pettigrew (1979) notes, the ultimate attribution error tends to occur when someone from a high-status group is judging the behavior of someone from an out-group, but not as much when someone from a low-status group is judging out-group members. But Pettigrew is quick to add that the ultimate attribution error is in no way limited to high-status groups, such as those who are wealthy, well-educated, or male, but probably occurs most when there is strong identification with an in-group and clear differentiation from out-groups.

Illusory Correlations

Another phenomenon that can influence our social judgments is illusory correlation. An **illusory correlation** is the assumption that a relationship exists between two variables, even though there is no statistical evidence to support that relationship (Spears, Eiser, & Van Der Pligt, 1987). If you have taken a statistics class, perhaps you remember that a correlation is a statistical analysis that shows a relationship between two variables. For instance, a person's shoe size and foot size are related: People with bigger feet wear bigger shoes. In contrast to valid correlations, illusory correlations may seem true, but they are not.

One commonly held illusory correlation is that Emergency Room (ER) visits increase during a full moon. Ask any ER nurse or doctor and he or she will swear that the ER is always busier the night of a full moon. Despite the pop-

Zacarias Pereira da Mata/Shutterstock.com

ularity of the myth that the ER is busier during a full moon, research shows that there is no correlation. A study published in the *American Journal of Emergency Medicine* looked at 150,999 records of ER admissions and found no significant difference between full moon nights versus other nights (Thompson & Adams, 1996).

If full moons do not actually correspond to busier nights, why do health professionals believe this illusory correlation? It may have to do with the fact that full moons are relatively rare events, occurring only once a month, and that makes them distinctive. If a nurse has worked a chaotic and busy night and then realizes there is a full moon, he or she is likely to see a relationship between the distinctive state of the moon and his or her crazy night. Even though health professionals have probably had busy nights when the moon is not full, humans are inclined to look for connections.

Another common illusory correlation is that flying is more dangerous than driving. In fact, flying is much safer than driving. In 2008, the National Highway Traffic Safety Administration compiled statistics across the country for vehicle and air traffic accidents and fatalities. There were 5 million accidents involving vehicles and only 20 accidents involving air travel, with no fatalities for air travel. The odds of dying in a car accident are 1 in 98 in a lifetime. The odds of dying in a plane crash are 1 in 7,178 (Locsin, 2014).

Ultimate Attribution Error
The tendency to give in-group, but not out-group, members the benefit of the doubt when they do something negative.

Illusory Correlation
The assumption that a relationship exists between two variables, even though there is no statistical evidence to support that relationship.

Despite these data, many people still refuse to fly. One reason may be the lack of control you have when flying. In a plane, you give all control over to a pilot, whom most of the time you never even see, and fly over 30,000 feet in the air. In a car, you are on the ground and you have control or know the person in control. You can also see what's in front of you.

Beyond these concerns about control is, again, the issue of distinctiveness. When a plane does crash, it is catastrophic. Falling 30,000 feet usually results in death. Very few people survive a plane crash, but how many people do you know who have walked away from a car wreck? When a plane crashes, it is all over the news and we are often bombarded with images of burning wreckage and grieving families. Most car wrecks, unless they are local or 30 car pile-ups, rarely make the evening news. Ironically, the very thing that reflects how safe flying is, the infrequency of plane crashes, contributes to the illusory correlation that flying is unsafe. We notice and remember plane crashes because they are rare.

Being biased against full moons or airplanes is one thing, but illusory correlations can also contribute to stereotypes and biases against groups of people (e.g., Risen, Gilovich, & Dunning, 2007). Out-groups, particularly if they are minorities, tend to be distinctive because they are encountered fairly infrequently. Negative behavior also tends to be distinctive because it generally occurs less frequently than positive behavior. When these two distinctive things are paired, people are more likely to notice them and overestimate how frequently they occur together. Like the ER nurse who swears the hospital is busier on full moons, people may be convinced that women talk more than men or that teenagers are lazy, but these stereotypes are based on illusory correlations.

Stereotype Threat

To this point, we have considered how being part of an in-group influences our interactions with others. In this section about stereotype threat, the focus shifts to how identifying with an in-group can influence our own individual performance on a task. To begin, there are obvious disparities in achievement between various groups in our society. As Inzlicht and Schmander (2012) note, there is a large gap between men and women's performance on the math section of college entrance tests like the Scholastic Achievement Test (SAT), for example, and men are over-represented in the fields of science, technology, math, and engineering. Also, at all age levels, Latinos and Blacks are behind Whites on standardized measures of math and reading. These sorts of achievement and socioeconomic gaps are not unique to the United States, and similar gaps occur across the globe.

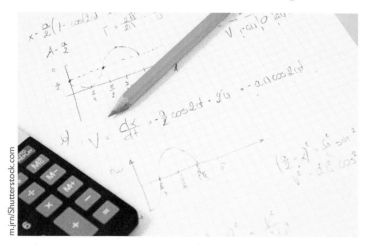

Explanations for why these differences exist have tended to blame either genetics (nature) or society (nurture). In terms of genetics, an explanation for the gender-based math achievement gap would be along the lines that women's brains just are not as good at math as men's brains. According to a society-based reason, this gap would be seen as a product of women's environment and how parents and teachers, perhaps unwittingly, might discourage their interest in math. What both types of explanations share, as

Inzlicht and Schmader (2012) point out, is (a) an assumption that the poorer performing groups lack the potential to achieve the same degree of success as the better performing groups because of either genetic differences or societal pressures and (b) a belief that scores on standardized tests fairly and accurately reflect a person's true ability.

Research on stereotype threat has given us a different way to examine these types of disparities. **Stereotype threat** is a situational predicament in which a person is "at risk of confirming, as self-characteristic, a negative stereotype about one's group" (Steele & Aronson, 1995, p. 797). To return to the math example, stereotype threat occurs when a woman sits down to take the math section of the SAT: She knows that the test is measuring her math ability, and she may fear confirming the stereotype that women are not good at math. That fear can, in turn, disrupt her cognitive performance, and the result is a lower test score.

Does stereotype threat sound far-fetched? Who believes in all those short-sighted stereotypes, anyway? And even if you thought you were not so great at math because you were a girl, that would not actually *lower* your performance below what you might otherwise have achieved, right?

Wrong. A couple of decades of research on stereotype threat have shown that stereotype threat is real, and it really does affect people from children to the elderly, males, females, and various ethnic groups, in a wide variety of performance situations. For instance, researchers have found that stereotype threat contributes to low performance among Blacks, Latinos, women, the elderly, and even White males in domains ranging from academic performance to athletic ability to driving (Inzlicht & Schmader, 2012). From the hundreds of studies on stereotype threat, we will consider just a few. These examples allow us not only to understand the methodology behind research on stereotype threat but also to clarify when and how stereotype threat occurs.

Stereotype Threat

When a person is at risk of confirming a negative stereotype about his or her group; the person may or may not feel the "threat," but their performance reflects the threat because it is lower than it would otherwise be.

Seminal Study: Steele and Aronson (1995)

Claude Steele and Joshua Aronson's (1995) seminal study introduced the concept of stereotype threat. They hypothesized that whenever Black students perform an intellectual task, they confront the threat of being judged by the negative stereotype about their group's intellectual abilities. This threat could interfere with their performance. To investigate this hypothesis, Steele and Aronson designed several experiments in which White and Black participants completed a verbal test taken from the Graduate Record Examination (GRE), as well as other questionnaires about their perceived performance, feelings of self-worth, and demographic information.

Lisa F. Young/Shutterstock.com

One independent variable Steele and Aronson (1995) manipulated was the instructions they gave participants. In the diagnostic condition, groups were told that the test would measure their verbal abilities, and they could receive feedback about their strengths and weaknesses after completing the study. This condition was intended to establish a testing situation similar to that faced during standardized testing of academic abilities; a situation in which participants might be judged by the negative intellectual stereotype about blacks. In the nondiagnostic condition, groups were told the test did not measure ability, and the study was about psychological or cognitive processes. The nondiagnostic condition was intended to minimize the idea that participants were taking a "test," and to avoid the pressure associated with having one's abilities assessed.

Steele and Aronson (1995) found that Black participants in the diagnostic condition performed worse than Black participants in the nondiagnostic condition and worse than White participants in either condition. White participants' performance was not affected by condition. In other words, when Black participants were put in a testing situation that purportedly measured their abilities, their performance suffered.

In a final experiment, Steele and Aronson (1995) gave everyone the same set of instructions, but varied whether participants had to report their race on a questionnaire they filled out before taking the test. Although the instructions did not mention anything about ability, merely having participants report their race affected the Black participants' performance: Black participants who reported their race performed significantly worse than Black participants who did not report their race, and worse than White participants who did report their race. Apparently reminding participants of their race, by having them indicate it on the questionnaire, was enough to trigger the stereotype of poor intellectual abilities for the Black participants, and their performance declined.

This initial study by Steele and Aronson (1995) established that a group's performance could be negatively affected by either the situation (describing the task as a test that measures ability) or by reporting one's race (a reminder of one's in-group). It is important to note that, in all cases, the test was the same and the groups were randomly assigned, so differences in performance were not due to differences in ability or test difficulty, but rather to stereotype threat. These results are summarized in Figure 10.5.

Conditions	Race	Results	Did stereotype threat occur?
Diagnostic (groups were told the test measured ability) vs. **Nondiagnostic** (groups were told the test did NOT measure ability)	Blacks	Blacks in the diagnostic condition performed worse than Blacks in the nondiagnostic condition, and worse than Whites in either condition.	Yes
	Whites	Whites performed similarly, regardless of condition.	No
Reported race (questionnaire required participants to indicate their race) vs. **Did not report race** (questionnaire did not ask about participants' race)	Blacks	Blacks who reported their race performed worse than Blacks who did not report their race and worse than Whites who did report race.	Yes
	Whites	Whites performed similarly, regardless of condition.	No

Figure 10.5. Summary of the results from Steele and Aronson's (1995) study.

Children and Math Ability

When Steele and Aronson (1995) first proposed the concept of stereotype threat, they assumed that individuals affected by stereotype threat would not only be aware of a particular stereotype about their group, but would also believe it to some extent, at least unconsciously. However, recent research suggests that even when people do not endorse the stereotype, it can still affect their performance. For instance, Galdi, Cadinu, and Tomasetto (2014) point out how research has indicated that young girls appear to be influenced by a math-gender stereotype threat, even when they show no awareness of the math-gender stereotype and do not personally believe girls are bad at math. Like these researchers, you may be wondering, "How could that possibly be? If a girl thinks that boys and girls are equal at math, and does not seem aware that others believe boys are better, why would that girl face stereotype threat?"

Galdi et al. (2014) suggest that the answer may lie in implicit associations, such as those measured with the IAT (which was introduced in Chapter 6 and discussed earlier in this chapter). They used a version of the IAT designed for children in their study and found that 6-year-old girls (but not 6-year-old boys) showed automatic associations between *girl* and *language*, and *boy* and *mathematics*, consistent with the math-gender stereotype. Importantly, however, when explicitly asked whether a boy or a girl is better at math, girls did not endorse the math-gender stereotype. Boys and girls both favored their own gender, with 57% of each gender claiming that their own gender was the one superior at math. The rest of the children either thought both genders were equal or that the opposite gender was better at math. But, only 22% of girls thought boys were better, compared to 31% of boys who thought girls were better.

Before the children took a math test, Galdi et al. (2014) had them color a picture which, depending on the condition, was designed to either prompt stereotype threat or not. In the stereotype-consistent condition, the picture was of a boy correctly solving a math problem on a blackboard while a girl fails to respond. In the stereotype-inconsistent condition, the picture showed the girl correctly solving the problem while the boy does not respond. A control condition had a picture of a landscape.

Results showed that girls in the stereotype-consistent condition performed worse than girls in the stereotype-inconsistent condition; boys performed similarly across conditions. In other words, girls showed the typical decrease in performance due to stereotype threat, despite their lack of conscious endorsement of that stereotype. Galdi et al. (2014) conclude that the implicit associations of the girls must be the source of their stereotype threat. One final thing Galdi et al.'s study demonstrates is how stereotype threat can be triggered by reminding participants of the content of the negative stereotype, in this case, coloring a picture of a boy succeeding at math while a girl does not.

Older People and Driving

Stereotype threat is not just something that affects people in academic settings, as Joanisse, Gagnon, and Voloaca's (2013) study of older drivers attests. They looked

at the simulated driving performance of participants who were over 65 years old, splitting participants into two conditions. In the stereotype threat condition, they reminded participants of the negative stereotype about older drivers by indicating that the study was investigating why older adults were at fault in more on-road accidents. In the control condition, participants were told the study was about the underlying processes involved in driving.

Joanisse et al. (2013) found that participants in the stereotype threat condition made more mistakes driving than those in the control condition, the most common of which was, interestingly, speeding. However, they were not more likely to have a car crash. These effects were found only for the participants who identified driving as "extremely important" in their life; participants who placed less importance on driving did not show increased mistakes in the stereotype threat condition.

In discussing their results, Joanisse et al. (2013) point out the serious implications that stereotype threat can have for older drivers. Reminders of the negative view of older drivers come from the media, such as news stories that demean older drivers, and even from governmental policies, such as requirements that people past a certain age take a driving test, regardless of their driving record. These reminders can negatively influence older drivers' performance, to the detriment of us all.

Reducing Stereotype Threat

The good news of stereotype research is that, just as it can be induced by reminding people of negative stereotypes about their in-group (see Figure 10.6 for a summary of the research), it can also be reduced or eliminated. In one study (McGlone & Aronson, 2006), for example, when women were reminded that they were female, their performance on a math test suffered, but when they were reminded that they were students at a private school, their performance was much

Methods	Examples
Describe the task as a test of the ability related to the negative in-group stereotype.	▪ Steele and Aronson's (1995) instructions that the test measured participants' verbal abilities.
Make the in-group identity salient.	▪ Steele and Aronson's (1995) questionnaire asking participants to identify their race.
Make the content of the negative stereotype salient.	▪ Galdi et al.'s (2014) task of coloring a picture depicting a boy solving a math problem while a girl did not respond.
	▪ Joanisse et al.'s (2013) description of their study as investigating why older drivers are at fault in more accidents.

Figure 10.6.   Methods of inducing stereotype threat.

better. These results suggest that because we all belong to many social groups, one way to counteract stereotype threat is to keep in mind our membership in groups that have neutral or positive stereotypes related to the task at hand.

Other research, such as that of Danaher and Crandall (2008), indicates that simply asking demographic questions about race and gender after the test, instead of before it, can reduce stereotype threat. Danaher and Crandall go as far as suggesting that if the Educational Testing Service changed their testing procedure and asked for demographic information after their tests, almost 5,000 additional female students would receive AP credit in calculus each year.

What Can We Do About Prejudice?

We have shared a lot of information about prejudice, most of which suggests that it is a very natural behavior that any individual is susceptible to. So what does that mean for ourselves and our society? It does not mean that humans are not responsible for their behaviors nor does it justify any discrimination or violence toward those who are different than us. What it does is give us an understanding of why we do what we do, and with that understanding we can find solutions to the problem.

The American Psychological Association (APA, 2012) published the report *Dual Pathways to a Better America: Preventing Discrimination and Promoting Diversity*. In the report, one strategy suggested is education. The APA proposes multicultural and diversity education begin as early as preschool. They recommend creating a standard curriculum that "includes case vignettes" and "exercises to demonstrate the biasing effects" (p. 74). This curriculum should be made available to all teachers and college professors. A national networking linkage for teachers to share ideas and activities they have used in their classroom should be created. Additionally, the APA feels that creating interactive web-based trainings could be another way to encourage young children to learn about prejudice and diversity.

Using education to overcome prejudice is not a new concept. During the civil rights movement, Martin Luther King Jr., made the same plea to social scientists at the 1967 APA annual convention. In his speech he stated:

> *All too many White Americans are horrified not with conditions of Negro life but with the product of these conditions—the Negro himself …. White America has an appalling lack of knowledge concerning the reality of Negro life. One reason some advances were made in the South during the past decade was the discovery by northern whites of the brutal facts of southern segregated life. (King, 1967, paras. 4 & 6)*

As King's statement implies, a key piece of educating people about prejudice is empathy. Learning dry facts or abstract ideas about prejudice is not enough. To truly understand the nature of prejudice and to be inspired to reduce our own prejudices, we need to know what it feels like to be the object of prejudice.

Reducing Prejudice Through Empathy

One school teacher, Jane Elliott, took it upon herself to do exactly that: show her students what it felt like to be discriminated against. Elliot was a third-grade teacher in Iowa during the civil rights movement. Her students were all White, and after the assassination of Martin Luther King, Jr., she wanted her students to learn about prejudice.

The statue memorial for Martin Luther King Jr. in West Potomac Park, Washington, DC.

Elliott began class the Friday after King's assassination by dividing the students into groups based on their eye color: brown-eyed, green-eyed, and blue-eyed students (Bloom, 2005). She made the blue-eyed students wear green arm bands to distinguish them from the other students. She then proceeded to tell the students that the brown-eyed people in the room were better, cleaner, and smarter. As she explained the link between brown eyes and intelligence, pointing out that blue-eyed people were lazy and wrecked nice things, "she could feel a chasm forming between the two groups of students" (p. 1). Elliott then set separate rules for the students, giving the brown-eyed students more privileges and the blue-eyed students more restrictions. Almost instantly students gave in to their prejudices against each other and also toward themselves. Previously confident, well-performing blue-eyed students started to question their abilities.

The following Monday, Elliott reversed the exercise, making the blue-eyed students the superior group. Interestingly, she found the blue-eyed students' discrimination was less nasty toward the brown-eyed students, perhaps because they knew what it meant to be discriminated against? Elliot was "dumbfounded" at

Jane Elliott.

http://www.corbisimages.com/stock-photo/rights-managed/42-15947805/former-school-teacher-jane-elliott?popup=1

the effectiveness of the exercise, which she thought had served its purpose of allowing students who had never experienced prejudice to understand what it felt like to be discriminated against (Bloom, 2005, p. 2). The exercise made for a couple of traumatic days in the classroom, but afterward, students had a different perspective on racism, and some, years later, would say with gratitude that it had changed their lives.

Elliott's landmark exercise made her famous, even landing her a spot on "The Tonight Show" with Johnny Carson. But not everyone was enthusiastic about her experiment. In fact, hundreds of "Tonight Show" viewers sent letters saying that they were appalled by her work, and some of her fellow teachers gave her the cold shoulder (Bloom, 2005). Despite the backlash, Elliott continued to teach and to carry out her exercise every year for almost two decades until she left teaching to share her experience and knowledge nationally.

People continue to disagree about the appropriateness and effectiveness of Elliott's exercise (e.g., Bloom, 2005; Diversity Gains, 2010; Stewart, Laduke, Bracht, Sweet, & Gamarel, 2003), but what is becoming more clear from research is that exercises inviting empathy with an out-group can be very effective in reducing prejudice (e.g., Dovidio et al., 2004; Todd, Bodenhausen, & Galinsky, 2012). For example, watching a video in which racial discrimination occurred did not, on its own, reduce prejudice; however, when participants were instructed to imagine the victim's feelings, their prejudice was significantly reduced (Dovidio et al., 2004). This type of activity, which relies on participants' imagining the victim's perspective, is less invasive and traumatic than Elliott's exercise, and therefore not ethically objectionable. Thus, it is encouraging that simply imagining what it feels like to be discriminated against can be an effective way of reducing prejudice.

Reducing Prejudice Through Contact

Another way to reduce prejudice is through contact. As we have seen, issues like out-group homogeneity bias are more severe when people are less familiar with an out-group, so it seems intuitively obvious that connecting people from different groups would lessen prejudice. However, as Allport (1954) observed early on, it is not as simple as throwing two groups of people together: People need to experience the right sort of contact in order for that contact to be a positive encounter that reduces prejudice. Allport explains that the principle characteristics of positive contact are

a) Equal status between groups
b) Pursuit of common goals
c) Perception of a common humanity (so people get to know each other as people)
d) Institutional support (such as laws, customs, or an environment that supports the contact)

Research has confirmed Allport's observations. In the decades since Allport laid out these characteristics, hundreds of studies have consistently shown that the more closely the contact between groups follows Allport's conditions, the more effectively it reduces prejudice (Pettigrew & Tropp, 2006).

Travel is fatal to prejudice, bigotry, and narrow-mindedness, and many of our people need it sorely on these accounts. Broad, wholesome, charitable views of men and things cannot be acquired by vegetating in one little corner of the earth all one's lifetime.

Mark Twain (a.k.a. Samuel Clemens)

Clemens, 2008, p. 650

The Robbers Cave Study One classic example of how Allport's (1954) characteristics can be seen in a contact situation is the Robbers Cave study by Muzafer Sherif and his colleagues (Sherif, M., Harvey, White, Hood, Sherif, C. W., 1954/1961). Sherif et al. invited 22 fifth-grade boys to participate in a two-week summer camp. The campers were randomly separated into two groups, the Eagles and the Rattlers, and at first each group did not know of the other's existence. Once they learned of the other group, prejudice began to form. This prejudice was strengthened by competitions between the two groups, such as tug-of-war and contests to see who could pitch a tent the fastest. By the beginning of the second week of camp, the campers in both groups were quite hostile toward out-group members: calling them by derogatory names, refusing to sit near them at meal times, and stealing from them.

During the second week of camp, the Eagles and Rattlers were given the opportunity to have contact with the other group in noncompetitive situations, such as waiting in line for dinner and shooting off firecrackers. Yet, the rivalry and prejudice continued unabated until Sherif et al. (1954/1961) introduced several challenges that required the cooperation of both groups in order to be solved. First, the camp counselors announced that there was something wrong with the camp's water supply. Both groups had to search for leaks, eventually ending up together at the main water tank, where they found and repaired the problem. Other challenges involved a truck that was apparently having engine trouble and would not start, and pooling money to get a movie to watch. After solving a number of problems together, the hostility of the two groups diminished, so that by the last day of camp, no trace of it remained.

The Robbers Cave study (Sherif et al., 1954/1961) provides evidence that equality between two groups, institutional support for friendliness, and opportunities to get to know out-group members as people—three of Allport's (1954) four characteristics—are not enough to produce positive interactions between groups that have a strong negative prejudice against each other. A key element for group contact that reduces prejudice is pursuit of common goals. Working together to accomplish a task almost inevitably breaks down barriers and brings people together, especially if Allport's other three characteristics are already in place.

The Jigsaw Method Elliot Aronson (2012) describes how this sort of collaboration can take place in a classroom. In the 1970s, Aronson and several colleagues developed the **jigsaw method** of teaching. They developed this method to alleviate racial tensions and competitiveness in a school district that had recently been desegregated, and they found that the positive effects of the jigsaw method reached far beyond the classroom walls.

In the jigsaw method, students are divided into groups. Each member of the group has a different piece of information that is needed to accomplish a task, so collaboration with group members becomes essential. Aronson (2012) gives an example of a jigsaw task that involved learning facts about Joseph Pulitzer for an upcoming test. Each student in a six-person learning group was given a different paragraph about Pulitzer's life. The students had to share their information with

Jigsaw Method
Dividing students into groups in which each person must share his or her piece of information in order for everyone in the group to have the complete information they need; this method encourages collaboration.

THINKING CRITICALLY (C)

Look again at the quotes (all of which were retrieved from www.brainyquote.com) that were presented at the beginning of the chapter; by applying what you learned in this chapter, can you identify what is wrong with them?

1. Prejudice is a learned trait. You're not born prejudiced; you're taught it.
   ~ Charles R. Swindoll

2. The less secure a man is, the more likely he is to have extreme prejudice.
   ~ Clint Eastwood

3. If people are informed they will do the right thing. It's when they are not informed that they become hostages to prejudice.
   ~ Charlayne Hunter-Gault

   See the end of the chapter for sample answers.

their groups, and, importantly, they had to listen carefully while group members shared what they knew. The students soon realized that it was more effective to encourage and help students who were having trouble communicating than it was to ridicule or dismiss them. After all, they needed to know that information for the test.

As research on reducing prejudice has shown, education, empathy, contact, and collaboration all have a role in decreasing prejudice and promoting the kind of society where different groups can live, work, and play together, to everyone's benefit.

Conclusion

This chapter began by defining prejudice, stereotype, and discrimination, describing how the three terms are related to each other and how stereotypes and discrimination can be considered cognitive and behavioral aspects of prejudice, respectively. Because people are often reluctant to admit their negative biases and because prejudice may be implicit, researching prejudice is challenging. To get accurate information about people's prejudices, researchers often evaluate self-reported information in light of participants' behaviors or the results of implicit tests of prejudice, such as the IAT.

Prejudice is not so much something that children are taught (nurture) as it is a natural byproduct of the way the brain categorizes the world and the way the evolutionary drive to survive leads us to favor our in-group (nature). Terror Management Theory explains hostility and violence toward out-group members in terms of fear: When we feel threatened, we are more likely to cling to our worldview and lash out at those who do not share it.

Categorizing people into in-groups and out-groups influences our perceptions and judgments. Out-group homogeneity bias leads us to see out-group members as perceptually similar, to assume that they share the same characteristics, and to make the ultimate attribution error of thinking that the negative behavior of one member is representative of how all members act. Furthermore, illusory correlations can make it seem that negative behaviors occur more frequently with minority groups, leading to stereotypes about those groups. We ourselves are not immune to the stereotypes about our in-group. Whether we believe them or not, being reminded of these stereotypes can affect our performance, as research on stereotype threat shows.

Although prejudice is a natural consequence of our human nature, that does not absolve us from responsibility for our own biases or mean we are helpless to confront and change them. Being in situations, real or imagined, in which we empathize with the targets of prejudice and discrimination reduces our own prejudice. Also, working with out-groups and getting to know their members as people can eliminate prejudice on both sides.

Thinking Critically Answers

Thinking Critically (A)

1. Regardless of whether you agree with your results or not, think about *why* you agree or disagree. Are you annoyed that your results show an implicit bias, although you strive to be unprejudiced and think of yourself as a fair person? Are you secretly pleased that you "passed" the test and your implicit associations indicate that you are a good person without prejudice? Consider also not just how you *want* to act, but how you really feel around others who are different from yourself. Do you feel a bit like an outsider? Slightly uncomfortable? Completely at ease? How you feel may be based on implicit associations.

2. If you were unsuccessful in your attempt to fake the Race IAT, check out the tips that Fiedler and Bluemke (2005) gave their participants on how to change their results. A version of their paper is available at http://faculty.washington.edu/agg/IATmaterials/PDFs/Fiedler%26Bluemke.BASP(in%20press).pdf. Then try again and see if you, too, can fake your results, keeping in mind what scores might give away your faking.

3. In thinking about insights from this exercise, consider not just who you want to be, but also the social environment you were raised in, as well as the environment you are in now. If your home neighborhood was racially and culturally diverse, you probably have fewer racial implicit biases simply because you have been exposed to a wide range of people, good and bad, from a wide range of groups (see the section on "How categorization influences our perceptions and judgments," this chapter). On the other hand, if your experience of other races or cultures has come primarily from the media, you may have stronger implicit biases.

Thinking Critically (B)

1. The Black community in Baltimore. More specifically lower class Blacks.
2. Caucasian police force/local government/city officials.
3. According to TMT when an in-group's survival is threatened they will engage in "worldview bolstering" and out-group discrimination. The quote by Reverend Delman Coates suggests that the Black population of Baltimore does feel like their in-group's survival is threatened. Lack of jobs, education, and healthcare are all threats to survival in our society. After the death of Freddie Gray, they may feel like they are all at risk of being harmed by the out-group, making their mortality very much a salient threat. Their protests and signage "BLACK LIVES MATTER" would fall under the behavior of "worldview bolstering." Violence toward the police and city officials would be out-group discrimination.

Thinking Critically (C)

Suggested answers are below, but they are starting points for discussion rather than the final critique of the quotes.

1. Actually, people are born with an innate drive to categorize, and this leads to prejudice and discrimination even in very young babies, who cannot have been "taught" those behaviors.

2. Identification with an in-group has more to do with a person's prejudices than feeling secure. When people have a strong identification with an in-group, they are more likely to show out-group homogeneity bias and to have illusory correlations that lead to negative prejudices about out-groups. In terms of Terror Management Theory, fearing death and feeling our survival is threatened can lead to clinging to our beliefs and to discrimination, so to a certain extent Clint Eastwood has a point.

3. Just learning about prejudice is not enough. We have to actually experience positive contact with out-groups and/or empathize with what is like to be in a negatively impacted group.

Additional Resources

Topics Not Addressed in the Chapter

Gender prejudices in higher education:

- If you'd like to know how male professors are rated more positively that female professors on everything from intelligence to personality, check out this website: http://benschmidt.org/profGender/. It gives an interactive chart based on RateMyProfessor.com that represents how many times a word, such as "smart" or "disorganized," is used to describe male and female professors.
- For a more scholarly approach to the same topic, see the article: MacNell, L., Driscoll, A., & Hunt, A. N. (2015). What's in a name: Exposing gender bias in student ratings of teaching. *Innovative Higher Education, 40*, 291–303. doi:10.1007/s10755-014-9313-4

Historical perspectives on racial prejudice:

- This book explains how the initial encounters between Blacks and Whites in the ancient world were contacts between equals: Snowden, F. M., Jr. (1991). *Before color prejudice: The ancient view of Blacks.* Cambridge, MA: Harvard University Press.
- To learn how American and Japanese stereotypes about each other have changed over the years, see this article: Weisman, S. R. (1991, October 19). Japanese coin word for their unease about U.S. *The New York Times.* Retrieved from http://www.nytimes.com

The relationship of personality and prejudice:

- A book that looks at how the authoritarian personality is related to prejudice is: Adorno, T. W., Frenkel-Brunswik, E., Levison, D. J., & Sandord, R. N. (1950). *The authoritarian personality.* New York: Harper. Available online at the American Jewish Committee Archives: http://www.ajcarchives.org
- This article evaluates the relationship between Big Five personality dimensions and prejudice: Ekehammar, B., & Akrami, N. (2003). The relation between personality and prejudice: A variable- and person-centered approach. *European Journal of Personality, 17*, 449–464. doi:10.1002/per.494

Topics Addressed in the Chapter

Implicit biases:

- The *What Would You Do?* bike thief video is available at http://www.you-tube.com/watch?v=8ABRlWybBqM
- A discussion of conscious and unconscious mental processes and how they can influence people is found in the article: Uhlmann, E. L., Pizarro, D. A., & Bloom, P. (2008). Varieties of social cognition. *Journal for the Theory of Social Behavior, 38,* 293–322. doi:10.1111/j.1468-5914.2008.00372.x

Babies and categorization:

- Paul Bloom and Karen Wynn discuss their research with Lesley Stahl in this section of *60 Minutes*: http://www.cbsnews.com/news/babies-help-unlock-the-origins-of-morality/
- Paul Bloom summarizes the findings about babies' judgments of right and wrong in this article with embedded video footage of one experiment: http://www.cnn.com/2014/02/12/opinion/bloom-babies-right-wrong/index.html?hpt=hp_t4

Terror Management Theory:

- Landau, M. J., Greenberg, J., & Sullivan, D. (2009). Managing terror when self-worth and worldviews collide: Evidence that mortality salience increases reluctance to self-enhance beyond authorities. *Journal of Experimental Social Psychology, 45,* 68–79. doi:10.1016/j.jesp.2008.08.007
- Das, E., Bushman, B. J., Bezemer, M. D., Kerkhof, P., & Vermeulen, I. E. (2009). How terrorism news reports increase prejudice against outgroups: A terror management account. *Journal of Experimental Social Psychology, 45,* 453–459. doi:10.1016/j.jesp.2008.12.001

Stereotype threat:

- This episode of "Stossel in the Classroom," a section of ABC's *20/20* show, discusses stereotype threat in academic and athletic domains, and explores how Jane Elliott's work also demonstrated stereotype threat: https://www.youtube.com/watch?v=ASDzcvyatgw
- The website http://www.reducingstereotypethreat.org contains a wealth of information about stereotype threat, including ways of reducing or eliminating it.

Resources related to Jane Elliott's work:

- This Frontline show, "A Class Divided," gives footage from one of Jane Elliott's third-grade classes experiencing her brown-eyed versus blue-eyed demonstration, as well as comments of class members 14 years later, and footage from Elliott's workshops with adults: http://www.pbs.org/wgbh/pages/frontline/shows/divided/etc/view.html
- One scholarly evaluation of Elliott's work is: Stewart, T. L., Laduke, J. R., Bracht, C., Sweet, B. M., & Gamarel, K. E. (2003). Do the "eyes" have it? A program evaluation of Jane Elliott's "Blue-Eyes/Brown-Eyes" diversity training exercise. *Journal of Applied Social Psychology, 33,* 1898–1921. doi:10.1111/j.1559-1816.2003.tb02086.x

References

Allport, G. W. (1954). *The nature of prejudice*. Cambridge, MA: Addison-Wesley.

American Psychological Association (APA). (2012). *Dual pathways to a better America: Preventing discrimination and promoting diversity*. Retrieved from http://www.apa.org/pubs/info/reports/promoting-diversity.aspx

Aronson, E. (2012). *The social animal* (11th ed.). New York, NY: Worth.

Becker, E. (1971). *The birth and death of meaning: An interdisciplinary perspective on the problem of man* (2nd ed.). New York, NY: Free Press.

Blanton, H., & Mitchell, G. (2011). Reassessing the predictive validity of the IAT II: Reanalysis of Heider & Skowronski (2007). *North American Journal of Psychology, 13*, 99–106. Retrieved from http://ssrn.com/abstract=2558807

Bloom, P. (2013). *Just babies: The origins of good and evil*. New York, NY: Crown.

Bloom, S. (2005, September 1). Lesson of a lifetime. *Smithsonian Magazine*. Retrieved from http://www.smithsonianmag.com

Clemens, S. (2008). *The innocents abroad or, The new pilgrim's progress* (Illustrated ed.). Scituate, MA: Velvet Element Books.

Cvencek, D., Greenwald, A. G., Brown, A. S., Gray, N. S., & Snowden, R. J. (2010). Faking of the Implicit Association Test is statistically detectable and partly correctable. *Basic and Applied Social Psychology, 32*, 302–314. doi:10.1080/01973533.2010.519236

Danaher, K., & Crandall, C. S. (2008). Stereotype threat in applied settings re-examined. *Journal of Applied Social Psychology, 38*, 1639–1655. doi:10.1111/j.1559-1816.2008.00362.x

Darwin, C. (1896). *The origin of species by means of natural selection or the preservation of favored races in the struggle for life, with additions and corrections from the sixth and last English edition, in two volumes*. Retrieved from http://oll.libertyfund.org/titles/2185

Defense of Marriage Act of 1996, 1 U.S.C. § 7 and 28 U.S.C. § 1738C (1996).

Diversity Gains. (2010). *Diversity training: Learning from failure to succeed in the future*. Retrieved from http://www.diversitygains.com/DiversityGains/home.aspx

Dovidio, J. F., & Gaertner, S. L. (2000). Aversive racism and selection decisions: 1989 and 1999. *Psychological Science, 11*, 315–319.

Dovidio, J., Hewstone, M., Glick, P., & Esses, V. (2010). Prejudice, stereotyping and discrimination: Theoretical and empirical overview. In J. Dovidio, M. Hewstone, P. Glick, & V. Esses (Eds.), *The SAGE handbook of prejudice, stereotyping and discrimination* (pp. 3-29). London, England: Sage. doi:http://dx.doi.org/10.4135/9781446200919.n1

Dovidio, J. F., ten Vergert, M., Stewart, T. L., Gaertner, S. L., Johnson, J. D., Esses, V. M., ... Pearson, A. R. (2004). Perspective and prejudice: Antecedents and mediating mechanisms. *Personality and Social Psychology Bulletin, 30*, 1537–1549. doi:10.1177/0146167204271177

Fiedler, K., & Bluemke, M. (2005). Faking the IAT: Aided and unaided response control on the Implicit Association Tests. *Basic and Applied Social Psychology, 27*, 307–316. doi:10.1207/s15324834basp2704_3

Fiske, S. T. (1998). Stereotyping, prejudice, and discrimination. In D. T. Gilbert, S. T. Fiske, & G. Lindzey (Eds.), *Handbook of social psychology* (4th ed., Vol. 2, pp. 357–411). New York, NY: McGraw-Hill.

Galdi, S., Cadinu, M., & Tomasetto, C. (2014). The roots of stereotype threat: When automatic associations disrupt girls' math performance. *Child Development, 85*, 250–263. doi:10.1111/cdev.12128

Graham, D. (2015, April 22). The mysterious death of Freddie Gray. *The Atlantic*. Retrieved from http://www.theatlantic.com

Greenberg, J., & Arndt, J. (2012). Terror management theory. In P. M. Van Lange, A. W. Kruglanski, E. T. Higgins (Eds.), *Handbook of theories of social psychology* (Vol. 1, pp. 398–415). Thousand Oaks, CA: Sage.

Greenwald, A. G., Poehlman, T. A., Uhlmann, E. L., & Banaji, M. R. (2009). Understanding and using the Implicit Association Test: III. Meta-analysis of predictive validity. *Journal of Personality and Social Psychology, 97*, 17–41. doi:10.1037/a0015575

Greenwald, A. G., McGhee, D. E., & Schwartz, J. L. K. (1998). Measuring individual differences in implicit cognition: The Implicit Association Test. *Journal of Personality and Social Psychology, 74,* 1464–1480.

Hamlin, J. K., Wynn, K., & Bloom, P. (2010). Three-month-olds show a negativity bias in their social evaluations. *Developmental Science, 13,* 923–929. doi:10.1111/j.1467-7687.2010.00951.x

Hamlin, J. K., Wynn, K., Bloom, P., & Mahajan, N. (2011). How infants and toddlers react to antisocial others. *Proceedings of the National Academy of Sciences, 108,* 19931–19936. doi:10.1073/pnas.1110306108

Inzlicht, M., & Schmader, T. (2012). *Stereotype threat: Theory, process, and application.* New York, NY: Oxford University Press.

Joanisse, M., Gagnon, S., & Voloaca, M. (2013). The impact of stereotype threat on the simulated driving performance of older drivers. *Accident Analysis and Prevention, 50,* 530–538. doi:10.1016/j.aap.2012.05.032

Khan, M., & Ecklund, K. (2012). Attitudes toward Muslim Americans post-9/11. *Stigma, 7,* 1–16. doi:http://dx.doi.org/10.3998/jmmh.10381607.0007.101

King, M. L., Jr. (1967). The role of the behavioral scientist in the civil rights movement. Retrieved from http://apa.org/monitor/features/king-challenge.aspx

Krupp, D. B., & Taylor, P. D. (2015). Social evolution in the shadow of asymmetrical relatedness. *Proceedings B of the Royal Society Publishing, 282,* 20150142. doi:10.1098/rspb.2015.0142

Linville, P. W., Fischer, G. W., & Salovey, P. (1989). Perceived distributions of the characteristics of in-group and out-group members: Empirical evidence and a computer simulation. *Journal of Personality and Social Psychology, 57,* 165–188.

Liptak, A. (2015, June 26). Supreme Court ruling makes same-sex marriage a right nationwide. *The New York Times.* Retrieved from http://www.nytimes.com

Locsin, A. (2014). Is air travel safer than car travel? *USA Today.* Retrieved from http://traveltips.usatoday.com

Mahajan, N., & Wynn, K. (2012). Origins of "us" versus "them": Prelinguistic infants prefer similar others. *Cognition, 124,* 227–233. doi:http://dx.doi.org/10.1016/j.cognition.2012.05.003

McGlone, M., & Aronson, J. (2006). Stereotype threat, identity salience, and spatial reasoning. *Journal of Applied Developmental Psychology, 27,* 486–493. doi:10.1016/j.appdev.2006.06.003

Mullen, B. (2015, June 5). Museum to celebrate Flag Day throughout June. Retrieved from http://recordherald.com/news/home_top-news/153927533/Museum-to-celebrate-Flag-Day-throughout-June

Pettigrew, T. (1979). The ultimate attribution error: Extending Allport's cognitive analysis of prejudice. *Personality and Social Psychology Bulletin, 5,* 461–476.

Pettigrew, T., & Tropp, L. R. (2006). A meta-analytic test of intergroup contact theory. *Journal of Personality and Social Psychology, 90,* 751–783. doi:10.1037/0022-3514.90.5.751

Pyle, J. (Ed.) (2010, May 6). Lost key or bike thief: What would you do? [Television broadcast]. In Van Gilder, B. (Producer), *What would you do?* New York, ABC News.

Quotes. (2015). Retrieved from http://www.brainyquote.com/

Risen, J. L., Gilovich, T., & Dunning, D. (2007). One-shot illusory correlations and stereotype formation. *Personality and Social Psychology Bulletin, 33,* 1492–1502. doi:10.1177/0146167207305862

Schevitz, T. (2002, November 26). FBI sees leap in anti-Muslim hate crimes / 9/11 attacks blamed for bias – blacks still most frequent victims. *SFGate.* Retrieved from http://www.sfgate.com/

Shalby, C., & Barajas, J. (2015, April 30). Here's the real reason people in Baltimore are protesting [Web log post]. Retrieved from http://www.pbs.org/newshour/rundown/freddie-grays-death-baltimore-community-speaks-citys-future/

Sherif, M., Harvey, O. J., White, B. J., Hood, W. R., & Sherif, C. W. (1954/1961). *Intergroup conflict and cooperation: The Robbers Cave experiment.* Retrieved from http://psychclassics.yorku.ca/Sherif/

Smith, J. (2014, August 17). In Ferguson, black town, white power. *The New York Times.* Retrieved from http://www.nytimes.com

Snyder, R. C. (2006). *Gay marriage and democracy: Equality for all.* Lanham, MD: Rowman & Littlefield.

Spears, R., Eiser, J. R., & Van Der Pligt, J. (1987). Further evidence for expectation-based illusory correlations. *European Journal of Social Psychology, 17,* 253–258. doi:10.1002/ejsp.2420170211

Spencer, H. (1851). *Social statics; Or, the conditions essential to human happiness specified, and the first of them developed.* Retrieved from http://oll.libertyfund.org/titles/273

Stahl, L. (2012, November 18). The baby lab. [Television broadcast]. In Finkelstein, S. (Producer), *60 Minutes*. New York, CBS Broadcasting.

Steele, C. M., & Aronson, J. (1995). Stereotype threat and the intellectual test performance of African Americans. *Journal of Personality and Social Psychology, 69*, 797–811.

Steinfels, P. (2007, June 23). A liberal explains his rejection of same-sex marriage. *The New York Times*. Retrieved from http://www.nytimes.com

Stewart, T. L., Laduke, J. R., Bracht, C., Sweet, B. A. M., & Gamarel, K. E. (2003). Do the "eyes" have it? A program evaluation of Jane Elliott's "blue-eyes/brown-eyes" diversity training exercise. *Journal of Applied Social Psychology, 33*, 1898–1921. doi:10.1111/j.1559-1816.2003.tb02086.x

Tajfel, H., Billig, M. G., Bundy, R. P., & Flament, C. (1971). Social categorization and intergroup behaviour. *European Journal of Social Psychology, 1*, 149–178.

Taylor, S. E., Fiske, S. T., Etcoff, N. L., & Ruderman, A. J. (1978). Categorical and contextual bases of person memory and stereotyping. *Journal of Personality and Social Psychology, 36*, 778–793.

Thompson, D. A., & Adams, S. L. (1996). The full moon and ED patient volumes: Unearthing a myth. *The American Journal of Emergency Medicine, 14*, 161–164. doi:10.1016/S0735-6757(96)90124-2

Todd, A. R., Bodenhausen, G. V., & Galinsky, A. D. (2012). Perspective taking combats the denial of intergroup discrimination. *Journal of Experimental Social Psychology, 48*, 738–745. doi:10.1016/j.jesp.2011.12.011

Tracking the events in the wake of Michael Brown's shooting. (2014, November 8). *The New York Times*. Retrieved from http://www.nytimes.com

Weiser, C. (Ed.). (2015). God bless the USA songfacts. Retrieved from http://www.songfacts.com/detail .php?id=3263

Zelizer, G. (2002, January 7). Quick dose of 9-11 religion soothes, doesn't change. [Editorial]. *USA Today*. Retrieved from http://usatoday30.usatoday.com/news/comment/2002/01/08/ncguest2.htm

Chapter Eleven
Love and Attraction

Dr. Lora Adair

Lyon College

Learning Objectives

- Compare and contrast "liking" and "loving"
- Understand the primary theories of love, including Sternberg's Triangular Theory of Love, prototype models of love, and Fisher's three phases of love
- Explore current debates within the field of love and attraction, including the definition of love as an emotion or a drive and the prevalence of sexual fluidity
- Understand how human love and attraction fits within a larger phylogenetic context by discussing love and attraction within other species
- Discuss the effect of our social world on our expectations regarding romantic relationships and the roles of each sex within romantic relationships

Chapter Outline

· Attraction

- "… I like you, I like-like you, and I love you"
  - The distinction between "liking" and "loving"
    - Types of love and their theoretical foundations
      - Sternberg's Triangular Theory of Love
- What attracts us?
  - Proximity
    - The mere exposure effect
  - Similarity
    - Assortative mating and the role of similarity in attraction
  - Sexual orientation
    - Measurement of sexual orientation
      - The Kinsey Scale
      - The Klien Sexual Orientation Grid
    - Sexual fluidity
  - Sex differences in attraction
    - Parental Investment Theory
    - Heteronormativity
  - The biology of attraction
    - Pheromones
    - Waist-to-hip ratio
    - Shoulder-to-hip ratio
    - Body size preferences

· Love

- What is love?
  - Love as a drive vs. love as an emotion
- What are we like when we are "in love?"
  - Idealizing the object of our affections
  - Focused attention (and ignoring rivals)
  - Intrusive thinking
- Love: What's sex got to do with it?
  - The relationship between sexual satisfaction and relationship satisfaction
- Phylogenetic evidence: Love and attraction in non-human animals
  - Harlow on attachment and bonding
  - Monogamy and pair-bonding
  - Uni-directional and bi-directional attraction
- Myths about love
  - Galician on mass media and love

Love and Attraction

According to Shakespeare (see Shakespeare & Durband, 1985), love is:

> *. . . a smoke raised with the fume of sighs;*
> *Being purged, a fire sparkling in lovers' eyes;*
> *Being vex'd a sea nourish'd with lovers' tears;*
> *What is it else? a madness most discreet,*
> *A choking gall and a preserving sweet.*

We are fascinated and perplexed by love. We are obsessed with love. Humans are apt to be found writing about love, singing about love, creating films about love, reading advice regarding how to find love, and searching for love through their social connections (both on- and off-line). Throughout this chapter, we will explore what we, as psychologists, have come to understand about attraction, liking, and loving. We will explore theories that classify various types of love, how love changes over time, and our understanding of why we fall in love with the ones we do. We will go on to elucidate some of the ongoing debates within the field of love and attraction, and end with a discussion of the darker side of love—including intimate partner violence and the dissolution of romantic relationships. Throughout, we will use a comparative eye to better understand the evolutionary roots of human love and attraction, by investigating similar phenomenon in nonhuman mateships.

Attraction

At some point, we have all done it: described our perfect partner, the traits that attract us. This description often includes mention of humor, intelligence, physical attractiveness, ambitiousness, among others. In the field of psychology, there is an increasing appreciation for the surprising consistencies and patterns in the traits that attract us to a potential mate. Here, we will explore various theories describing attraction from social, biological, physiological, and behavioral perspectives:

". . . I Like You, I Like-Like You, and I Love You"

As this chapter explores psychology's current understanding of love and attraction, it is critical to begin with the distinction between "liking" and "loving." This is a distinction that has been much debated in the field of social psychology, with some arguing that the two phenomena represent different points on a single continuum (Brehm, 1985; Clore & Byrne, 1974; Lott & Lott, 1968, 1974) where "loving" simply refers to feeling more strongly toward someone the same feelings of attraction that comprise "liking," but to a greater degree (see Figure 11.1). In this perspective, as attraction grows, "like" transforms into "love." However, these perspectives on "liking" and "loving" tend to oversimplify the relationship between these two constructs; for example, it does not seem, in practice, to be true that "loving" relationships are simply more pleasant and more reinforcing than friendships. In fact, it could be argued that romantic relationships are composed of both higher highs and lower lows than friendships (Hessick, 2007).

Alternatively, some theorists argue that "liking" and "loving" are two distinct concepts, with none (Hazan & Shaver, 1987; Wilson, 1981), or perhaps only

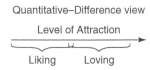

Figure 11.1. "Liking" and "loving" as concepts on a single continuum (Sternberg, 1987).

some (Sternberg & Grajek, 1984), common features (see Figure 11.2). What these perspectives have in common is that they espouse that "liking" and "loving" are categorically, and functionally, distinct concepts. For example, an evolutionary perspective on "liking" and "loving" distinguishes these concepts on a functional basis; contending that our various interpersonal attachments, including our attachments to offspring, mates, and friends or kin, serve distinct functions, and therefore the psychological features of these attachments are also distinct. The distinct features of "liking" and "loving" have served as advantageous in categorically disparate situations, where aspects of "liking" may foster reciprocal relationships between individuals in our social environment ("I loan my neighbor sugar when they need it," "My friend feeds my cat when I am out of town," etc.), "loving" (in the sense of romantic love) promotes relationships that may result in the production and shared care of offspring. The primary issue with theories of love that treat "liking" and "loving" as completely (or almost completely) disjointed is that they very well describe romantic love: love which is characterized by passion, a relationship characterized by sexual and emotional bonds. When it comes to love between intimate partners, which is nonsexual, or companionate love, for example, the love that characterizes many aging, long-term relationships where the initial passionate, physical attraction is dampened, these theories are largely silent (Sternberg, 1987).

The commonly accepted alternative to these theoretical perspectives on the distinction between "liking" and "loving" is Robert Sternberg's Triangular Theory of Love. According to Sternberg (1987), "liking" and "loving" share a set-subset relationship, where "loving" is a larger concept, which may or may not include aspects of "liking" (see Figure 11.3). By viewing "liking" as an aspect of some, but not all, "loving" relationships, Sternberg's Triangular Theory of Love has overcome many of the inadequacies of alternative theories of "liking" and "loving." Its primary strength is that Sternberg's Triangular Theory of Love describes well both "liking", nonsexual relationships, as well as passionate,

Qualitive–Difference view

A. Disjoint set relation

B. Overlaping set relation

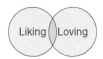

Figure 11.2. "Liking" and "loving" as concepts which share none (A) or some (B) attributes (Sternberg, 1987).

Subset-set relation

Figure 11.3. "Liking" and "loving" as concepts which have a set-subset relationship (Sternberg, 1987).

and romantic "loving" relationships, and many things in-between. According to Sternberg, we can best understand the distinction between "liking" and "loving" through his eight types of love, which are presented in Table 11.1.

In sum, the distinction between "liking" and "loving," much like many psychological concepts, is the subject of much debate between scientists in the field. Some argue that "loving" someone simply describes a relationship where one

Table 11.1.   Eight Types of Love as Proposed By Sternberg

Nonlove: Acquaintances, or brief social encounters, which do not involve intimacy, passion, or commitment.

Infatuation: What is often described in romantic films and stories as "love at first sight," characterized by arousal and physical attraction only.

Empty love: Commitment to stay with one's intimate partner, in the absence of emotional closeness and physical attraction; describing relationships in which partners may be "staying together for the kids" or perhaps arranged marriages, where partners commit to one another before establishing physical or emotional closeness.

Liking: Friendships, which do not involve passion or necessarily a commitment to remain close in the distant future, but are nonetheless emotionally close and intimate.

Romantic love: Often described as the "Romeo and Juliet" kind of love; a relationship characterized by both physical attraction and emotional closeness, without any long-term commitment to one another.

Companionate love: Relationships in which the participants have made the decision to stay together in the long term, and the individuals share an emotional closeness with one another. The absence of physical attraction, or passion, in these relationships makes them descriptive of long-term intimate partnerships in which the passion has faded.

Fatuous love: As Sternberg (1987) describes them, these relationships are "whirlwind" romances or even "shotgun marriages"; in both cases, physical attraction and the decision to commit to one's partner in the long term are present, but an emotional closeness has not yet developed.

Consummate love: Relationships characterized by all of Sternberg's (1987) three attributes of love: intimacy, passion, and commitment. Partners are physically attracted to one another, emotionally close and vulnerable with one another, and committed to remain together.

feels *more* of whatever "liking" entails. Others contend that "liking" and "loving" are distinct, and serve distinct functions—namely to create distinct types of relationships. A more popular theoretical perspective is that "liking" is one aspect of the psychological phenomenon that is "love"—when we **like** someone, we are referring to an emotional closeness, an intimacy, a bond that we have with that individual. This can refer to the way we feel toward a friend (a platonic relationship) or a lover (a sexual relationship). When we **love** someone, we are often referring to the experience of what Sternberg calls "romantic love," we feel not only an emotional closeness to this individual but also a physical attraction that can lead these relationships to become sexual in nature.

What Attracts Us?

In Hollywood it is referred to as a "meet cute": an aspect of a narrative that brings two characters together, and sparks a passionate connection. For example, the charmingly awkward interaction between Diane Keaton and Woody Allen in a tennis match in *Annie Hall* (1977). In the real world, we construct our own narrative, we are charged with creating our own charming, romantic, or awkward "aligning of the stars" in which we meet that next intimate partner. How do we do this? What attracts us to one another? We will explore several aspects of our social world that draw us together, and spark "liking" and even "loving."

Proximity One aspect of our social environment that can explain, at least in part, what attracts us to one another is a simple one: physical closeness or proximity. We are far more likely to begin a romantic relationship with someone who goes to the same school that we do, or works at the same business that we do, than someone we do not see regularly. Our tendency to be more likely to begin a romantic relationship with someone who is physically close to us, whom we regularly see, is described by a psychological phenomenon called the **mere exposure effect**. The mere exposure effect (Zajonc, 1968) refers to an increased liking of a person, a symbol, or an object, to which we are frequently exposed. This tendency to increase liking of a thing after "mere exposure" to that thing was initially identified by Robert Zajonc (1968) who found that participants increased their positive attitudes, or liking, of both words and nonsense syllables after simply being exposed to these words or syllables with an increased frequency. Zajonc referred to this pattern of findings as his "exposure-attitude" hypothesis, and since has been identified after repeated exposure to food and drink (Pliner, 1982), tones (Rajecki, 1974), images presented for such short durations that individuals cannot consciously recall seeing them (Zajonc, 2000), and faces (Rhodes, Halberstadt, & Brajkovich, 2001), to name a few. So, if you are looking for love, you may not have to look very far.

Similarity Let's begin with some colloquialisms that are actually a bit contradictory: how is it that "birds of a feather flock together" *and* "opposites attract?" It is not the case that both can be true, so which is it? Do (or don't) opposites attract? For the answer, we can look to evolutionary psychology and a concept known as **assortative mating**. To understand the concept of assortative mating, it is best to begin with the analogy of our social world as a "mating market," where we exchange goods in the form of our mating value. A "valuable" mate is physically attractive, has symmetrical facial features (Jones et al., 2001), is industrious/ambitious, and kind (Buss & Barnes, 1986), just to name a few traits that have been consistently, and cross-culturally (Buss

"Like"
Emotional closeness, intimacy, and body that we have with another individual. Typically a bond that is not sexual in nature.

"Love"
Emotional closeness, physical attraction, and physiological arousal that we feel in the presence of another individual.

Mere Exposure Effect
Increased liking of a person, symbol, or object to which we are frequently exposed.

Assortative Mating
The tendency for individuals to be paired with mates of a similar mate value, personality, height, attractiveness, and with similar values and interests.

et al., 1990), identified as important when choosing a mate. As in any market, the value of goods you can acquire depends on the value of goods you have to spend. In the case of a mating market, the concept of assortative mating explains that individuals tend to be paired with mates of similar mate value and other mating-relevant traits. In fact, individuals tend to be more likely to marry those with similar education levels, religious beliefs and practices (Hur, 2003), personality traits, weight, and height (Carmalt, Cawley, Joyner, & Sobal, 2008). Beyond this, couples who have more similar personalities, including similar levels of openness to experience (Jenkins, 2007), extraversion, agreeableness, and neuroticism (Gonzaga, Carter, & Buckwalter, 2010), tend to also report higher relationship satisfaction. However, there is a bit of debate within the field of psychology on this topic; some contend that it is our similarity to our potential mate that attracts us to them, called *positive assortment* (Gonzaga, Campos, & Bradbury, 2007). Others argue that it is through the process of being together that individuals in a relationship become more like one another, called *convergence* (Anderson, Keitner, & John, 2003). Either way, overwhelming evidence indicates that it is likely that "birds of a feather" do indeed "flock together."

Sexual Orientation

An umbrella term referring to several aspects of our sexual identity, including the sex (or sexes) to whom we are attracted sexually, romantically, and emotionally.

Sexual Orientation   In this section, we will explore the potential roots of our patterns of attraction—namely the biological sex to whom we are sexually and romantically attracted. The term **sexual orientation** refers to several aspects of our sexual identity, including the sex (or sexes) to whom we are attracted sexually, romantically, *and* emotionally (Rosenthal, 2013). However, psychological science has not always treated sexual orientation as a multidimensional construct of human attraction, our measurement of sexual orientation began with questions of sexual behavior only. Alfred Kinsey developed a widely used measure of sexual orientation in 1948, called the Kinsey Scale, which asks individuals to self-report their sexual behavior and experiences on a scale ranging from "0: Exclusively heterosexual" to "6: Exclusively homosexual" (Kinsey, Pomeroy, & Martin, 1948; see Figure 11.4 and Table 11.2).

Now, the Klien Sexual Orientation Grid (Klein, 1990) offers a much more complex, and inclusive, view of sexual orientation (see Table 11.3). Klein's scale captures patterns of emotional attraction (the sex or sexes to which one prefers to develop close emotional relationships), sexual attraction (the sex or sexes that are the object of one's sexual fantasies, behaviors, and physical desires, and one's

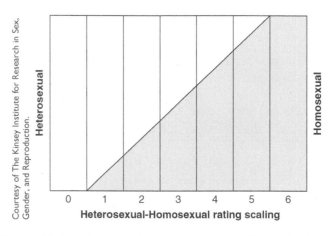

Figure 11.4.   A single-dimension measure of sexual orientation, The Kinsey Scale (© The Kinsey Institute).

Table 11.2:   Kinsey Scale of Sexual Orientation

0: Exclusively heterosexual

1: Predominantly heterosexual, only incidentally homosexual

2: Predominantly heterosexual, but more than incidentally homosexual

3: Equally heterosexual and homosexual

4: Predominantly homosexual, but more than incidentally heterosexual

5: Predominantly homosexual, only incidentally heterosexual

6: Exclusively homosexual

Table 11.3:   Klien Sexual Orientation Grid

A. Sexual attraction

B. Sexual behavior

C. Sexual fantasies

D. Emotional reference

E. Social preference

F. Self-identification

G. Heterosexual/homosexual lifestyle

Note. This table is adapted from *A Multi-dimension Measure of Sexual Orientation, The Klein Sexual Orientation Grid* (Klein, Sepekoff, & Wolf, 1985).

inner sense of sexual orientation (the sexual orientation one primarily identifies as). Beyond this, Klein's measure of sexual orientation allows for variation across time, as well as the inclusion of both the "ideal" and "actual" objects of one's attractions.

Why might it be insightful to include measures of both past and present patterns of attraction? Increasing evidence suggests that the measurement and theoretical treatment of sexual orientation as a construct must take into account change and development over time, in order to most accurately capture and describe sexual orientation. For example, a longitudinal study of 156 adolescents in New York City (ages 14–21) that identified as gay, lesbian, or bisexual found that 43% of these individuals experienced changes and transitions in their self-reported sexual orientation over time (Rosario, Schrimshaw, Hunter, & Braun, 2011). Psychologists that study sex and sexuality refer to this phenomenon as **sexual fluidity**, or the tendency for one's sexual identity, sexual behaviors, and/or sexual and romantic attractions to change over time. It is not uncommon for both men and women who identify as heterosexual to also report experiencing same-sex attractions and sexual experiences (and vise versa for many of those who identify as homosexual). Many recent studies have found that women are much more likely to report sexual fluidity in their attractions and behaviors, compared to men (Chandra, Mosher, Copen, & Sionean, 2011; Vrangalova

Sexual Fluidity
The tendency for ones sexual identity, sexual behaviors, and/or sexual and romantic attractions to change over time.

& Savin-Williams, 2010). It is possible that a disproportionate tendency toward sexual fluidity and/or bisexuality has been adaptive for women throughout our evolutionary past, as some evolutionary psychologists suggest; according to the alloparenting hypothesis, women's same-sex attractions may have helped them foster bonds with other women for assistance in caring for their offspring and providing for their families (Kuhle & Radtke, 2013). Alternatively, it is possible that men (who identify as heterosexual) experience same-sex attractions and behaviors just as frequently as women, but face stronger social pressures to conform to a heterosexual, masculine norm and therefore are less likely to report these same-sex attractions, fantasies, and/or behaviors. Indeed, increasing work in the area of sexual orientation and sexual fluidity suggests that it is rarely true that individual's sexual attractions can be accurately described as 100% heterosexual, or 100% homosexual, as photographer iO Tillett Wright finds in her art project photographing individuals who identify as falling somewhere on the LGBT spectrum—nearly all of her participants reported some degree of sexual fluidity in their attractions. As she (Wright, 2012) puts it,

> *Most people fall on a spectrum of what I have come to refer to as "grey" . . . In no way am I saying that preference doesn't exist . . . what I am saying, though, is that human beings are not one-dimensional . . . If you have gay people over here, and you have straight people over here, and while we recognize that most people identify as somewhere closer to one binary or another, there is this vast spectrum of people that exist in between.*

It is worth noting that the existence of sexual fluidity does not serve as evidence that sexual orientation is a choice—one's patterns of sexual and romantic attraction are determined by a complex interaction of genetic factors, social factors, situational factors, neurobiological factors, and hormonal factors. Therefore, viewing the issue of one's sexual attractions, behaviors, and identity as either biologically determined *or* shaped by one's own volition is inherently flawed, as it is both social and biological factors that seem to shape our sexual orientations and identities. These various types of influences that shape our patterns of sexual attraction are inextricably woven together, and through the use of twin studies researchers have found that siblings tend to display the same sexual orientation due to both shared environmental and genetic influences (Bailey, Dunne, & Martin, 2000; McGuire, 1995). In (at least partial) response to the question of why we are attracted to whom we are attracted, we can conclude that our patterns of attraction are shaped by a complex collection of factors, typically shared with our genetic relatives, and are formed throughout our lives. This paints a complex, and beautiful, picture of human relationships.

Sex Differences It is the premise driving many a romantic comedy plot—men and women are never looking for the same thing. What attracts and what satisfies men and women in a romantic relationship is often regarded as completely different; he is looking for something casual, someone attractive, and doesn't really care for emotional intimacy, and she is looking for something meaningful, someone funny and kind, and isn't looking for physical intimacy before emotional closeness has been established. But. . . is it true? Are men and women attracted to different traits in a romantic partner? The answer that has been arrived at after much debate is, perhaps disappointingly, *it depends*. For this image to begin to come into focus, let's begin with an interesting study performed by Clark and Hatfield in 1989. In this study, young adults were approached by an opposite-sex stranger and propositioned for casual sex. To this invitation, *not one* female participant said "yes"; 75% of male participants accepted. This example illustrates one consistent sex difference found in the psychology literature regarding sex and sexual attraction—men are more comfortable with casual sexual encounters, and are more likely to report seeking casual sexual encounters, compared to women (Buss & Schmitt, 1993).

Additionally, sex differences exist in the traits that are prioritized when searching for a mate; this difference has been demonstrated across several studies and even across cultures. In fact, females tend to prioritize traits that are indicative of a mate's ability to acquire resources, including ambition, industriousness, and earning capacity (Buss, 1989), which is consistent with an evolutionary theory called Parental Investment Theory (Trivers, 1972). Parental Investment Theory (Trivers, 1972) explains that many of the sex differences that persist today have roots in the different challenges faced by males and females for the past several thousand years, specifically that females (of many species, including humans) have the highest minimum parental investment in potential offspring, compared to men, given that females are required to commit to 9 months of gestation and subsequent lactation. Since females are required to invest more in potential offspring, females tend to be the choosier sex, and they tend to prioritize traits indicative of an individual's ability to provide for potential offspring (see Figure 11.5). Alternatively, males are only required to invest in a single sexual encounter; therefore, they are free to prioritize traits that are indicative of a mate's ability to produce healthier offspring—including youth and attractiveness (Buss, 1989). While both males and females tend to search for traits like kindness, humor, and intelligence

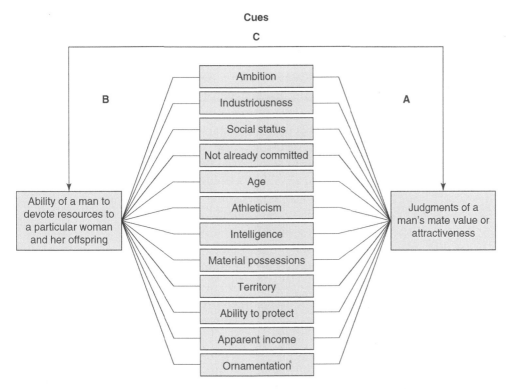

Figure 11.5. The traits prioritized by women when searching for a potential mate, which in turn contribute to a potential mate's perceived value (Buss & Schmidt, 1993).

THINKING CRITICALLY (A)

Take a moment to explore your own ideas about sexuality. Heteronormativity is not only observable in certain psychological and biological theories, it is a *cultural bias* that presents heterosexuality as "normal" or natural.

In fact, cultural expectations and norms—including the expectation that it is normal and common to identify as heterosexual—are communicated through various social routes. Specifically, we can obtain normative information through our family, our friends and acquaintances, the media, our morality or religiosity, and through government policy and law. Consider these sources of normative information when you ask yourself some questions relevant to heteronormativity.

Questions:

1. Consider your beliefs about sexuality—do you endorse the idea that heterosexual behavior and identity are "normal" and natural?
2. Consider the causal explanation—where did your beliefs about sexuality and sexual orientation come from? How does an individual learn that heterosexuality is the "normal" sexual orientation?
3. What do you feel are the potential problems associated with a cultural bias that presents heterosexuality as "normal"?

Heteronormative
Referring to ideas, theories, language, and concepts that treat heterosexuality as ubiquitous, morally right, and "normal."

in a potential mate, the traits that they view as most important when searching for a new mate are actually quite different. It is worth noting that Parental Investment Theory is **heteronormative**, meaning that this theory treats heterosexuality as ubiquitous and "normal" while not explaining the nature of mate choice in same-sex relationships. However, the availability of theoretical and empirical works in evolutionary psychology that are more inclusive of all sexual orientations is steadily increasing in recent years. More on the concept of heteronormative can be found in the Thinking Critically Box above.

Above, we mentioned that the answer to the question of "do men and women search for different things in a potential romantic partner" is *it depends*. Indeed, it seems that just how different men and women's mate preferences are depends on *what type* of relationship they are looking for. While men tend to be more likely to indicate interest in short-term, casual mateships than do women, and women tend to be more likely to employ long-term mating strategies than do men, both men and women search for both long-term and short-term pairings. And, as you might expect, when searching for a short-term mate, men and women's preferences tend to be more similar—both men and women, in short-term contexts, prioritize traits related to physical attractiveness and youth (Buss & Schmidt, 1993). Further, when searching for a long-term mate, men and women tend to similarly prefer traits such as humor, intelligence, and kindness (Buss & Schmidt, 1993). So, when it comes to sex differences in attraction, it depends on what you are looking for.

The Biology of Attraction   So far, we have discussed social and evolutionary components of attraction, but there are important biological substrates of the psychological experience of attraction. Here, we will explore the significance of the senses, namely visual attention and scent, in attraction, as well as the importance of our neural reward circuitry. How does our biology pull us together?

Our senses play an important role in the process of attraction. For example, sense of smell is critical in the process of attraction and mate selection in nonhuman animals: the use of chemical signals called **pheromones** (secreted through the skin) to determine if another organism (a) is a member of the same species, (b) is a potential mate, and (c) is a high-quality (or "attractive") mate has been identified in many species with *extremely* simple social systems (Johansson & Jones, 2007). What is surprising is that primates, including humans, in spite of having developed incredibly complex social systems and bi-directional mate choice, are still capable of sensing and using pheromonal communication in the process of attraction and mate selection. In one fascinating study (Wedekind, Seebeck, Bettens, & Paepke, 1995), men were asked to sleep for two nights in t-shirts provided by the researchers. Importantly, these men were instructed not to use any deodorant, antiperspirant, or cologne while wearing the t-shirts. These t-shirts were then presented to women, whom were asked to indicate how appealing or pleasant they found the odor of the t-shirts. Wedekind and colleagues found that naturally cycling women (women who were not using any kind of hormonal contraceptive) preferred the odor of t-shirts worn by men who were more genetically *dissimilar*, specifically men with dissimilar MHC or major histocompatibility complex. These molecules are responsible for identifying pathogens and protecting our bodies from disease and infection, and when two individuals with dissimilar MHC produce offspring, that offspring will enjoy the benefits of stronger immune function and more diverse immunities. Interestingly, Wedekind and colleagues also found that women taking hormonal contraceptives, which model, to a certain extent, the experience of pregnancy in the body through hormones like progesterone and estrogen, preferred the odor of genetically *similar* men. This seemingly counterintuitive preference for genetically similar men has been subsequently explained thusly; in our evolutionary past, pregnant women relied heavily upon the support and shared contributions of their kin to provide for their growing family. Therefore, it is hypothesized that the hormonal experience associated with taking hormonal contraceptives closely enough mimics the experience of pregnancy to facilitate the adaptive preference for kin and genetically similar social connections.

In another interesting observational study, Miller, Tybur, and Jordan (2007) asked 18 erotic dancers to record their tip earnings after every shift they worked, for two months. They also measured (a) whether or not the dancers were using hormonal contraceptives and (b) the phase of their menstrual cycle the dancers were experiencing. They found that naturally cycling dancers made their highest tip earnings when experiencing peak fertility (see Figure 11.6). Therefore, we may conclude that (while likely consciously unaware) humans *can* and *do* use their sense of smell in the process of attraction and mate selection. Evidence suggests that we can detect fertility and genetic "compatibility"/similarity through our sense of smell. So, the next time you reach for deodorant before stepping out for a date, perhaps you decide against covering up your natural odor.

Our vision and attention also have an important part to play in the process of attraction. The obvious relationship between our vision and the process of attraction is that many of the traits that attract us are assessed visually, including facial symmetry (mentioned above; Jones et al., 2001), clear and youthful skin, blushed cheeks and lips (hypothesized to have evolved as a signal of fertility in primates), high vocal pitch in women and low vocal pitch in men (Collins, 2000) and body shape, including waist-to-hip ratio and shoulder-to-hip ratio (Singh, 2004). Evolutionary theory suggests that these universal cues of attractiveness are likely perceived as attractive due to their association with good health, youth, and fertility.

One of the physical traits associated with attractiveness is waist-to-hip ratio in women, and shoulder-to-hip ratio in men. Interestingly, this specific aspect of

Pheromones
Chemical signals often secreted through the skin, which can affect the behavior of other members of the same species.

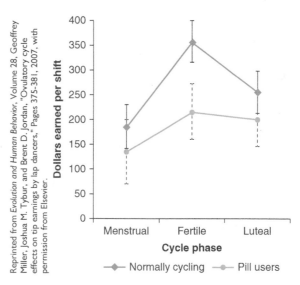

Reprinted from *Evolution and Human Behavior*, Volume 28, Geoffrey Miller, Joshua M. Tybur, and Brent D. Jordan, "Ovulatory cycle effects on tip earnings by lap dancers," Pages 375-381, 2007, with permission from Elsevier.

Figure 11.6. Evidence for chemical signaling in humans: an increase in tip earnings observed in naturally cycling dancers experiencing peak fertility (Miller et al., 2007).

body shape and size seems to be more important in determining attractiveness of a potential mate than body size, or body mass index (BMI). In other words, whom we are attracted to is more clearly shaped by the relative size of their waist to their hips, or their shoulders to their hips, than simply their weight and their height. Although, it is worth noting that there are interesting regional preferences for size, such that individuals living in the United States tend to prefer thinness and individuals living in areas characterized by food scarcity and extreme poverty tend to prefer heavier mates (Sobal & Stunkard, 1989; Swami, Knight, Tovée, Davies, & Furnham, 2007). Recent work has even identified within-nation variation in body size preferences, such that (for example) what has been regarded as a Western universal preference for thinness is absent in low socioeconomic status (SES) regions of the United States and Britain; in these areas, where resources are scarce, a heavier body size is indicative of wealth and success. As Singh (1993, p. 304) puts it:

> *Human societies that face frequent food shortage or must depend primarily on hard labor to acquire and store food may find strong legs and arms or overall plumpness of the body more attractive. Other societies may not find such features attractive because of different environmental conditions and constraints in which their society evolved. The degree of affluence of a society . . . may, to a large extent, determine the prevalence and admiration of fatness. A majority of studies investigating the relationship between socioeconomic status (SES) and obesity have found a positive relationship between SES and obesity in both sexes in developing societies, whereas a negative relationship between SES and obesity is found in developed societies.*

Likely more important than body size or height in determining women's physical attractiveness is waist-to-hip ratio (WHR), a measure of women's weight distribution that critically changes after puberty, with fat deposits increasing in the hips after experiencing puberty (Marti et al., 1991). Furthermore, lower WHR has been associated with increased fertility—married women with lower WHR report greater ease in becoming pregnant (Kaye, Folsom, Prineas, Potter, & Gapstur, 1990). *Recall that traits that are universally perceived as physically attractive tend*

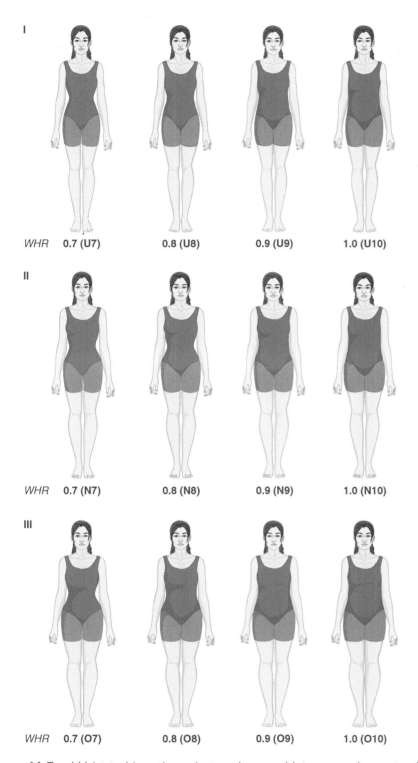

Figure 11.7. Waist-to-hip ratio and attractiveness: Heterosexual men tend to prefer women with lower WHR regardless of their body size, or BMI (Singh, 1993).

to be indicative of health, youth, and/or fertility. Indeed, when presented with images of women with varying waist-to-hip ratios, heterosexual men tend to prefer low WHR (around .7) in women, regardless of weight. Although, ratings of attractiveness did vary less across WHR for women with higher BMI, meaning that discriminations based on WHR are strongest in women that are underweight or of "average" size (see Figure 11.7).

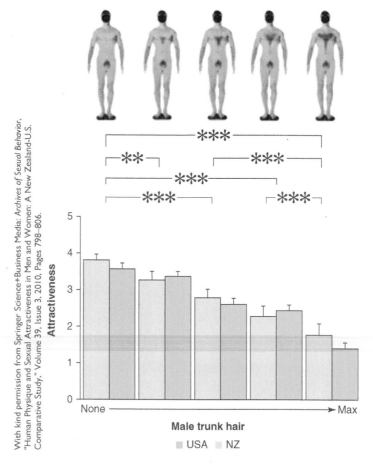

With kind permission from Springer Science+Business Media: *Archives of Sexual Behavior*, "Human Physique and Sexual Attractiveness in Men and Women: A New Zealand-U.S. Comparative Study," Volume 39, Issue 3, 2010, Pages 798–806.

Figure 11.8. Less body hair is associated with greater perceived physical attractiveness in men (Dixson, Dixson, Bishop, & Parish, 2010).

Male's physical attractiveness is strongly linked with a similar measure of relative size, termed shoulder-to-hip ratio (SHR). Similarly, SHR shifts as a result of puberty, and is therefore a reliable signal of fertility and health to potential mates (Dixson, Halliwell, East, Wignarajah, & Anderson, 2003). Where *lower* WHR is typically perceived as more physically attractive, *higher* SHR is typically perceived as more physically attractive (around 1.6). Broader shoulders, slimmer hips, and a muscular build (referred to as mesomorphy) have been found to be associated with higher physical attractiveness in men across several studies (Dixson et al., 2003; Dixson, Dixson, Morgan, & Anderson, 2007). Furthermore, *less* body hair has been found to be perceived as more physically attractive in men (see Figure 11.8).

Many of the universal traits associated with physical attraction we have explored here pull and shape the direction of our attention. While we tend to pay close attention to faces generally, compared to other features of our visual world (Ro, Russell, & Lavie, 2001), attractive faces are particularly magnetic. Attractive faces tend to hold our visual attention for longer than unattractive faces (Aharon et al., 2001), and this even happens without our conscious awareness. When involved in a completely different visual task, such as determining whether a letter is presented upright or upside down, our performance is disrupted and slowed by the presence of an attractive face (Sui & Liu, 2009). That is, attractive faces pull our attention and hold our attention, a phenomenon known as attentional adhesion (Maner, Gailliot, Rouby, & Miller, 2007). The sensation that we can't seem to take our eyes off of the object of our affection is an example of attentional adhesion, and studies have found that when a separate visual task requires that we switch the location of our attention (for example, from one quadrant to another quadrant of a computer screen), this switch of our attention takes longer when it involves pulling our gaze away from an attractive potential mate that has been pictured. Furthermore, we also tend to pay less attention to other potential mates when we are in a relationship with a romantic partner. When it comes to the process of attraction, it seems true to say that we are indeed "glued" to the object of our affection.

Love

So far, we have explored the psychological, social, and biological processes associated with attraction to a potential mate. Now, we will transition to the phenomenon called "love." As we discussed earlier in the chapter when we distinguished "liking" from "loving," "love" refers to not only an experience of emotional closeness to someone (which can be descriptive of platonic friendships or romantic relationships) but also a physical attraction that may lead these relationships to become sexual in nature. While the experience of "love" can be interpreted as many things, including the feelings of attachment and intimacy we feel for friends and family, for our purposes we will use the term "love" to be indicative of "romantic love": a bond characterized by both emotional intimacy and physical passion (Sternberg, 1987).

Although expressions of love are somewhat culturally dependent—for example, emotional intimacy and self-disclosure seem to be more important indicators of relationship satisfaction in individualistic cultures, compared to collectivistic cultures (Dion & Dion, 1993), the concept of romantic love seems to be a human universal. In a massive cross-cultural study of 166 different societies, Jankowiak and Paladino (2008) found that 90.9% of these social groups feel and express romantic love.

What Is Love?

When we feel or experience love, when we say that we are "in love," is this experience a *drive* or an *emotion*? In psychology, when we refer to a drive, we are typically describing something with roots deep into our evolutionary past. A **drive** motivates us to act, often referring to behaviors that have been critical to the survival and perpetuation of our genes; for example, we possess drives that motivate us to obtain food, sex, and escape physical danger. Can we best describe the experience of love as merely a biological drive to obtain a romantic partner? There is brain imaging data which suggests that certain aspects of love are associated with the activation of brain areas associated with motivation and drive, such as the hypothalamus and the amygdala (Arnow et al., 2002; Beauregard, Levesque, & Bourgouin, 2001).

But, in some ways the experience of love seems very much like an emotion—when we say that we are "in love," are we not typically describing how we *feel*? In psychology, when we refer to an **emotion**, we are typically describing a judgment or an evaluation about something complex (are we satisfying our goals, achieving what we want/need?) or something simple (am I experiencing a physiological change, like an increase in my heart rate? This can then be interpreted

Drive
Motivation to action, motivation to perform behaviors that have been critical to the survival of a species, and the perpetuation of an individual's genes into subsequent generations.

Emotion
A judgment or an evaluation about something complex (goal satisfaction and attainment) or something simple (changes in our physiology, increases in heart rate, sweat, etc.).

as a specific emotion). Can we best describe the experience of love as this kind of appraisal, a feeling, an emotion? Interestingly, many emotion theorists and researchers within the field of psychology do not include "love" in their lists of the "basic human emotions" (see Table 11.4). Additionally, while most so-called basic emotions are associated with a specific facial expression—and these facial expressions are even present in humans as early as 60 minutes after birth, and are shared with nonhuman primates (Ekman, 2006)—there doesn't seem to be a facial expression that would be uniquely associated with the feeling of being "in love." One theory of love, Fisher's Three Phases of Romantic Love (Fisher, 2004), marries these two perspectives on what love is. As Fisher (p. 89) describes her theory:

> *In fact, I have come to believe that romantic love is one of three discrete, interrelated emotion/motivation systems that all birds and mammals have evolved to direct courtship, mating, reproduction, and parenting . . . (lust, attraction, and attachment) Each brain system is associated with different feelings and behaviors; each is associated with a different (and dynamic) constellation of neural correlates; each evolved to direct a different aspect of reproduction; and each interacts with the other two in myriad combinations to produce the range of emotions, motivations, and behaviors associated with all types of love.*

According to this theoretical perspective (Fisher, 2004), romantic love is best described as three distinct phases, (a) Lust, (b) Attraction, and (c) Attachment. The first phase, *lust*, describes the experience of our deeply, biologically rooted sex drive—a motivation to seek out sexual experiences. This phase is likely maintained and initiated by sex hormones, including estrogens and androgens (Fisher, 2004; Van Goozen, Wiegant, Endert, Helmond, & Van de Poll, 1997). According to Fisher (2004), this is, chronologically, the initial phase of romantic love, and contrary to subsequent phases of romantic love, lust can be directed toward many targets, or many potential romantic partners.

Table 11.4:   Basic Human Emotions Identified By Various Researchers

Reference	Basic Human Emotions
Ekman (1992)	anger, disgust, fear, sadness, enjoyment, contempt, surprise, guilt, interest, shame, embarrassment, awe, and excitement
Izard (1991)	anger, contempt, disgust, sadness, enjoyment-joy, fear, interest-excitement, surprise-astonishment, guilt, shame, and shyness
Oatley and Johnson-Laird (1987)	anger, disgust, fear, happiness, and sadness
Panksepp (1998)	expectancy, fear, rage, panic, joy, lust, nurturance, greed, and dominance
Plutchik (1980)	acceptance, anger, anticipation, disgust, joy, fear, sadness, and surprise
Tomkins (1984)	anger, interest, contempt, disgust, distress, fear, joy, shame, and surprise
Weiner and Graham (1984)	happiness and sadness

Note. This table is adapted from Shaver, Morgan, and Hu's (1996, p. 82) and Ortony and Turner's (1990, p. 316) review articles.

The second phase, *attraction*, characterizes the many efforts and behaviors aimed at winning a specific, chosen romantic partner (Fisher, 2004). During this phase, we describe ourselves as being "in love," and we focus our attention and our efforts on the object of our affection. Fisher's (1998, 2004) work has also found that this focused phase of love, where we guard against potential rivals and express our love to our chosen romantic partner, is likely maintained by the reward pathways in our brain, specifically the "feel good" neurotransmitters: dopamine, serotonin, and norepinephrine (Fisher, 2004).

If the first two phases of love (lust and attraction) brings us together, then it is the third phase (*attachment*) keeps us together. During this phase, neurotransmitters like oxytocin promote affiliative behaviors (Lim, Murphy, & Young, 2004). In the attachment phase, we feel emotionally connected to our partner, physically attracted to our partner, and committed to our partner. This phase is characterized by feelings of never wanting to be apart, feelings of security within one's romantic relationship, and the sharing of chores, responsibilities, and often a living space (Fisher, 2004).

According to this perspective on love, all three of the phases of love have evolved to serve a specific function; *lust* drives us to seek out sexual encounters, *attraction* focuses our mating efforts on a specific individual and often results in the production of offspring (in the case of heterosexual pairings), and *attachment* maintains our romantic bond so that we may, together, provide for one another and any offspring. Together, we have a complex system of drives and emotions, each driven and maintained by different hormones and neurotransmitters, combining to describe the chronological experience of falling in love, and being in love. Importantly, we can see that there is an empirically supported alternative to settling on love as *either an emotion or a drive*; we can instead characterize it as both, with the lust phase of romantic love serving as the drive, and the attraction and attachment phases, including the emotions that characterize being "in love."

What Are We Like When We Are "in Love"?

Imagine—for a moment—how you would answer the following questions:

What does it feel like to be "in love"?
How do you know when you are "in love"?
How does being "in love" change you, if at all?

After introspecting, you may find that these questions are difficult to answer. It may seem as though it is difficult to find the words to explain exactly how this business of being "in love" feels, what it does to you. Psychological scientists have been at these questions for decades, and answers are taking shape. In a nutshell, the experience of being "in love" can be described as the feeling that the object of your affection has changed; this person has become special, unique, and especially meaningful to you. You know you are "in love" when:

It seems that your attention is focused, solely, on your beloved—and all other people seem to disappear. Individuals "in love" tend to idealize the object of their affection, by inflating their positive traits, and underrating their negative traits or flaws (Murray, Holmes, & Griffin, 1996). In fact, couples that idealize one another tend to remain together longer, and partner's even begin to internalize their loved one's esteemed versions of themselves; in other words, they begin to see themselves the way their partner sees them. Further, when induced to feel love for their romantic partner, by writing a short essay about their love for their partner, individuals were better able to suppress thoughts of an attractive potential mate, and were less able to remember what was appealing about that potential mate (Gonzaga, Haselton, Smurda, sian Davies, & Poore, 2008). Interestingly, this effect was *not* present when individuals were induced to feel sexual desire for their romantic partner, by writing a short essay about their physical, sexual desire for their partner, so it seems that this "zooming in" or increased attention towards the object of our love may be an effect unique to the experience of being "in love." It also becomes more difficult for individuals to discriminate the scents of other potential mates when they are "in love," as their attention and perceptual systems all seem to be focused on their beloved.

You experience intense physiological arousal, which is heightened activity of your sympathetic nervous system, including feeling excited, increased heart rate and breathing rate, sweaty palms, and flushed skin (Menchaca & Dehle, 2005). Indeed, when asked what being "in love" feels like, we are likely to describe the experience as feeling happy when the object of your love is with you, feeling that you can trust the person you love, and feeling aroused around the person you love (Lamm & Wiesmann, 1997). You feel emotionally dependent upon the object of your love, you experience high levels of empathy (feeling what your partner feels) when you are "in love," and often you find that you can't *not* think about your partner (Fisher, 1998). Your mind is drawn, seemingly involuntarily, to your beloved, over and over again, a phenomenon referred to as **intrusive thinking** (Gray & Garcia, 2013).

When you are in love, you feel as if the person you love has acquired "special meaning" to you (Gray & Garcia, 2013), you see them through "rose-colored glasses" until they begin to see themselves that way (Murray et al., 1996), you find yourself thinking of them all the time, and no one else, in fact you seem to forget or ignore all other potential partners (Gonzaga et al., 2008), you feel your beloved's pain and joy, and you feel happy and excited when in the presence of the one you love (Fisher, 1998; Harris, 1995). It is a complicated collection of psychological experiences, being "in love," all designed to draw us to one another, and keep us together.

Intrusive Thinking
The drawing of the mind, involuntarily, to a specific idea, thought, image, or person.

Love: What's Sex Got to Do with It?

We only have to travel as far as the checkout line at the grocery store to find out "How often you and your partner should be having sex" or "How often the happiest married couples have sex" or "How sex can keep your relationship alive." But what does psychological science have to say about love, relationship satisfaction, and sex? Is sex really that important in loving relationships? In one survey, the great majority of men (91%) and women (95%) disagreed with the statement: "The best thing about love is sex."

Taken together, evidence seems to suggest that the relationship between sex and relationship satisfaction depends on the desires of the individuals in that particular couple. Individuals who are dissatisfied with how often they have sex with their partner are also likely to indicate that they are dissatisfied and unhappy in their relationship (Smith et al., 2011). While many studies have identified a relationship between sexual satisfaction and relationship satisfaction (see Sprecher, Cate, Harvey, & Wenzel, 2004, for a review), attempts to determine a causal link between sexual satisfaction and relationship satisfaction have been inconclusive (Byers, 2005), not demonstrating strong evidence suggesting that low sexual satisfaction causes low relationship satisfaction *or* that low relationship satisfaction causes low sexual satisfaction. Perhaps critical in explaining the relationship between sexual satisfaction and relationship satisfaction is the nature of each partner's sexual desires, for example, disparate levels of sexual desire have been demonstrated to explain the link between sexual satisfaction and relationship satisfaction (Davies, Katz, & Jackson, 1999). In heterosexual couples, relationship satisfaction seems to be particularly low when females report lower levels of sexual desire than their partners (Davies et al., 1999).

It is possible that there is little compelling evidence of a strong *causal link* between sexual frequency or sexual satisfaction and relationship satisfaction because there are several psychological and behavioral variables that contribute to overall relationship satisfaction. For example, feeling satisfied with communication in one's relationship and sharing values about communication (Burleson, Kunkel, & Birch, 1994), having similar values and interests (Neimeyer, 1984), feeling highly invested and committed, as well as feeling high levels of intimacy (Rusbult & Buunk, 1993) within one's romantic relationship are all strongly predictive of relationship satisfaction. Perhaps unsurprisingly, the most critical predictor of relationship satisfaction seems to be *how a couple communicates* (and how they *perceive* their communication patterns to be): over time, couples that feel that their communication is unrewarding or negative are more likely to develop relationship stress (Markman, 1979). Individuals who feel that they are better *understood* by their partner tend to report being happier in their relationship (Cahn, 1990). Perhaps the best thing about love isn't sex, perhaps the best thing *for* your loving relationship isn't sex, it is feeling that you can trust, empathize, and communicate openly with your partner. This emphasis on the nonsexual elements of a romantic relationship, and the long-term context of a romantic relationship is uniquely human. By contrast, love and attraction in nonhuman animals (while quite complex and similar in many respects) is focused on sexual encounters and the production of offspring.

Love and Attraction in Nonhuman Animals

The fields of comparative psychology and evolutionary psychology teach us that there is much to be learned about our contemporary experiences as humans from nonhuman animal models. In many ways, the simpler biological and social systems of nonhuman animals provides insights into our evolutionary history and allows us to investigate human processes with more scientific control. For example, while it would be unethical to remove infant humans from their mothers to study the nature of attachments and bonding, Harry Harlow's (1958) work on attachment was the first evidence suggesting that it was *not* the providing of nutrition but of physical nurturance that fosters the formation of bonds between mother and child. Unlike humans, pair bonds in nonhuman animals are often (a) short-term mateships, (b) formed and maintained for the purpose of the production of offspring (although same-sex pairings are very common in nonhuman animals as well), and thus focused on sexual encounters, and (c) attraction and mate choice is often uni-directional.

Pair bonds are often formed and maintained in the short term in nonhuman animals—variation in the length of relationships in nonhuman animals seems to be dependent upon the time it takes for offspring to reach maturity. When offspring require more time, support, and investment before they can separate from their parents and provide for themselves, long(er)-term pair bonds are observed.

Furthermore, when offspring require more time and investment to mature, monogamous pair bonds are often favored (Kleiman, 1977). Several studies using nonhuman animal models, which follow these animals over long periods of time, have indeed found that the longer a bonded pair remains together, the more successful and healthy their offspring will be (Black, 2001; Ens, Choudhury, & Black, 1996). For example, pair bonds are often monogamous and long term in several species of elephant, as their calves require 16 to 17 years of investment until they reach sexual maturity and are capable of providing for themselves. By contrast, mating in the *Antechinus agilis*, a small marsupial (about the size of a mouse) takes place in very short-term pair bonds and is characterized by high levels of promiscuity, notably, their offspring are weaned and self-sufficient in a matter of days (Fisher, Double, & Moore, 2006).

In nonhuman animals, attraction and mate choice is also (almost exclusively) uni-directional, compared to human mate choice and attraction, which is bi-directional, where *both* mates feel attraction to one another, and evaluate one another to determine if they will be selected to form a pair bond or romantic relationship. Bi-directional mate choice often only occurs in species where (a) offspring require high levels of investment to reach maturity and (b) both individuals in the relationship are required to invest highly in the success of their family. In many nonhuman animal models (in heterosexual pairings), males only invest in one sexual encounter, whereas females invest in gestation and subsequent lactation when offspring are produced from a pairing (Adair, Dillon, & Brase, 2015). These differences in minimum parental investment also predict interesting differences in mating and attraction; for example, in most nonhuman animal species, the female is required to invest more in the production and care of potential offspring. Since females are often required to invest more in a specific pairing, they are also often the "choosier" sex (Trivers, 1972). The theoretical reasoning here is this: since females are required to invest more *if* offspring are produced from a specific pairing, *then* they have more to lose if they choose a poor-quality mate. Alternatively, since males are not required to invest in the gestation and postnatal care of offspring, *then* they have little to lose if they choose a poor-quality mate. This difference in parental investment, and therefore choosiness in the sexes (Trivers, 1972), explains why uni-directional mate choice is often observed in nonhuman animals. For examples, in some species of bird, mate choice and attraction happens in the contexts of leks. Leks refer to a mate-choice environment where many males collect and put on mating displays for on-looking females. Males compete with one another, engage in mating displays or dances to demonstrate their genetic fitness, and sometimes even construct elaborate "houses," as in the case of the bowerbird, the males construct "homes" adorned with colorful objects from their environments to impress females (see Figure 11.9), to attract the "*choosy*" females (Adair et al., 2015; Noe, 2015).

Myths About Love

It may not be surprising to you that we can acquire a host of inaccurate information about love and romantic relationships from our social world. We learn much about what "love" and "romantic love" is supposed to be like from our social world, as Bloch (2009, p. 11) puts it:

> . . . *the articulation of love as an ideal, which is what we mean by romantic love, is the product of a historical process, of material conditions of a contingent set of circumstances and even personalities, belonging to a specific time and place.*

Figure 11.9.   Nest created by male bowerbird to attract potential mates.

Bring to mind the narrative of almost any romantic tale, love story, or "Rom Com" (romantic comedy), and you will likely find examples of the following myths about love (see Table 11.5):

It is important to be aware of these myths about love, and realize that while early relationships are characterized by lust, physiological arousal ("butterflies," increased heart rate and breathing rate), happiness, a desire to be with your

Table 11.5:   Myths About Love

Myths about love
You have one "soul mate" that is cosmically predestined, you are "meant to be" so nothing can tear you apart
Love happens "at first sight"
If your partner is your "soul mate," then they will know what is wrong with you or what you want without you having to say so
If your partner is your "soul mate," sex will come easily to you and be wonderful
(If you are a woman) To keep your partner with you and keep your partner happy, you should "fit" the beauty ideal—being thin, having a small waist and large hips, tan skin, etc.
(If you are a man) You should not be less successful in your career, be less educated, earn less, or be shorter or weaker than your partner
You can change your partner, and (if you are a heterosexual woman) you can transform your "beast" into a gentleman
(If you are a heterosexual woman) You do not have to work to maintain your relationship, the man you are with will be responsible for all romantic gestures, including proposing, buying flowers, and buying dinner when you go on a date

Note. This table is adapted from Galician's (1995) Mass Media Love Quiz and Galician's (2004) collected works on the subject of love and the media.

THINKING CRITICALLY (B)

Explore your own ideas about love by taking Galician's (1995) Mass Media Love Quiz for yourself at http://www.realisticromance.com/quiz.html.

After you finish the quiz and consider your results, ask yourself some questions regarding normative information and social expectations regarding love in Western culture.

Questions:

1. Consider your score—which (if any) of the statements about love did you agree with? How many "myths" about love do you feel you endorse?
2. Consider the causal explanation—where do these messages about love come from? How does an individual learn what love and "romance" are supposed to be like?
3. What do you feel are the potential problems associated with the messages about romantic love perpetuated by the media?

partner all the time, and thinking about your partner all the time, often long-term romantic relationships transition into a bond characterized by commitment, attachment, and emotional intimacy. Satisfying relationships change over time, and require the efforts, trust, and openness (particularly in communication) of both partners to remain satisfying and healthy. Love and attraction make us happy, they are all around us, in the media that we consume, in our daily lives in the expressions of love that we give and receive, they characterize a collection of complex social and biological processes that pull us together and keep us together. Altogether, we can conclude that they keys to long-lasting love seem to be mutual trust, communication, and emotional intimacy.

References

Adair, L. E., Dillon, H. M., & Brase, G. L. (2015). I'll have who she's having: Mate copying, mate poaching, and mate retention. In M. L. Fisher (Ed.) *Handbook on women and competition.* New York, NY: Oxford University Press.

Aharon, I., Etcoff, N., Ariely, D., Chabris, C. F., O'Connor, E., & Breiter, H. C. (2001). Beautiful faces have variable reward value: fMRI and behavioral evidence. *Neuron, 32*(3), 537–551. doi:http://dx.doi.org/10.1016/S0896-6273(01)00491-3

Anderson, C., Keltner, D., & John, O. P. (2003). Emotional convergence between people over time. *Journal of Personality and Social Psychology, 84*(5), 1054–1068. doi:http://dx.doi.org/10.1037/0022-3514.84.5.1054

Arnow, B. A., Desmond, J. E., Banner, L. L., Glover, G. H., Solomon, A., Polan, M. L., ... Atlas, S. W. (2002). Brain activation and sexual arousal in healthy, heterosexual males. *Brain, 125,* 1014–1023. doi:http://dx.doi.org/10.1093/brain/awf108

Bailey, J. M., Dunne, M. P., & Martin, N. G. (2000). Genetic and environmental influences on sexual orientation and its correlates in an Australian twin sample. *Journal of Personality and Social Psychology, 78*(3), 524–536. doi:http://psycnet.apa.org/doi/10.1037/0022-3514.78.3.524

Beauregard, M., Levesque, J., & Bourgouin, P. (2001). Neural correlates of conscious self-regulation of emotion. *Journal of Neuroscience, 21,* 165.

Black, J. M. (2001). Fitness consequences of long-term pair bonds in barnacle geese: Monogamy in the extreme. *Behavioral Ecology, 12*(5), 640–645. doi:10.1093/beheco/12.5.640

Bloch, R. H. (2009). *Medieval misogyny and the invention of Western romantic love.* Chicago, IL: University of Chicago Press.

Brehm, S. S. (1985). *Intimate relationships.* New York, NY: Random House.

Burleson, B. R., Kunkel, A. W., & Birch, J. D. (1994). Thoughts about talk in romantic relationships: Similarity makes for attraction (and happiness, too). *Communication Quarterly, 42*(3), 259–273. doi:10.1080/01463379409369933

Buss, D. M. (1989). Sex differences in human mate preferences: Evolutionary hypotheses tested in 37 cultures. *Behavioral and Brain Sciences, 12*(01), 1–14. doi:http://dx.doi.org/10.1017/S0140525X00023992

Buss, D. M., & Barnes, M. (1986). Preferences in human mate selection. *Journal of Personality and Social Psychology, 50*(3), 559–570. doi:http://psycnet.apa.org/doi/10.1037/0022-3514.50.3.559

Buss, D. M., & Schmitt, D. P. (1993). Sexual strategies theory: An evolutionary perspective on human mating. *Psychological Review, 100*(2), 204–232. doi:http://psycnet.apa.org/doi/10.1037/0033-295X.100.2.204

Buss, D. M., Abbott, M., Angleitner, A., Asherian, A., Biaggio, A., Blanco-Villasenor, A., . . . Yang, K. S. (1990). International preferences in selecting mates a study of 37 cultures. *Journal of cross-cultural psychology, 21*(1), 5–47. doi:10.1177/0022022190211001

Byers, E. S. (2005). Relationship satisfaction and sexual satisfaction: A longitudinal study of individuals in long-term relationships. *Journal of Sex Research, 42*(2), 113–118. doi:10.1080/00224490509552264

Cahn, D. D. (1990). Perceived understanding and interpersonal relationships. *Journal of Social and Personal Relationships, 7*(2), 231–244. doi:10.1177/0265407590072005

Carmalt, J. H., Cawley, J., Joyner, K., & Sobal, J. (2008). Body weight and matching with a physically attractive romantic partner. *Journal of Marriage and Family, 70*(5), 1287–1296. doi:http://dx.doi.org.er.lib.k-state.edu/10.1111/j.1741-3737.2008.00566.x

Clore, G. L., & Byrne, D. (1974). A reinforcement-affect model of attraction. In T. L. Huston (Ed.), *Foundations of interpersonal attraction* (pp. 143–170). New York, NY: Academic Press.

Collins, S. A. (2000). Men's voices and women's choices. *Animal Behavior, 60*, 773–780. doi:http://dx.doi.org/10.1006/anbe.2000.1523

Davies, S., Katz, J., & Jackson, J. L. (1999). Sexual desire discrepancies: Effects on sexual and relationship satisfaction in heterosexual dating couples. *Archives of Sexual Behavior, 28*(6), 553–567. doi:10.1023/A:1018721417683

Dion, K. K., & Dion, K. L. (1993). Individualistic and collectivistic perspectives on gender and the cultural context of love and intimacy. *Journal of Social Issues, 49*(3), 53–69. doi:10.1111/j.1540-4560.1993.tb01168.x

Dixson, B. J., Dixson, A. F., Bishop, P. J., & Parish, A. (2010). Human physique and sexual attractiveness in men and women: A New Zealand–US comparative study. *Archives of Sexual Behavior, 39*(3), 798–806. doi:10.1007/s10508-008-9441-y

Dixson, A. F., Dixson, B. J., Morgan, B., & Anderson, M. J. (2007). Studies of human physique and sexual attractiveness: Sexual preferences of men and women in China. *American Journal of Human Biology, 19*, 88–95. doi:10.1002/ajhb.20584

Dixson, A. F., Halliwell, G., East, R., Wignarajah, P., & Anderson, M. J. (2003). Masculine somatotype and hirsuteness as determinants of sexual attractiveness to women. *Archives of Sexual Behavior, 32*(1), 29–39. doi:10.1023/A:1021889228469

Ekman, P. (2006). *Darwin and facial expression: A century of research in review.* Los Altos, CA: Malor Books.

Ekman, P. (1992). An argument for basic emotions. *Cognition & Emotion, 6*(3–4), 169–200.

Ens, B. J., Choudhury, S., & Black, J. M. (1996). Mate fidelity and divorce in monogamous birds. *Oxford Ornithology Series, 6*, 344–401.

Fisher, H. (1998). Lust, attraction, and attachment in mammalian reproduction. *Human Nature, 9*, 23–52. doi:10.1007/s12110-998-1010-5

Fisher, H. (2004). *Why we love: The nature and chemistry of romantic love.* New York, NY: Henry Holt.

Fisher, D. O., Double, M. C., & Moore, B. D. (2006). Number of mates and timing of mating affect offspring growth in the small marsupial Antechinus agilis. *Animal Behaviour, 71*(2), 289–297.

Gallo, F. T., Greenhut, R., & Joffe, C. H. (Producers), & Allen, W. (Director), (1977). *Annie Hall* (Motion picture). United States: United Artists.

Galician, M. L. (1995). Galician's Mass Media Love Quiz. Retrieved from http://www.realisticromance.com/quiz.html

Galician, M. L. (2004). *Sex, love, and romance in the mass media: Analysis and criticism of unrealistic portrayals and their influence.* London, England: Routledge.

Gonzaga, G. C., Campos, B., & Bradbury, T. (2007). Similarity, convergence, and relationship satisfaction in dating and married couples. *Journal of Personality and Social Psychology, 93*(1), 34–48. doi:http://psycnet.apa.org/doi/10.1037/0022-3514.93.1.34

Gonzaga, G. C., Carter, S., & Buckwalter, J. G. (2010). Assortative mating, convergence, and satisfaction in married couples. *Personal Relationships, 17*(4), 634–644.

Gonzaga, G. C., Haselton, M. G., Smurda, J., sian Davies, M., & Poore, J. C. (2008). Love, desire, and the suppression of thoughts of romantic alternatives. *Evolution and Human Behavior, 29*(2), 119–126. doi:http://dx.doi.org/10.1016/j.evolhumbehav.2007.11.003

Gray, P. B., & Garcia, J. R. (2013). Evolution and human sexual behavior. *History and Anthropology, 24*(4), 513–515. doi:10.1080/02757206.2013.841682

Harlow, H. F. (1958). The nature of love. *American Psychologist, 13*(12), 673–685. doi:http://psycnet.apa.org/doi/10.1037/h0047884

Hazan, C., & Shaver, P. (1987). Love conceptualized as an attachment process. *Journal of Personality and Social Psychology, 52,* 511–524. doi:http://psycnet.apa.org/doi/10.1037/0022-3514.52.3.511

Hessick, C. B. (2007). Violence between lovers, strangers, and friends. *Washington University Law Review, 85,* 343–407.

Hur, Y. M. (2003). Assortative mating for personality traits, educational level, religious affiliation, height, weight, and body mass index in parents of a Korean twin sample. *Twin Research, 6*(06), 467–470.

Izard, C. E. (1991). *The psychology of emotions.* New York, NY: Plenum Press.

Jankowiak, W. R., & Paladino, T. (2008). Desiring sex, longing for love: A tripartite conundrum. In W. R. Jankowiak (Ed.), *Intimacies: Love and sex across cultures* (pp. 1–36). New York, NY: Columbia University Press.

Jenkins, J. (2007). *An investigation of marital satisfaction: Assortative mating and personality similarity.* ProQuest Dissertations and Thesis Database. Retrieved from http://search.proquest.com.er.lib.k-state.edu/docview/622023221?accountid=11789

Johansson, B. G., & Jones, T. M. (2007). The role of chemical communication in mate choice. *Biological Reviews, 82*(2), 265–289. doi:10.1111/j.1469-185X.2007.00009.x

Jones, B. C., Little, A. C., Penton-Voak, I. S., Tiddeman, B. P., Burt, D. M., & Perrett, D. I. (2001). Facial symmetry and judgements of apparent health: Support for a "good genes" explanation of the attractiveness-symmetry relationship. *Evolution and Human Behavior, 22,* 417–429.

Kaye, S. A., Folsom, A. R., Pineas, R. J., Potter, J. D., & Gapstur, S. M. (1990). The association of body fat distribution with lifestyle and reproductive factors in a population study of postmenopausal women. *International Journal of Obesity, 14,* 583–591.

Kinsey, A. C., Pomeroy, W. B., & Martin, C. E. (1948). Sexual behavior in the human male. *British Medical Journal, 11,* 1–3.

Kleiman, D. G. (1977). Monogamy in mammals. *Quarterly Review of Biology, 52*(1), 39–69. doi:http://www.jstor.org/stable/2824293

Klein, F. (1990). The need to view sexual orientation as a multivariable dynamic process: A theoretical perspective. In D. P. McWhirter, S. A. Sanders, & J. M. Reinisch (Eds.), *Homosexuality/heterosexuality: Concepts of sexual orientation.* New York, NY: Oxford University Press.

Klein, F., Sepekoff, B., & Wolf, T. J. (1985). Sexual orientation: A multi-variable dynamic process. *The Journal of Homosexuality, 11,* 35–49. doi:10.1300/J082v11n01_04

Kuhle, B. X., & Radtke, S. (2013). Born both ways: The alloparenting hypothesis for sexual fluidity in women. *Evolutionary Psychology: An International Journal of Evolutionary Approaches to Psychology and Behavior, 11*(2), 304–323.

Lamm, H., & Wiesmann, U. (1997). Subjective attributes of attraction: How people characterize their liking, their love, and their being in love. *Personal Relationships, 4*(3), 271–284.

Lim, M. M., Murphy, A. Z., & Young, L. J. (2004). Ventral striatopallidal oxytocin and vasopressin V1a receptors in the monogamous prairie vole (*Microtus ochrogaster*). *Journal of Comparative Neurology, 468*(4), 555–570. doi:10.1002/cne.10973

Lott, A. J., & Lott, B. E. (1968). A learning theory approach to interpersonal attitudes. In A. G. Greenwald & T. M. Ostrom (Eds.), *Psychological foundations of attitudes* (pp. 67–88). New York, NY: Academic Press.

Lott, A. J., & Lott, B. E. (1974). The role of reward in the formation of positive interpersonal attitudes. In T. L. Huston (Ed.), *Foundations of interpersonal attraction* (pp. 171–189). New York, NY: Academic Press.

Maner, J. K., Gailliot, M. T., Rouby, D. A., & Miller, S. L. (2007). Can't take my eyes off you: Attentional adhesion to mates and rivals. *Journal of Personality and Social Psychology, 93*(3), 389–416. doi:http://psycnet.apa.org/doi/10.1037/0022-3514.93.3.389

Markman, H. J. (1979). Application of a behavioral model of marriage in predicting relationship satisfaction of couples planning marriage. *Journal of Consulting and Clinical Psychology, 47*(4), 743–749. doi:http://psycnet.apa.org/doi/10.1037/0022-006X.47.4.743

Marti, B., Tuomilehto, J., Saloman, V., Kartovaara, L., Korhonen, H. J., & Pietinen, L. (1991). Body fat distribution in the Finnish population: Environmental determinants and predictive power for cardiovascular risk factor levels. *Journal of Epidemiology and Community Health, 45*, 131–137. doi:10.1136/jech.45.2.131

Menchaca, D., & Dehle, C. (2005). Marital quality and physiological arousal: How do I love thee? Let my heartbeat count the ways. *The American Journal of Family Therapy, 33*(2), 117–130.

McGuire, T. R. (1995). Is homosexuality genetic? A critical review and some suggestions. *Journal of Homosexuality, 28*, 115–145. doi:10.1300/J082v28n01_08

Miller, G., Tybur, J. M., & Jordan, B. D. (2007). Ovulatory cycle effects on tip earnings by lap dancers: economic evidence for human estrus? *Evolution and Human Behavior, 28*(6), 375–381. doi:http://dx.doi.org/10.1016/j.evolhumbehav.2007.06.002

Murray, S. L., Holmes, J. G., & Griffin, D. W. (1996). The self-fulfilling nature of positive illusions in romantic relationships: Love is not blind, but prescient. *Journal of Personality and Social Psychology, 71*(6), 1155–1180.

Neimeyer, G. J. (1984). Cognitive complexity and marital satisfaction. *Journal of Social and Clinical Psychology, 2*(3), 258–263.

Noe, R. (2015). Animal architects: Bowerbirds design and build showy, colorful homes to attract mates. Retrieved from http://www.core77.com/posts/26541/animal-architects-bowerbirds-design-build-showy-colorful-homes-to-attract-mates-26541

Oatley, K., & Johnson-Laird, P. N. (1987). Towards a cognitive theory of emotions. *Cognition & Emotion, 1*, 29–50.

Ortony, A., & Turner, T. J. (1990). What's basic about basic emotions? *Psychological Review, 97*(3), 315. doi:http://psycnet.apa.org/doi/10.1037/0033-295X.97.3.315

Panksepp, J. (1998). *Affective neuroscience: The foundations of human and animal emotions.* New York, NY: Oxford University Press.

Pliner, P. (1982). The effects of mere exposure on liking for edible substances. *Appetite, 3*, 283–290.

Plutchik, R. (1980). A general psychoevolutionary theory of emotion. In R. Plutchik & H. Kellerman (Eds.), *Emotion: Theory, research, and experience: Vol. 1. Theories of emotion* (pp. 27–48). Hillsdale, NJ: Erlbaum.

Rajecki, D. W. (1974). Effects of prenatal exposure to auditory or visual stimulation on postnatal distress vocalizations in chicks. *Behavioral Biology, 11*, 525–536.

Rhodes, G., Halberstadt, J., & Brajkovich, G. (2001). Generalization of mere exposure effects to averaged composite faces. *Social Cognition, 19*, 57–70. doi:10.1521/soco.19.1.57.18961

Ro, T., Russell, C., & Lavie, N. (2001). Changing faces: A detection advantage in the flicker paradigm. *Psychological Science, 12*(1), 94–99. doi:10.1111/1467-9280.00317

Rosario, M., Schrimshaw, E. W., Hunter, J., & Braun, L. (2006). Sexual identity development among lesbian, gay, and bisexual youths: Consistency and change over time. *Journal of Sex Research, 43*(1), 46–58.

Rosenthal, M. (2013). *Human sexuality: From cells to society.* Belmont, CA: Wadsworth.

Rusbult, C. E., & Buunk, B. P. (1993). Commitment processes in close relationships: An interdependence analysis. *Journal of Social and Personal Relationships, 10*(2), 175–204. doi:10.1177/026540759301000202

Shakespeare, W., & Durband, A. (1985). *Romeo and Juliet.* Woodbury, NY: Barron's.

Shaver, P. R., Morgan, H. J., & Wu, S. (1996). Is love a "basic" emotion? *Personal Relationships, 3*, 81–96.

Singh, D. (1993). Adaptive significance of female physical attractiveness: Role of waist-to-hip ratio. *Journal of Personality and Social Psychology, 65*(2), 293–307. doi:http://psycnet.apa.org/doi/10.1037/0022-3514.65.2.293

Singh, D. (2004). Mating strategies in young women: Role of physical attractiveness. *Journal of Sex Research, 41,* 43-54. doi: 10.1080/00224490409552212

Smith, A., Lyons, A., Ferris, J., Richters, J., Pitts, M., Shelley, J., & Simpson, J. M. (2011). Sexual and relationship satisfaction among heterosexual men and women: The importance of desired frequency of sex. *Journal of Sex & Marital Therapy, 37*(2), 104–115.

Sobal, J., & Stunkard, A. J. (1989). Socioeconomic status and obesity: a review of the literature. *Psychological Bulletin, 105*(2), 260–275. doi:http://psycnet.apa.org/doi/10.1037/0033-2909.105.2.260

Sprecher, S., Cate, R. M., Harvey, J. H., & Wenzel, A. (2004). Sexual satisfaction and sexual expression as predictors of relationship satisfaction and stability. *The Handbook of Sexuality in Close Relationships,* 235–256.

Sternberg, R. J. (1987). Liking versus loving: A comparative evaluation of theories. *Psychological Bulletin, 102,* 331–345.

Sternberg, R. J., & Grajek, S. (1984). The nature of love. *Journal of Personality and Social Psychology, 47,* 312–329.

Sui, J., & Liu, C. H. (2009). Can beauty be ignored? Effects of facial attractiveness on covert attention. *Psychonomic Bulletin & Review, 16*(2), 276–281.

Swami, V., Knight, D., Tovée, M. J., Davies, P., & Furnham, A. (2007). Preferences for female body size in Britain and the South Pacific. *Body Image, 4*(2), 219–223.

Tomkins, S. S. (1984). Affect theory. In K. R. Scherer & P. Ekman (Eds.), *Approaches to emotion* (pp. 163–195). Hillsdale, NJ: Erlbaum.

Trivers, R. (1972). Parental investment and sexual selection. *Sexual Selection & the Descent of Man, Aldine de Gruyter, New York,* 136–179.

Van Goozen, S. H., Wiegant, V. M., Endert, E., Helmond, F. A., & Van de Poll, N. E. (1997). Psychoendocrinological assessment of the menstrual cycle: The relationship between hormones, sexuality, and mood. *Archives of Sexual Behavior, 26*(4), 359–382. doi:10.1023/A:1024587217927

Vrangalova, Z., & Savin-Williams, R. C. (2010). Correlates of same-sex sexuality in heterosexually identified young adults. *Journal of Sex Research, 47,* 92–102.

Wedekind, C., Seebeck, T., Bettens, F., & Paepke, A. J. (1995). MHC-dependent mate preference in humans. *Proceedings of the Royal Society of London B, 260,* 245–249.

Weiner, B., & Graham, S. (1984). An attributional approach to emotional development. In C. E. Izard, J. Kagan, & R. B. Zajonc (Eds.), *Emotions, cognition, and behavior* (pp. 167–191). New York, NY: Cambridge University Press.

Wilson, G. (1981). *The Coolidge effect: An evolutionary account of human sexuality.* New York, NY: William Morrow.

Wright, T. (Photographer). (2012). *Self evident truths.* Santa Monica, CA: Fractured Atlas.

Zajonc, R. B. (1968). Attitudinal effects of mere exposure. *Journal of Personality and Social Psychology, 9,* 1–27.

Zajonc, R. B. (2000). Feeling and thinking: Preferences need no inferences. *American Psychologist, 35,* 151–175.

INDEX

A

Accommodation
  definition, 170, 171
  schemas, 27, 28
Actor-observer difference, 38–39
Actor-observer effect, 59
Actual self, 57
Agender, 73
Aggression, 23
  agreeableness, 154–155
  alcohol consumption, 148
  continuum and frequency pyramid, 143–144
  definition, 142
  examples, 142
  exposure to weapons, 148–149
  general aggression model (GAM), 144–146
  heat, 149, 150
  hostile attributions, reduction of, 155
  media violence exposure, 150–151
  narcissism, 147–148
  physical aggression, 143
  re-appraisals, 153–154
  reduction techniques, 153–155
  relational aggression, 143
  risk and resiliency approach, 151–152
  sex differences, 147
  verbal aggression, 143
  violence escalation model (VEM), 152–153
  violent crimes, in United States, 142
Agreeableness, 154–155
Alcohol consumption, 148
Alloparenting hypothesis, 200
All-or-nothing thinking, 44
Altruistic motivation, 118–119
American Psychological Association (APA), 8, 9, 22
Amnestic heterosexism, 76
Anchoring bias, 14
Anchorman, 68
Anger, 35, 36, 208
Annihilation, 170, 171
Anxiety

automatic and controlled thinking, 30
  mortality, 61, 169–170
  self-consciousness, 55
Applied research
  definition, 15
  focus of, 14
  pros and cons of, 15
Archival research, 21–22
Aronson, Joshua, 177–178
Arousal cost-reward model, 120
Assimilation
  definition, 170, 171
  schemas, 27, 28
Assortative mating, 197–198
Attentional adhesion, 206–207
Attention allocation model, 148
Attitude change
  definition, 94
  direct experiences, 94–95
  indirect sources of information, 95
  researching, 100–102
Attitudes. *See also* Persuasion
  definition, 82
  explicit (*see* Explicit attitudes)
  formation, 91–94
  Genderism and Transphobia Scale (GTS), 73
  implicit (*see* Implicit attitudes)
  mere exposure, 83
  negative, 82
  neutral, 82
  positive, 82
  postpersuasion manipulation attitude
    measurements, 101–102
  self-awareness, 54
  strength of, 82–83
Attraction. *See also* Love
  assortative mating, 197–198
  attentional adhesion, 206–207
  "liking" and "loving," distinction between,
    194–197
  mere exposure effect, 197
  pheromones, 202–203